Moravian Christmas
in the South

by
Nancy Smith Thomas

Old Salem
MUSEUMS & GARDENS

Old Salem Museums & Gardens
Winston-Salem, North Carolina

Distributed for Old Salem by
The University of North Carolina Press
Chapel Hill, North Carolina

Moravian Christmas in the South
© 2007 Nancy Smith Thomas
Published by Old Salem Museum & Gardens, Winston-Salem, North Carolina

Distributed by
University of North Carolina Press,
116 South Boundary St.
Chapel Hill, North Carolina 27514

Additional copies of this publication may be ordered by calling
1-800-848-6224 or from the Press's website,
www.uncpress.unc.edu

LIBRARY OF CONGRESS CATALOGING-IN-PUBLICATION DATA

Thomas, Nancy Smith.
  Moravian Christmas in the South / by Nancy Smith Thomas.
      p. cm.
  Includes bibliographical references and index.
  ISBN-13: 978-0-8078-3181-6
  1. Christmas. 2. Moravian Church. I. Title.
  BV45.T45 2007
  263'.9150882846756—dc22
                              2007034149

Dedication

To my dear, supportive, indulgent, and greatly cherished family as well as my best friends: my husband Charlie, our daughter Laura Melanie, our son John Charles and his wife Amanda Minger; and in loving memory of my parents, Charles Milton and Hazel Laura Oliver Smith.

Table of Contents

Supporters

of *Moravian Christmas*
in the South

*This book was made possible through the generous support
of two of our corporate friends:*

Frank L. Blum Construction Company

Winston-Salem, NC

Henderson Bromstead Art

Winston-Salem, NC

Preface

On Christmas Eve some decades ago, a nurse at North Carolina Baptist Hospital in Winston-Salem handed a five-pound bundle to my mother and said, "Well, Mrs. Smith, you have just got yourself a real live baby doll!" That "Night Before Christmas" story was repeated to me each December 24th—my birthday—as long as my mother lived. It was undoubtedly the beginning of my enduring love for Christmas. When I was seven or eight, I was first allowed to read from my father's collection of the Harvard Classics kept in the living room secretary. Two favorites, whose bindings today show the countless perusals, were the fairy tales of Hans Christian Andersen and the folk tales of the Brothers Grimm. Thus began my lifelong passion for books. Looking back it seems that I was destined to someday write a book about Christmas.

After graduating from Wake Forest University I boarded the train to New York City to work for a publishing company. It was in New York that I met my future husband, Charlie, and also started my library and Christmas collection, buying the first box of German glass ornaments in an import shop on lower Fifth Avenue. My fascination with the holiday souvenirs of the past has never abated.

As our family grew, we made homes in the beautiful states of West Virginia and Connecticut. During these years I often reminisced with fondness about the poignant Christmas celebrations of the Moravians in my hometown of Winston-Salem. My youthful memories were soon joined by more happy Moravian associations when our daughter Laura attended Salem Academy and our son John graduated from Lehigh University in Bethlehem, Pennsylvania. By some unexpected coincidence our children had chosen to study in the two largest Moravian centers in the country! It shouldn't be a surprise then that when I moved back home to North Carolina with Charlie that I wanted to work at the Moravian living history museum now known as Old Salem Museums & Gardens. Being involved in interpretation at this priceless treasure of preservation for eighteen years has given me the opportunity to research many aspects of the social history of the Moravians, especially their Christmas traditions.

Although my background is neither theological nor Moravian, my interest in the topic of Christmas in general and Moravian culture in particular has been greatly piqued by my experiences at Old Salem. It was through the questions of museum visitors that I was able to discern those elements of life in Salem and Wachovia that people find enlightening and interesting. As part of my professional responsibilities and for my personal edification, I have read widely on the subjects of Christmas and Moravian social history and collected innumerable books on related topics. Along the way, I have gained enormous respect for the Moravian Church, its members, and its extensive archives.

Entire volumes have been written on the subjects presented in each of the chapters that follow, so the reader will understand the necessity of brevity and the occasional broad statement when a more complex or nuanced explanation could be made. Moravian music alone has been the subject of many scholarly examinations, which may be explored in depth elsewhere (see the Bibliography for suggested reading). What makes this work unique, however, is that it has more unpublished material about the nineteenth century Christmas of Salem, the surrounding tract of Wachovia, and the Springplace (Georgia) Moravian Indian Mission than any other book yet produced. It emphasizes that the first Christmas tree in America was almost surely erected by Moravians and that the earliest positively identified Christmas tree in the South was put up by Moravians—both significant landmarks in the history of the American holiday.

It is appropriate that this book begins with an Introduction that provides a concise background of the Protestant Moravians, their culture, and how they came to the American South, particularly Salem, North Carolina. The first chapter begins with engaging vignettes of an early Christmas in Salem and goes on to explore greater themes of how Moravian values informed the developing American Christmas. Chapter Two discusses the history of the German-based traditions of the Christmas tree and the pyramid.

Moravian Christmas decorations, including the unique *Putz*, form the core of Chapter Three. Chapter Four examines the European and American evolution of the various gift bringers and the Moravian tradition of Christmas gifts. Chapter Five focuses on celebratory foods, beverages, and related customs of Moravian communities, with particular references to the ubiquitous apple, ever present pork, and beloved Christmas cakes. The final chapter explores the ways music, church services, and both formal and informal gatherings brought Moravians in the South together during Christmastime.

The Christmas traditions of early Moravians were neither created nor practiced in a vacuum. In this book the juxtaposition of Moravian customs with occasional "outsider" references provides context for the celebration of the American Christmas that became an invented tradition for a new republic that needed reliable pillars of stability found in the church and home. The focus of the book is that of the Moravians' social history as it relates to Christmas and how the traditional celebrations unified and bonded members to their church and to their families, providing continuity and meaning to their lives and establishing a respected presence outside their church. They, as do we all, sought enrichment and fulfillment at a time when those occurrences were rare in the repetitive monotony of often difficult daily living.

The Moravians have long been known for bringing children to the forefront in their celebration of Christmas, so a thread that runs through the narrative is the kindly and nurturing attitude concerning children embraced early by the Moravian Church and gradually by other thoughtful adults of the nineteenth century. Such an attitude was initiated by a seventeenth-century Moravian bishop, John Amos Comenius, often called the "Father of Education," who wrote, "The principal guardianship of the human race is in the cradle, as testified by God." In a similar vein he added, "Lo, children are the heritage of the Lord." In fact, my first idea for this book was to focus on Moravian children at Christmas, but as I researched, gathered, and organized material my original intent gave way in some part to broader topics relevant to the Moravian Christmas traditions. This change of course was prompted by limited information: We do not always know as many of the specifics about children in the South at Christmas as we would like to know. Consequently the book presents the occasional snippet of how young Moravians were included in this important holiday, but the content is not exclusively focused on the Christmas of those children.

There is nothing more powerful in experiencing history than reading the exact words of those long ago people in the colorful nuances of their language, so a number of quotations, some of them translations from the German, have been liberally sprinkled throughout the book. Charles Francis Adams (1835-1915), great-grandson of John Adams, said in writing about the past: "One accustomed to the variety, luxury and refinement of modern life, if carried suddenly back into the admired existence of the past, would, the moment his surprise and amusement had passed away, experience an acute and lasting attack of home-sickness and disgust." Thus, out of many things I have learned in the absorbing years of studying the Moravians and their neighbors, one of the most important is that one must suspend modern prejudices, views, personal opinions, or biases when looking at the past. We are not those people, and we did not walk in their shoes or live their lives. We can learn much about our ancestors through their words, but we should not use today's standards to judge their actions.

As I reflect on my own past, little would I have thought years ago when as a child riding with my parents through the streets of the historic community of Salem and staring in awe at the town's iconic Coffee Pot trade sign with all its titillating imaginative possibilities, that I would draw such pleasure as an adult in exploring local traditions. Having desired a historic "Moravian connection" of my own, through my research I did discover an ancestor who attended the Salem Girls' Boarding School in the early part of the nineteenth century. (Her mother found the school to be excellent although the cost high.) I have realized that history with all of its artifacts is a treasure hunt worth pursuing, and the paths down which it leads us immeasurably alter our thinking and enrich our lives forever. I hope you will enjoy the reading of this volume as much as I have enjoyed researching and creating it, and perhaps you, too, will find your own special connection to the past within its pages.

Acknowledgments

It was at the home of special friends Jack and Diane Snyder in Charleston, West Virginia, that I beheld for the first time the splendor of a candlelit tree in the German style, around which we played stimulating games of charades at New Year's. It was there also that I tasted such early family holiday treats as Aunt Louise Anna's Raisin Nut Cookies and Cassoulet. Appreciation is extended to Jack in particular, who generously offered to me much valuable advice on the legalities of writing a book.

Gourmet cook Paula Saylor McKenney and her husband Ron introduced me to the gastronomic delights of German *stollen* and gingerbread houses, along with many other delicacies in years of family Christmas gatherings. My special interest in the backcountry foods of the South began when Paula and I collaborated to edit *Mountain Measures*, a regional Appalachian cookbook published by the Charleston, West Virginia, Junior League, a book that is now in its tenth printing.

On returning to Winston-Salem, we became fast friends with Joyce and Barry Kingman when they were assigned to be our fellowship friends at church. On Christmas Eve for years we have gathered with our families to celebrate friendship, Christmas, and my birthday with such treats as Brunswick stew and ham biscuits. Although both Joyce and Barry have now passed on, I remember them with deep affection.

The seeds for writing a book on early Christmas were planted in my mind years ago by some outstanding teachers who themselves loved books: Mrs. Alice Tucker, Miss Louise Smith, Miss Joanne Scott, Mrs. Beulah Raynor, Dr. E. E. Folk, and Dr. Edwin Wilson.

Old Salem Museums & Gardens staff members have provided invaluable support and encouragement. Space prevents me from listing here all of the talented, dedicated Historic Town of Salem interpreters, Single Brothers' Workshop guides, and MESDA guides that have assisted me. I thank them all. In particular, my appreciation is extended to Sally Gant, June Lucas, Katie Schlee, Martha Rowe, Zara Phillips, Linda Gardner, Johanna Brown, Abigail Linville, Paula Locklair, Peggy Parks, Mary Armitage, Mel White, June Edwards, Mary Hartung, Irma Muetzel, Joy Reich, Tom and Bonnie Tomchik, Lori Keiper, Mary Helen Boone, Jean Smith, Linda Sheffield, Gary Rohrer, Ruth Brooks, Sandy Hegstrom, Jeri Harrell, Sue Brehme, Jean Thomas, and Nat Norwood and the Historic Trades staff.

Former colleagues Gene Capps and Carol Hall merit special mention for their many productive years at Old Salem Museums & Gardens, during which they established a background of accuracy in interpreting the Moravian story, including Christmas. Gene is also a Christmas aficionado, and he shared some significant pictures and details from his files that appear in this book.

Longtime Salem resident and friend Flora Ann Bynum, who wrote *The Christmas Heritage of Old Salem* in 1982, provided inspiration and set high standards for subsequent Moravian Christmas books.

At the serene, beautiful, and treasure-filled Moravian Archives building in Winston-Salem, I relied on the expertise of Richard Starbuck and Dr. C. Daniel Crews. Dr. Nola Knouse at the Moravian Music Foundation in Winston-Salem also provided able assistance. For his enlightening lectures at Old Salem and insightful comments, I thank Moravian scholar Dr. Craig Atwood. Dr. Paul Peucker of the Moravian Archives in Bethlehem, Pennsylvania, provided images of excellent quality. The Herrnhut Moravian Archives in Saxony, Germany, shared images of some early paintings and prints.

At Salem College, help was liberally given by librarians Susan Taylor and Dr. Rose Simon, and publishing advice by Penelope Niven, Salem College's writer-in-residence, is very much appreciated. Herb and Frances Vogler entrusted me with papers from their ancestor Elias A. Vogler. The collection at Historic Bethabara Park contained invaluable background material, and the Museum of the Cherokee Indian at Cherokee, North Carolina, has long been an inspiration. Kay Moss of the Schiele Museum in Gastonia, North Carolina, led me to some additional research possibilities.

Enjoyable and instructive time was spent in various study programs and the libraries at the Winterthur Museum & Country Estate in Delaware and Colonial Williamsburg Foundation in Virginia. In particular, I thank Susan Moqtaderi at Winterthur for allowing me access to Christmas interpretive material during a four-week study course at the museum. I unearthed useful material in the Southern Historical Collection at the Louis Round Wilson Library of the University of North Carolina at Chapel Hill and the North Carolina State Archives in Raleigh. Valuable information came from the North Carolina Room and the reference section of the Forsyth County Public Library in Winston-Salem through John Via.

Springplace, Georgia, scholar Dr. Rowena McClinton verified a crucial translation. Justine Landis of the Historical Society of York County enlightened me on certain aspects of Lewis Miller's life. Kathy Staples, textile expert, examined some early needlework examples on Christmas subjects.

My friends at the retail stores of Old Salem Museums & Gardens and the Moravian Book and Gift Shop in Salem have provided me with many pleasurable hours of searching for current books and treasures. Each year I look forward to going to another favorite store, the historic Moravian Book Shop in Bethlehem, Pennsylvania.

Treasured friends and relatives with whom I have "kept Christmas" in one way or the other through the years are: my grandparents Virginia Brown and James Brush Oliver and Nan Nunn and Drury Smith; J. Harry Thomas; May, Carrie, Fan, Ruby, and Tom Oliver; Frances, Charles, Roger "Chip," and David Chandler; Margaret, Jim, Melissa, Maurice, and Lillian Morgan; Joan Mallonee and William Doty; Vann and Anne Carroll; Jeanette and Ray Graves and family; Joanna and Wesley Bailey; Maude and Reid Simmons, Etta Ray, Drury, and Loretta Smith, Frank and Beulah Smith, Dick and Annie Smith, Arthur and Jessie Smith, Tom and Daisy Smith, and all of their special descendants; Eloise Wolfe; Lollie Mickey and Austin Collins; Lola and Bill Hodgin; Mary Shirey; Barbara and Jim Smith; Dr. Les and Lyn Pitman; Gale, Miller, Tim, Melissa, and Ted Porterfield; Andy and Betty Comcowich; Marian and Joe Nicastro; Fran Tilton Nystrom; Jeanie and Pat McAward; Mary and John Myers; Louise Thomas; Betsy and Walt Nading; Nancy and Harry Underwood; Nancy and Jerry Warren; Linette Harrill; Betsy Clark; Shirley Blakley; Becky Minnix; Betty and Tom Damewood; Linda Ellis; Leigh and Susan Taylor; Jane and Bob McEldowney; Dr. C. G. and Pat Moyers; Kitty and John Cornell; Dr. Jay and Lucy Kauh; Ann Patterson; Caroline Green and Gravely Reid; Nancy Marshall; Jane Walsh; Mary King; Ken Thomas; Ann Fain; Anne and Tom Pierce; Thornie and Hal Worley; Dr. Gerald Taylor; Charlotte and L. C. Beckerdite; Anna Smith; and Ed Crissman.

During my research, I renewed the acquaintance of my remarkable Revolutionary War ancestor, Colonel Jack Martin (1756-1822) of the historic Rock House in Stokes County. His granddaughter attended Salem Academy, thus providing me with a personal link to the early Moravians

I remember with especial fondness deceased friends with whom I have shared Christmas memories: H.L. "Jack" Snyder; Paula McKenney; Lola Monk; Dorothy Smith; Harvey Joe Lynch; Christine Dearmin; Joyce and Barry Kingman; Margaret Snow; Mary Ellen Loftis Sims; Betty Colmer Bond; Donna Shores; Dr. Mary Ann Taylor; Dr. Joseph Moriarty; Jean and Bob Marshall; Dr. Rosemary Estes; and Mary Louise Thomas.

A large thank you is offered to Jean Walser and Tracy and Ed Matthews, who provide help year after year in the arranging of fresh greenery with the kaleidoscopic Christmas decorations and books in our authentic colonial house, which was enhanced by Steven Cole and meticulously conceived by Buffa Entwistle, someone I would like to have known.

Appreciation for their exceptional professional abilities is extended to Old Salem Museums & Gardens's Wes Stewart, staff photographer, who captured many of the beautiful images that grace this book; Jennifer Bean Bower, associate curator of photographic collections, who provided the engaging historical prints and coordinated the photography; and Betsy Allen, editorial associate, whose expertise is evident in this book. Book designer Claire Purnell of Annapolis, Maryland, deserves praise for expertly bringing words and images together to create the artistically arranged pages that follow. Gina Mahalek and Meagan Bonnell of UNC Press kept in constant touch for the promotion of the book.

Most particularly, with a grateful heart, I acknowledge editor and friend Gary Albert who promoted a succinct "focus and flow" for the manuscript. With thoughtful insight, style, and wisdom he has helped me bring this dear book to fruition. Our hope is that Moravians as well as non-Moravians, including Christmas aficionados and social historians, will find inspiration and knowledge within the pages.

All authors must fear the lack of acknowledgment of some special person who helped them along the way. I hope that all the many individuals and organizations that assisted me in the process resulting in this book will forgive me if I have inadvertently failed to mention their names. My gratitude is extended to everyone for each bit of wisdom and word of support offered.

Finally, for all of us, whatever our religious bent, whether at Christmas or not, there are certain times in our lives when at a particular "golden fruiting of the year...the best that is in us ripens, and falls into our neighbor's heart" (*The Moravian*, vol. 14, no. 52, 30 December 1869, 206). That quote is especially meaningful to me, for in any era and at any time of the year, not just Christmas, it conveys a thought worthy of reflection and action. My hope is that this book captures that indomitable spirit of generosity and good will.

Nancy Smith Thomas
Winston-Salem, North Carolina
20 June 2007

Introduction

The Moravians in the South

On Christmas Eve 1753 a small group of stalwart settlers assembled in the North Carolina Piedmont wilderness to celebrate the birth of the Baby Jesus. The gathering that they held to commemorate Christ's birth was called a lovefeast, a simple Bible-based service of fellowship, music, and perhaps some food. This particular Christmas lovefeast was the first in North Carolina and marked the beginning in the state of a Moravian tradition that continues today.

The long journey of the Moravians from the beginning of the church to the backcountry of North Carolina started in Prague in 1415 with the martyrdom of a Catholic priest named Jan Hus ("John Huss" in English). Huss advocated widespread reform within the church and its clergy. For such heresy he was burned at the stake. Although his tongue was silenced, the fervent spirit he created was not. Those inspired by his convictions fought and died for religious reform through many years of persecution.

In 1457 a group of Huss's followers organized the *Unitas Fratrum* (Latin for "Unity of Brethren") and ordained its first ministers. In spite of continual harassment, imprisonment, and torture, the Unity of Brethren slowly grew in size and reputation. Building churches, schools, and printing houses, they reached

a population of 200,000 by the time of Martin Luther, an outspoken German who shared many religious grievances with the Brethren. In 1517 Luther nailed his theses on ecclesiastical abuses to the church door in Wittenberg, thus precipitating the Protestant Reformation. Some historians have remarked that if there had been a printing press in the time of John Huss the Reformation might very well have taken place a hundred years sooner with the Unity of Brethren at the forefront.

The Thirty Years' War (1618-1648) between Protestants and Catholics increased the persecution of the Brethren, forcing them to seek refuge in remote areas of Bohemia, Moravia, and Poland. During this period John Amos Comenius (1592-1670), an intellectual leader and bishop in the church, nourished the seed of their faith and encouraged a renewal. In 1722 an emissary for a group of Brethren approached a German nobleman named Count Nicholas Ludwig von Zinzendorf to ask for refuge on his Saxon estate. Thus began the town of Herrnhut, where the German language and traditions became prevalent among the Bretheren even though by then church members came from such diverse areas as Holland, Russia, Ireland, Switzerland, England, and what is now the Czech Republic.

Zinzendorf, a magnetic and devout Lutheran, offered the Brethren structure, financial support, and spiritual guidance. Under his leadership the church celebrated its renewal and rebirth on 13 August 1727. The Count also instituted a strong missionary program, which began with enslaved Africans in the West Indies in 1732 and gradually spread to Africa, Greenland, Lapland, Ceylon (now Sri Lanka), South America, and the Far East. It was during this period, after establishing an English presence, that the Brethren came to be known as "Moravians" in English-speaking countries, due, of course, to the church's origins in Moravia (now the Czech Republic).

Wanting to create a base in North America for the church's economic and mission initiatives, Zinzendorf negotiated a grant from the Georgia Trustees to establish a settlement in Savannah in 1735. Unfortunately, in that location the Moravians were frequently caught in conflicts between the Spanish and Georgia settlers, and in 1740 they decided to abandon their little community and travel north to the more peaceful colony of Pennsylvania.

In Pennsylvania, with the help of other Moravians migrating from Europe, the Brethren established the towns of Nazareth in 1740, Bethlehem in 1741 (still today the center of the Northern

Province of the Moravian Church), and Lititz in 1754. Their reputation as industrious, pious people quickly grew and by 1752 the Brethren had been approached by one of the Lords Proprietors of the Carolina Colony, who was searching for good, hardworking people to buy and settle his land. Very interested by the opportunity, a Moravian exploratory party traveled south in 1753 under the guidance of Bishop August Gottlieb Spangenberg, who upon reaching his destination exulted in his diary, "The land on which we are now encamped seems to me to have been reserved by the Lord for the Brethren." The almost 100,000 acres that they surveyed on the Three Forks of the Muddy Creek encompassed a good part of what is now Forsyth County, North Carolina. The Great Wagon Road, an important passage for trade and travel between the North and South, traversed a portion of the tract. The Moravians completed the transaction and named the area *die Wachau* in honor of Zinzendorf's ancestral estate on expansive meadows along the banks of the Wach River in Austria. The name was later anglicized to "Wachovia."

Thus, the overwhelming task of creating a southern Moravian base began. In 1753 the first town, Bethabara, meaning "house of passage," was established in Wachovia. As the name implies, Bethabara was intended to be a temporary community while a planned central congregation town was surveyed and built. The French and Indian War delayed the building of the proposed town so Bethabara grew in size and structure. In 1759 the Moravians established a farming community called Bethania about three miles north of Bethabara. In the coming years three other farming congregations would be founded on the southern edge of the Wachovia tract: Friedberg (1773), Friedland (congregation organized in 1780),

and Hope (also organized in 1780). These five settlements, along with the central town of Salem, comprised the communities of eighteenth-century Wachovia.

While the Moravians living in Bethabara (and some other Moravian towns in Pennsylvania and Europe) operated under an *Oeconomie*, a communal system of housekeeping and labor with all income going into a general fund, the residents of Bethania and the three farming congregations lived under a more loosely organized structure. The *Oeconomie* of Moravian communities provided spiritual, financial, and domestic support that enabled residents to place their faith and a Christian model of living above all other priorities. For this dedication from its congregation, the Moravian Church was able to provide for its members and also maintain and expand missionary efforts.

Bethabara remained the primary community in Wachovia for thirteen years before the beginning in 1766 of the planned central congregation town of Salem, named from the Hebrew word for "peace." In the spring of 1772, after six years of construction, approximately 120 people moved from Bethabara to inhabit the European-style buildings of Salem around a square—a model of town planning that mimicked the communities of the Old Country.

In addition to being the spiritual and administrative core for Moravians in Wachovia, Salem was also envisioned to be a trades center to serve its neighbors (both Moravian and non-Moravian). The town would retain some communal aspects of the *Oeconomie*, but families would live together. Because of its role as a center for trades, Salem would be very connected to the outside world by letters, papers, and a constant supply of goods brought by wagons from Charleston, Wilmington, Cross Creek (Fayetteville), Petersburg, New Bern, and Pennsyl-

vania. The necessary interaction with strangers or outsiders—as non-Moravians were called—would frequently disturb the insulated world sought by the new town's church elders. When strangers came to do business, they often brought their worldly influences with them. Consequently, they were welcomed for business purposes but otherwise discouraged from contact with the residents.

The craftsmen in Salem were organized somewhat in the manner of the European guild system with boys apprenticing to masters of trades shops. The activities of tradesmen and businesses were overseen by a board of supervision and enforcement. In contrast to this mainly secular business board, there were boards for spiritual matters and for general community issues. Residents of Salem leased the church-owned land but built and possessed their own board-approved houses. They rented lots outside town where they could farm, and in general labored for their own sustenance. The church managed many businesses—such as the tavern, mill, tannery, and pottery—which it ran for its own profit to further mission work and maintain solvency in the administration of the Unity of Brethren. In owning all the land, the church was able to keep a controlling and paternal eye on the residents and their behaviors. Salem was a theocracy, although citizens were always free to leave. In fact, some residents were asked to do so, if their behavior was unacceptable.

Some of Salem's residents were enslaved, at first bought or leased by the church, but in time also by individuals. In the early days of the town a few enslaved persons were accepted into the congregation; however, as the nineteenth century approached, attitudes about slavery gradually changed. Increasingly, the views of the Moravians in Wachovia reflected the stereotypical racist ones of the period and region. Consequently, owning slaves by individuals was permitted by the church in 1847.

As in other Moravian congregations, the church members in Salem were divided into groups called "choirs"—not in the sense of singing groups but in the role of religious support groups. Choirs were organized by age, gender, and marital status with the purpose of encouraging spiritual growth. In Salem there were choirs for the Little Boys, Little Girls, Older Boys, Older Girls, Single Sisters, Single Brothers, Married People, Widows, and Widowers. The members of the choirs sat together in church, met frequently, and served as reliable sustainers to each other through-out the vicissitudes of life, such as marriage, childbirth, illness, and death. The only vestige of the choir system remaining in the modern Moravian Church is in God's Acre, the graveyard. If church members choose to be buried in a Moravian cemetery, they are buried with congregation members of the same sex, not with their families. The belief is that, regardless of status, in death all are equal, so the tombstones are generally uniform and flat.

Boys and girls in early Salem were educated in separate schools. At the age of about fourteen, most boys went to live in the Single Brothers' House where they ate, slept, and worked under the watchful eyes of older men while being apprenticed to various tradesmen in town. Especially promising boys might be sent for additional schooling in Moravian schools in Pennsylvania, after which they could become teachers, ministers, doctors, or administrators in the congregation. Older girls generally went to live in the Single Sisters' House where they learned important domestic and hand skills that could help them in their roles of wives, mothers, and community participants. Some women became teachers, administrators, and sick nurses. No one was required to marry, although most did. If they chose to remain single, both women and men could live out their lives in the choir houses where they earned their keep.

The history of education for girls in Salem is a long and cherished one that resulted in the Salem Girls' School that would eventually become Salem Academy and College, one of the oldest in continuous operation in the country. Accepting students from outside the Moravian community, the school very early became a profitable enterprise for the church. Widely known for its instruction and reliable supervision of students as the nineteenth century progressed, the school received daughters from many families during the Civil War specifically because of its reputation as a safe haven.

Although one of the goals of the Moravians when they came to the New World was to bring their message of God's love to the American Indians, circumstances in the South had prevented any significant organized effort to reach out to native populations until 1801 when missionaries were sent to Georgia to evangelize amongst the Creeks and the Cherokees. The endeavor moved slowly but positively, especially under the guidance of the superbly talented Moravian couple Anna Rosina Gambold and her husband John, until President Andrew Jackson forcibly removed the Indians to Oklahoma in the late 1830s in what was a mass extradition known as "The Trail of Tears." Some Moravians went West with their American Indian friends and continued their mission work among indigenous peoples.

Ten years earlier, the Female Missionary Society in Salem laid the groundwork for ongoing mission work of another kind: a separate African American congregation in Salem. As segregation grew in the South, so it did in Salem. In 1822 the Female Missionary Society created a mission congregation for African Americans in Salem that met in a log building and sought to provide some education to the members in its Sunday School classes until a North Carolina law in 1831 forbade such educational endeavors. Eventually, during the Civil War, a larger brick church was erected. Named St. Philips, it is the oldest African American church in North Carolina and has been restored as an interpreted site at Old Salem Museums & Gardens.

While the first seeds of independence for African Americans in Wachovia came with the end of the Civil War and the Emancipation Proclamation, almost a hundred years earlier white Moravians in Carolina felt the same fervent spirit of American independence that swept through the country after the Revolution. As a result, many changes occurred in the controlling and somewhat restrictive structure of Salem's congregational society. One of the most obvious changes was that English began to supplant German as the dominant language in Wachovia. Another fundamental change was the less frequent use of the lot as an instrument to determine God's will when significant decisions had to be made by church elders. The lot had been an integral part of the early Moravian Church as a way to seek guidance from the Lord in large and uncertain decisions. Throughout the eighteenth century the lot was consulted by Moravians to determine the placement of a building, approve the requests of applicants into the church, and sanction marriage proposals. By the early-nineteenth century some Moravians began to see the lot as an unnecessary formality, if not simply a relic of an earlier time, and the practice began to wane. For instance, after 1816 marriage for lay people no longer required the use of the lot to approve the selection of a mate.

Change in Wachovia was initiated by outside communities as well. From its inception Salem was a bustling economic force in the region as one of the only towns where finely crafted and imported goods could be acquired. As small non-Moravian settlements in Piedmont North Carolina grew into substantial towns with economies of their own, Salem had to adjust to the growth and encroachment of civilization all around it. Also, the technologies of the Industrial Revolution could produce manufactured goods that were cheaper and sometimes more uniform than the handmade items in Salem. As a result the specialized trades shops gradually closed and woolen and cotton mills were built.

When the State of North Carolina created Forsyth County in 1849, Salem was expected to be its seat. Still attempting to control the interaction between its members and the outsiders, the church resisted having the county government centered in Salem and sold the state a parcel of land just north of the Moravian community for the county courthouse. Thus the town of Winston, so named for a Revolutionary War hero in 1851, was established, and Salem quickly felt its presence.

In 1856 the Moravian Church recognized that the continuing control of businesses and individuals in Salem was no longer viable and decided to cease congregational management of the town. Salem became a municipality of North Carolina in 1857

and continued to be a strong presence. Winston and Salem existed alongside one another—two entities with their own civil governments—for several decades, during which time they were often known as the Twin City. By 1913, when the two towns merged under the name of Winston-Salem, most of the economic growth in the form of the booming tobacco industry had migrated to Winston leaving the former Moravian town in a state of decline.

The unique personality of Salem began to fade as its longtime residents passed on, recognized businesses departed, and new enterprises formed. The meticulously constructed eighteenth- and nineteenth-century structures either fell into disrepair or were adapted for other uses. Despite the presence of Home Moravian Church, the offices of the church's Southern Province, and Salem College, the historic community was disintegrating at an alarming pace.

Fortunately, in 1950 some local, influential civic and business leaders came together to create a nonprofit organization to restore and preserve the historic town of Salem. Fifty-eight years later, Old Salem Museums & Gardens has restored or reconstructed more than 70 historic buildings and recreated acres of historic landscapes and gardens. The Historic Town of Salem and its sibling museums, the Museum of Early Southern Decorative Arts (MESDA), the Old Salem Toy

Museum, and the Old Salem Children's Museum, combine to make Old Salem Museums & Gardens one of America's most authentic and comprehensive history attractions.

Today, the Moravian Church is in the mainstream of the Protestant denominations with a membership of about 800,000 worldwide, one-half of that number in Tanzania in East Africa where mission work bore abundant fruit. In the United States there are about 26,000 members in the Northern Province and 18,000 in the Southern Province, concentrated in the area of North Carolina. The Moravian Church has long been known for diligent record keeping and saving of important papers, which have provided invaluable documents for historians. The Moravian Archives in Winston-Salem, North Carolina, and in Bethlehem, Pennsylvania, as well as the Moravian Music Foundation, all yield impressive treasures of regional as well as national importance.

Cherished traditions endure at Home Moravian Church, the religious center of Salem since its inception as a congregation in 1771 and construction of the church in 1800. At Christmas the congregation continues to celebrate the birth of Christ with a traditional lovefeast, just as did the hearty band of fearless men, who first gathered humbly in a primitive cabin in the middle of the North Carolina wilderness over 250 years ago.

"Salem Street Scene in Winter" by Pauline Bahnson Gray, 1940s. *Private collection.*

Chapter 1

Moravian Christmas Traditions and the Evolution of the Holiday

"The Moravians know how to keep Christmos [*sic*]."

— The Wachovia Moravian, *December 1894*

What was an early southern Moravian Christmas like? Nowhere did anyone write down in one place a detailed description of all of the activities at church and at home leading to the celebration of one of the most important events in Moravian church history: the birth of the baby Jesus. However, through diaries, journals, church reports, and letters, along with an informed speculation, we are able to piece together a narration. So, to begin, let us part the curtains to the past on an early southern Moravian Christmas.

It is a brisk, cold day in late November about two hundred years ago in Salem, North Carolina. The cacophony of tradesmen's tools, the creaking of wagon wheels, and the rhythmic clip-clopping of horses' hooves mingle with the shrill squeals of pigs being readied for butchering in several backyards along Main Street. Children scurry about to help their parents in this arduous, but necessary task, a job so essential that it takes precedence over school. In readiness for the making of cider, wine, and brandy, the pungent odor of fermenting apples wafts from the direction of the brewery and distillery west of town. Faint sounds of music issue from the church where the organist practices a special Advent anthem. The first whisper of Christmas is in the air.

As December 25th approaches, a rosy-cheeked girl, excused by her parents from school for the day, rushes importantly from one of the clapboard houses, quickly returning with a small collection of the neighbor's tin cookie cutters bundled in her checked apron. Eventually the spicy aroma of freshly baked Christmas cakes drifts from the outside oven sheltered in a lean-to at the back of the narrow lot. The mouth-watering smell mingles with the honeyed odor of warm beeswax emanating from a nearby shed where several women are dipping candles for the lovefeasts. Two young men emerge from the community store with some loosely-wrapped sugar candies, purchased for their godchildren, and walk briskly down the dirt street. As they stride along, deep in conversation, indistinct German phrases float upward, linger, and fade. All

through town households are being tidied and doorsteps and yards swept (if the mud is not too great). In between their everyday chores some mothers, older sisters, aunts, and grandmothers find time in their orderly houses to hem a small woolen petticoat or cut out a striped short gown for a little girl, knit some warm socks or sew up a new linen shirt for a growing boy. If they finish in time, these useful gifts may be placed on a table in the sitting room to be distributed when the family returns from the Christmas Eve lovefeast at the church.

A few days before Christmas the schoolteacher and some of his pupils, all wearing closely knit warm caps, pass by on a borrowed horse-drawn wagon bound for the country where they will seek out a supply of pine, cedar, laurel, and moss to use in the church decoration. When they return, the teacher and several adult friends from the Single Brothers' house begin to construct their essential Christmas decoration, the Putz. During the construction they hang some bedsheets to conceal the unfinished project. They painstakingly build a framework to be placed at the back of the minister's table and then piece together the green garlands, festoons, and swags, attaching to them large cut-out paper letters of German words that when translated read "Glory to God in the Highest." A small watercolor

Putz at the Salem Tavern, early twentieth-century. *Old Salem Historic Photograph Collection, Old Salem Museums & Gardens (hereafter OSHPC).*

transparency of the Holy family is placed in the center of the arrangement, and a number of candlesticks are arranged beside and behind it to effectively illuminate it when the time comes. After many hours or even days of work, on completion they celebrate at the afternoon vesper with a glass of wine, a slice of apple cake, coffee, and perhaps a good cigar.

Christmas Eve arrives at last. To simplify matters, a late vesper and early supper may be combined. As the afternoon fades, mothers with their babies and small children walk to the church at the corner of the square for the five o'clock lovefeast service especially designed for the little ones. Two hours later families, including their larger children, return for the Christmas Eve service. They divide into their special choir sections upon entering at the two separate doors, the men and older boys sitting on one side, the women and older girls on the opposite side. Children sit at the front. Led by the minister, who reads the Christmas story from the second chapter of Luke, they enjoy singing in unison as well as antiphonally (responsively) some carefully selected hymns accompa-

nied by musicians playing violins, a viola, trombones, clarinets, and French horns. There are a dozen or more visitors in the sanctuary, many of them guests at the tavern, and they sing the familiar tunes softly in their own language, while the enslaved African Americans seated on the long bench at the back of the church follow along as best they can, some in German and some in English. By the soft light of the golden-colored candles the devout group drinks warm tea or sugar-sweetened lovefeast coffee mixed with milk and savors the hearty and substantial yeast bread. The children receive gifts that have been neatly tied to two small evergreen trees arranged on either side of the nativity scene. Cries of delight indicate their appreciation of the printed Bible verses lovingly embellished by the minister's wife, shiny red apples, and spicy cakes (Lebkuchen). The older boys and girls recite their verses received at last year's celebration before they are all presented with lighted candles to represent Christ as the light of the world. It is quite dark now, and the flickering flames dance and weave, forming giant shadows on the walls. Stepping into the cold night air, the congregation observes snowflakes gently cloaking the trees in white. As they tread gingerly through the powdery mixture, some of the older adults reflect on their own long ago childhoods in Pennsylvania, as well as various countries of Europe, England, and Africa.

Upon reaching home, the parents stir up the coals from the ashes of the fireplace, add more wood, and observe that a bucket of water on the opposite wall has begun to freeze. While the children remove outer garments and nibble on their cache of sweet cakes from church along with apples and cider, a fire is built in the sitting room and finally that door, which had concealed the adults' Christmas preparations including the Putz and some small gifts, is opened with a flourish. Revealed on the table is a small carved wood or paper nativity set, lovingly unpacked from a chest in the garret and carefully nestled in moss and evergreens with a few sheep grazing close by on a rocky slope. The young people are mesmerized at the sight of such a diminutive scene highlighted by the tallow candles, and the parents are content with their efforts to bring the story of the beloved Jesus into their home. A song is sung, a prayer is said, and the young people may again repeat their memorized Bible verses. As the family retires, they hear the night watchman's voice calling the hour and chanting a verse from one of the hymns earlier sung at church. Tomorrow morning the children will carefully place the tiny infant in the empty crib and linger there, repositioning the animals and adding to the straw as they relish each tiny detail of their own Putz.

Christmas Day begins with chores and perhaps some work projects. There may be two morning church services, the first liturgical and the second a longer preaching service at which there are again some visitors to whom the minister may offer a portion of the sermon in

A few neighbors with their children may visit each other's Putz decoration.

English, and of course there is much music. At home for dinner served at about noon there is a piece of roasted pork, or maybe a turkey, sauerkraut or cabbage, potatoes, pickles, bread and butter, a fruit pie, pound cake, and beer, wine, or cider. Later in the afternoon there are short choir meetings where a vesper of coffee or tea with the Christmas ginger cakes is enjoyed. A few neighbors with their children may visit each other's Putz decoration. A supper of leftovers is taken in haste so as to hurry again to church for more music, worship, and fellowship. At this meeting perhaps some of the school girls present a well-rehearsed ode, a recitation and musical dialogue about the birth of Jesus, which has been prepared by the minister.

As Salem grows and evolves over time, the English language becomes

Salem *Putz* at Home Moravian Church's Candle Tea. *Courtesy of Women's Fellowship, Home Moravian Church.*

MORAVIAN CHRISTMAS TRADITIONS

prevalent and many more goods are brought from afar. As a result, sometime in the mid-century, Moravians in Carolina begin to observe increasingly elaborate Christmas traditions. However, the church services are still at the center of the celebration. The Fries children are curling up at home with a little book in which the gift bringer is pictured coming down the chimney with a pack of toys. Another picture book shows a decorated tabletop tree covered with small presents. The Putz grows to include buildings, running water, and an expanse of space. Trees are laden with homemade as well as store-bought gifts. A drink of eggnog is enjoyed upon arising on Christmas morning, and imported oysters, oranges, figs, nuts, and chocolates are part of the day's fare for those who can afford such extras. An assemblage of useful and edible items gathered for the few enslaved helpers is passed out in a little ceremony during the day.

The scene fades. The years pass. Additional elements of Christmas celebration are introduced.

The vignettes above illustrate the active participation of children in all of the Moravian Christmas traditions. Although the nineteenth century was the real beginning of the American model for Christmas as we recognize it today, the Moravians had indeed been known as participants in a meaningfully celebrated

Bethlehem: "The Christmas City"

Moravian archivist Dr. Adelaide Fries called Bethlehem's name "a Christmas souvenir."[i] Although contemporary historians have asserted that the name Bethlehem had already been picked in Europe, the following story is a charming one of the little settlement's first Christmas, as related by Fries:

"In 1741 Count Zinzendorf was spending the Christmas season with the Brethren in the log house which had been built near the banks of the Lehigh,—a house constructed Continental fashion, with dwelling rooms and stable under one roof. Following the custom of that day the Brethren on the Lehigh were holding a Christmas Eve Watch Service, the Count presiding. During the service, on a sudden impulse, the Count arose and led the company into the stable, there continuing the service and singing a very old Christmas hymn which began 'Not Jerusalem, Rather Bethlehem, Gave us that which Maketh life rich.' The little village, thus far without a name, took the name Bethlehem from this idea."[ii]

Engraving of Bethlehem, Pennsylvania, 1750-60, engraved by J. Noual, London. *Collection of Old Salem Museums & Gardens (hereafter OSMG).*

Christmas Day for much longer. As a writer in *The Moravian* in 1863 wrote, "In our own Church, it has ever been the custom to dedicate [the festival of Christmas] almost exclusively to [children's] instruction and enjoyment."[1] In 1870 the editor reminded adults "Let us rear the Christmas tree for them [the children], and make the house full of joy and Christmas warmth and light. But let us not neglect to tell them *what it all means* [emphasis added]."[2] The reason for that attention was well explained in the Southern Church publication some years later: "The manner in which the Son of God entered our human nature has sanctified the estate of childhood. He came as a babe laid in the manger in order that the little children might be loved and prized as they never had been before. If, therefore, in homes and Sunday schools we make children happy, we are doing what Jesus did in his birth at Bethlehem."[3]

Perhaps the greatest contributor to the value that Moravians gave to the nurturing and education of children was the prominent church leader and bishop John Amos Comenius (1592-1670). Comenius, known far and wide as the "Father of Education," instituted many positive and still enduring theories of an early and broad education for children. Teaching by pictures as well as by text and entertaining children as they were learning were creative approaches used by Comenius in his book *Orbus Pictus*, published in 1658 and considered the "first illustrated school book,"[4] or "the first children's picture book."[5]

Employing pictures, visual images, and even plays to mentally and emotionally teach and inspire churchgoers had long been a successful method of the Catholic Church, particularly for those who were illiterate. For example, it is said by many

OLD KRISSKINGLE.

YOU see here, a picture of good old Krisskingle, or Bellsnickle, as he is sometimes called; he is, as you all know, the good friend and patron of all good children at Christmas.

Early gift bringer image, mid-nineteenth century. Courtesy of the North Carolina Office of Archives & History.

historians that the miracle plays or "Moralities" presented in medieval European churches of Bible stories (such as Adam and Eve with a Paradise tree hung with apples) was the scene from which came the forerunner of the Christmas tree and probably the *Putz*. The Moravians were also adept at using these techniques effectively and meaningfully, not only with children but also with adults. They understood the impact of images and symbols and used such things as greenery-enhanced illuminated nativity scenes, colorfully executed

Bible verses, the light of candles, a star, a lamb, and even Christmas trees and pyramids to inform and enlighten.

Underscoring that the Moravians were always mindful of their children and of the importance of visual references to reinforce their faith, Bishop August Gottlieb Spangenberg, in his definitive exposition of Moravian beliefs published in 1778, wrote "God gives his angels to the service of children; and therefore children, who are of so much value with God, should likewise be precious and dear to us."[6] As a group in the church very young children themselves were known as angels.[7] Religious support groups called choirs were formed to correspond to the children's ages, and thus suitable instruction was ongoing in the progressing stages of life.[8] Angels were an important and common theme at that time; nineteenth-century Christmas pictures sometimes depicted children as angels and the gift bringer to the children as a young angel.[9]

The use of Christmas candles on 24 December 1747 in Marien-born (near Herrnhut, now in Germany) for a Christmas Eve watch service illustrates the Moravians' early use of visual symbols for children. Brother Johannes von Watteville, son-in-law of Count Zinzendorf, told the children of the birth of Jesus and to remind them of His great sacrifice presented each little one with a burning taper, tied with a red ribbon. Holding their lighted candles high as Brother Johannes sang, the children clearly grasped the symbolism of Christ's redemptive love as the light of the world in the hearts of people.[10]

Seemingly in contradiction to this long Moravian tradition of recognizing children as members of the congregation in need of special attention is the fact that the Moravians emerged from an unmistakable European communal society. In Salem, the Moravians had lived in family units from the beginning, but their strong sense of church and mission work had emphasized a Christ-centered focus above all else. In Europe, and even occasionally in Salem, to carry out God's work sometimes meant departure and separation from family for months or years, but with the secure understanding that other responsible adults were always available to act as surrogates for their children in choir groups, in the church, and in homes.[11]

While the communal aspects of eighteenth- and early-nineteenth century Salem made the Moravians distinct from their Carolina neighbors, by the mid-nineteenth century Salem society had changed significantly. The eighteenth-century model of a congregation town with service to God and the church placed above all else had all but disappeared and

A children's lovefeast, 1760, engraved by I. Rod Holzhalb, France or Germany. *OSMG.*

The Maxims for Parents on Rearing Children

The Moravian published some maxims for parents in 1863.[iii] Originally appearing in a handbill published in Birmingham, England, they began with a quote: "When the ground is soft and gentle, it is time to sow the seed; when the branch is tender, we can train it easiest; when the stream is small, we can best turn its course."

1. Begin to train your children from the cradle. From their earliest infancy, inculcate the necessity of obedience.

2. Unite firmness with gentleness.

3. Never give them anything because they cry for it.

4. Seldom threaten; and be always careful to keep your word.

5. Never promise them anything, unless you are quite sure, you can give them what you promise.

6. Always punish your children for willfully disobeying you; but never punish in a passion.

7. Do not be always correcting your children; and never use violent or terrifying punishment. Take the rod (so Solomon says,) let it tingle, and pray God to bless it.

8. On no account allow them to do at one time what you have forbidden under the same circumstances at another.

9. Teach them early to speak the truth on *all occasions.*

10. Be very careful what company your children keep.

11. Make your children useful as soon as they are able, and find employment for them as far as possible.

12. Teach your children not to waste any thing; to be clean and tidy; to sit down quietly and in good order to their meals; to take care of and mend their clothes, to have "a place for every thing, and every thing in its place." (I Cor. XIV, 40. John VI, 12.)

13. Never suffer yourself to be amused by an immodest action; nor, by a smile, encourage those seeds of evil which, unless destroyed, will bring forth the fruits of vice and misery.

14. Encourage your children to do well; show them that you are pleased when they do well.

15. Teach your children to pray, by praying with and for them yourself. Maintain the worship of God in your family, if you desire his blessing to descend on you and yours.

16. Impress upon their minds that eternity is before them, and that those only are truly wise who secure eternal blessings.

17. Above all, *let parents be themselves what they would wish their children to be."*

Maxim illustration, nineteenth century. *Author's collection.*

Emil De Schweinitz of Salem with his toy train, c. 1868. *OSHPC*.

Anna Paulina De Schweinitz of Salem with her doll in carriage, c. 1868. *OSHPC*.

"Marie Agnes von Zinzendorf" (1735-84) by Johann Valentine Haidt. *Courtesy of the Moravian Archives, Herrnhut, Germany.*

a recognizably American community emerged with the family unit as the focus. This movement away from communal organization was driven by gradual assimilation of southern Moravians into American society. And not only was the family receiving closer attention in Moravian communities in Wachovia, it was becoming more important in American homes in general. For both groups, the individual pockets of culture of eighteenth-century, backcountry America had often formed insulated units. By the later nineteenth century, for better or for worse, the American cultural "tossed salad" was beginning to be stirred into a "melting pot."[12] For the Salem Moravians, assimilation into American society had been occurring in increments since the town's beginnings, but officially took place in 1857 when Salem ceased to exist as a closed church community or theocracy, less than a century from its founding.[13]

As the nineteenth century progressed, the Moravians in Salem and their fellow Americans increasingly made a niche for family, friends, and charges to gather around the figurative hearth for bonding, fellowship, and conversation. Painful memories of the Civil War increased ties to home. "Let the fires of home religion be kindled anew," pled *The Moravian* of 1868.[14] The editor of *The Moravian* remarked in 1870, "Christmas is emphatically a home-festival."[15] "Home, sweet home" was becoming an American goal, although it poignantly had not always been so in the American reality. A Civil War soldier had written in 1863 in "The Children's Column" of *The Moravian* in Bethlehem to express his "New-Year's greeting from the army." He described his life as a soldier in realistic terms: the tent-covered "pine twigs" and "corn-blades" makeshift bed dug into a trench, and the "cracker-box" table on which he was writing. A positive touch was a "nice fire," so life was not totally unbearable, although he stated, "'Home, Sweet Home' is far preferable."[16] Religion was an integral and influential part of a large segment of eighteenth- and nineteenth-century life in America, especially as the country became more settled and traveled, industrialized, urban, and materially endowed. Many people were moving from rural farms to take jobs in factories in the cities. The middle class was expanding and becoming more educated and refined as it purchased cheaper and more affordable manufactured goods, thereby increasing its comforts and leisure. As some mothers had fewer children, and health care and improved sanitation helped those offspring to live longer, a heightened interest in the family emerged. The broader dissemination of printed materials in the form of books, periodicals, and newspapers increasingly served to inform and enlighten people on many topics. The results of the Industrial Revolution were more and more apparent in the various Moravian communities. The trades town of Salem found it harder to sell its more expensive handmade goods, and so mills and factories began to be established and manufactured goods were brought in from outside, thus contributing to the demise of the little church town as a closed community.

One national social trend that occurred was that children gradually began to receive more attention and status within the family from what had been a more repressed condition. Young mothers did not necessarily know how to cope with children in this new role, and so magazine and book writers dispensed needed advice not only in straightforward treatises, but in the guise of "domestic fiction," "woman's fiction," or "sentimental fic-

Home Sweet Home die cut decoration, Germany. *Author's collection.*

tion."[17] Such writers as Mrs. Lydia Maria Child, Marion Harland, and the Beecher sisters wrote manuals with compilations of recipes and remedies as well as advice on housekeeping, domestic economy, and raising children.[18] The Beecher sisters "affectionately inscribed" *The American Woman's Home* in 1869 to "The Women of America in whose hands rest the real destinies of the republic, as moulded by the early training and preserved amid the maturer influences of home."[19] Such books were immensely popular and sometimes went through as many as a dozen printings.

In 1856, in the first volume of the newly started paper *The Moravian*, "Mr. Moravian," the children's editor, highlighted the pleasures of winter, Christmas, and the comforts of home in the following passage: "Apples and grapes, and chestnuts, and hickory nuts, and Christmas and new-

year's gifts, and snow and ice, and sleds and skates, and warm firesides and home comforts rise up before you at the sound of their names."[20] A number of years later in a story in the same publication entitled "The Christmas Blessing," home was given its important place. "Christmas is preeminently also a family, as well as a Church, festival...celebrated in the domestic circle as in the Church with particular reference to the children... ."[21]

The loving scene described by Mr. Moravian did not always embrace America's early children, however. For them, life was sometimes a litany of "dos and don'ts" with their infrequent appearances at adult functions strictly controlled and regulated by the idea that children were often neither to be seen nor heard. Consider the 1805 edition (originally appearing in 1783) of a popular and widely used textbook for American students,

Adam and Eve Charger

This delftware charger "Adam and Eve" was made in Bristol, England, about 1650-1690 by an unknown potter. Polychromed dishes like this were more decorative and meant to be hung on the wall or prominently displayed as a sign of some affluence. The subject here is the fall of Man and includes an apple tree entwined by a serpent to represent evil. This motif was in part popular because of the publication in 1667 of John Milton's poetic immortalization "Paradise Lost." It also has a Christmas significance coming from the Christian medieval church "mystery" or "miracle" plays, popular in the fourteenth and fifteenth centuries, in which stories of the Bible were depicted with props to visually teach the mostly illiterate parishioners. Even after the plays were no longer performed sometime in the fifteenth century, people remembered the depiction of the "Paradise" tree representing immortality and the Tree of Life and Adam's fall, all as associations of Christmas. On the early saints calendar Adam and Eve Day was on December 24. It was, therefore, only natural to erect a tree decorated with apples for this significant event.

Noah Webster's *The American Spelling Book.* Some of the rules of behavior for children were outlined:

Be a good child; mind your book; love your school; and strive to learn. Tell no tales; call no ill names; you must not lie, nor swear, nor cheat, nor steal. Play not with bad boys; use no ill words at play; spend your time well; live in peace and shun all strife. This is the way to make good men love you, and save your soul from pain and woe... . As for those boys and girls that mind not their books, and love not the church and school, but play with such as tell tales, tell lies, curse, swear and steal, they will come to some bad end, and must be whipt till they mend their ways.[22]

An earlier edition of Webster's book was in use in Salem in May of 1791 when President George Washington visited the classroom of Samuel Kramsch where a reading session was in progress.[23] During this period Anna Rosina Gambold, at the remote Spring-place, Georgia, Cherokee Mission established by the Moravians, had thirty-eight books, which included Noah Webster's *The American Spelling Book.*[24]

Webster's occasionally laborious book nevertheless was considered a welcome respite from the even heavier scholastic materials formerly employed, with the exception of Comenius's writings. Books solely for the pleasure of children had only become available in the second half of the eighteenth century, and many of these "wagged their fingers in print" against anything "playful and imaginative," as the child had to be early converted to save him from a quick and unexpected death with the eternal accompanying damnation.[25]

Up until such books as Webster's, the catechism and hornbooks for learning the alphabet were considered the basics for the few children who were privileged to learn to read and write. Then chapbooks, religious and otherwise, often sold by peddlers and containing all kinds of stories, became very appealing and, thus, popular. Moral instruction was being encouraged by the Second Great Awakening, which swept through the country from 1795 to 1836 and hence promoted upright, enlightened living. The Sunday School movement, having started in England in the 1770s for underprivileged children, began in 1816 in Wachovia. It fostered memorization of Bible verses, as well as some general education.[26] Salem children, of course, already received both, so a local Sunday School for them was not begun until 1849.[27] The Sunday School Union and the American Tract Society both issued moralistic tracts, and churches sponsored men called colporteurs (an effort in which the Moravians participated), who traveled the countryside, passing out tracts, Bibles, and the dispensation of religion by word of mouth in order to reach each and every uninformed soul, including children.

An image of a family Christmas, early-nineteenth century, from an American Tract Society publication. *Author's collection.*

Long before the advent of Sunday Schools, however, Moravian children at Christmas had been given pretty colored or illuminated Bible verses as part of their gift from the church, along with the aforementioned candles and perhaps a tasty treat, like a ginger cake. They were encouraged to take the verses home and memorize them. When African Americans in Salem obtained their own church, they, too, benefited from some education. On 26 December 1841 at the African American log church, the children recited the Christmas verses they had learned and then received cakes.[28]

The Moravian Church believed that educated people could enhance their lives by reading the word of God directly from the Bible and thus become stronger Christians, so it is not surprising that schools were an early part of the establishment of their towns. As Comenius wrote in *The School of Infancy* about Solomon's wisdom, "A young man duly instructed as to his way, even when old will not depart from it."[29] The Moravians' "heart religion" encouraged a simple, direct, familiar, and joyful communion with God to whom one could always turn in times of need, whatever the age. In knowing God, one knew oneself and grew in that knowledge. This, not doctrine, was the essence of Moravian theology.

Such activities as singing together bound people to each other and to the church. They were used on a national scale by certain influential adults as a way of creating traditions meaningful to families and their children and bringing them not only to each other and the church, but to the larger community as a whole. For the Moravians, music was an essential ingredient in their faith.

Outside the church in the South, revelry associated with the holiday had long been manifested by such activities as shooting matches, fox hunts, cock fights, races, dances, balls, parties, dinners, games, lotteries, noise making, and the inevitable drinking, an issue that eventually led to the temperance movement. Some of these activities were escalating into what could become a population out of control, particularly in the cities. America needed its own solid,

Illustration from *Harper's Weekly*, December 1886. *Author's collection.*

suitable, inspiring celebrations for special occasions, not the drunken, boisterous, unruly, loud, and destructive behavior, which was increasingly becoming a problem, both locally and elsewhere. Social reform was required, and so a renewed interest in religion had developed, ranging from temperance meetings to Bible societies, missionary societies, Sunday Schools, and gospel tract ministries. Some local agnostics, like the outsider (non-Moravian)[30] Dr. George Wilson of Bethania, thought the proliferation of such organizations stifling, but many citizens thought them essential.[31]

The various tract and Sunday School writings, as we have noted, were particularly prolific in advancing the state of morality in children and adults. The earliest so-called Christmas books for children were usually filled with stories about naughty boys and girls who learned valuable lessons to improve and the good children who became better by example.

A poem (right) appeared in 1821 in *The Children's Friend*, a little illustrated volume in which "Santeclaus" arrived on Christmas Eve. It taught a number of lessons and warned of punishment for transgressions: the "birch, logic, and religion"[32] aspects sometimes delineated by well-meaning but autocratic adults.

This poem was only one in what proved to be an increasing abundance of Christmas material. In the 1820s, New Yorkers John Pintard, Washington Irving, and Clement Moore (responding to unseemly public rowdiness as well as the need for American traditions) had begun to lay the groundwork for the new American Christmas, and, in the 1840s, Charles Dickens's redemptive story of Scrooge's

change into a model of charity was very influential.[35] Pintard and Irving concentrated on Nicholas, the Dutch bringer of gifts, and Moore, of course, wrote the now immortal poem "An Account of a Visit from St. Nicholas,"[36] which may have had as one of its sources the poem from *The Children's Friend*, although Moore portrayed the gift-bringer as a genial and non-threatening character.

A Pennsylvania-published Christmas book said to have an enormous impact on the developing Christmas in America, according to that state's Christmas historian Alfred Shoemaker, was *Kriss Kringle's Christmas Tree*, published in 1845 and widely distributed. It validated Kriss Kringle as

Old SANTECLAUS with much delight
His reindeer drives this frosty night,
O'er chimneytops, and tracks of snow,
To bring his yearly gifts to you.

The steady friend of virtuous youth,
The friend of duty, and of truth,
Each Christmas eve he joys to come
Where love and peace have made their home.

Through many houses he has been,
And various beds and stockings seen,
Some, white as snow, and neatly mended,
Others, that seem'd for pigs intended.

Where e'er I found good girls or boys,
That hated quarrels, strife and noise,
I left an apple, or a tart,
Or wooden gun, or painted cart;

To some I gave a pretty doll.
To some a peg-top, or a ball;
No crackers, cannons, squibs, or rockets,[33]
To blow their eyes up, or their pockets.

No drums to stun their Mother's ear,
Nor swords to make their sisters fear;
But pretty books to store their mind.
With Knowledge of each various kind.

But where I found the children naughty,
In manners rude, in temper haughty,
Thankless to parents, liars, swearers,
Boxers, or cheats, or base tale-bearers,

I left a long, black, birchen rod,
Such, as the dread command of God
Directs a Parent's hand to use
When virtue's path his sons refuse.[34]

one of the gift bringers, including the names of Santa Claus and St. Nicholas, and even the antecedent of Kriss Kringle, *Christ-Kindlein* (the Christ Child who brought presents to Protestant children in Germany and in America).[37] This little book had on the cover the picture of an elfin gift-bringer in the act of placing toys on a small tabletop Christmas tree, thus introducing many American children who saw the book to some of the symbols associated with the secular Christmas.

One entry in the Kriss Kringle book is a poem called "The Christmas Gift" in which a boy is offered by a charitable lady his choice of one item from an array of "baubles and toys."[38] He is greatly attracted by a toy white horse, a warrior's accoutrements, and some books, but ultimately settles on a Bible, which he knows his mother loves most and that he can share with his siblings. Along with the obvious lesson of choosing the Bible over temporal objects, this story represents the charitable giving to underlings and the less privileged that became so prevalent as a theme in literature and in life of the nineteenth century. Chapter Three will explore some of the Moravian instances of youthful giving.

Emphasizing the good will towards children long expressed by the Moravian Church, Mr. Moravian wrote affectionately to his young readers on Christmas Day, 1857: "We haven't forgotten the delight with which we used to look forward to Christmas Eve and morning; and whilst the feeling has become deepened and hallowed, it is as joyous as ever.... It does us good to see your smiles, and to hear your merry, ringing laughter. It wakes up the memory of early days, when we used to run to our stockings, and tables, and Christmas trees, to see whether

Mr. Santa Claus had remembered us or not. He was sure to do it. Candies, cakes, nuts, fruits, wax-candles, books and gifts of all sorts for juveniles were there; and though we don't care quite as much for some of these things now, as we did then, we are glad to see you enjoy them, and are happy if you are happy."[39] In the middle of the Civil War in 1863, Mr. Moravian again reiterated, "It is a season rightly devoted to childish joy. Blessed are the children who are spending a happy Christmas... [as] they sported around the Christmas-tree... . The holiest asso-ciations of childhood cluster around this Christmas festival and influences proceed from it which are never lost."[40]

The development of the American Christmas is epito-mized by what many such writers as Mr. Moravian were promoting. One of them said it thusly:

Never deny the babies their Christmas! It is the shining seal set upon a year of happiness. If the preparations for it—the delicious mystery with which these are invested; the solemn parade of clean, whole stockings in the chim-ney corner; or the tree, decked in secret, to be revealed in glad pomp upon the festal day-if these and many other features of the anniver-sary are tedious or contemptible in your sight, you are an object of pity; but do not defraud your children of joys which are their right, merely because you have never tasted them. Let them believe in Santa Claus, or St. Nicholas, or Kriss Kringle, or whatever the name the jolly Dutch saint bears in your region. Some latter-day zealots, more puritanical than wise, have felt themselves called upon, in schools, and before other juvenile audiences, to deny the claims of the patron of merry Christmas to popular love and gratitude. Theirs is a thankless office; both parents and children feeling themselves to be aggrieved by the gratuitous disclosure, and this is as it should be. If it be wicked to encourage such a delusion in infant minds, it must be a transgression that leans very far indeed to virtue's side.

All honor and love to dear old Santa Claus! May his stay in our land be long, and his pack grow every year more plethoric! And when, throughout the broad earth, he shall find, on Christmas night, an entrance into every home, and every heart throbbing with joyful gratitude at the return of the blessed day that gave the Christ-child to a sinful world, the reign of the Prince of Peace shall have begun below; everywhere there shall be rendered, 'Glory to God in the highest,' and 'Good-will to men' shall be the universal law—we shall all have become as little children.[41]

This thought brings us back to the Moravian bishop Comenius's statement "The Lord himself declares 'Except ye be converted, and become as little children, ye shall not enter into the kingdom of heaven.' Since God thus wills that children be our precep-tors, we owe them the most diligent attention."[42] In addi-

Cover of *Kriss Kringle's Christmas Tree*, 1846. *Author's collection.*

tion, Comenius made another statement which the Moravians may well have taken to heart in regard to Christmas: "Parents ought to be especially careful never to allow their children to be without delights," for "the joy of the heart is the very lifespring of man."[43]

As a result of this recognition of children there was the development of a new kind of Christmas, one which centered on the family, the home, and the gifts that began to be offered as tokens of friendship and love. If happiness did not reign supreme at the hearth, which was the symbol of family bonding and togetherness, mothers were told how to achieve domestic bliss through the aforementioned religious tracts, advice books, magazines, and other publications. As the nineteenth

century progressed and as fewer fathers worked at home, the mother found herself as one of the cornerstones of family life, who came to be largely responsible for the religion, culture, behavior and manners, education, clothing, food, household furnishings, and management of her children. In essence, in the burgeoning middle class she was the managing partner, as her spouse was the financial partner.[44] Expansion of education in childhood would ultimately allow adults to be better equipped to act responsibly, a desirable goal in this growing republic. Carefully molding children with positive religious principles would assure success in our democracy. Just such a foundation was exemplified in a familiar classic of the period, *Little Women* by Louisa May Alcott, written in 1868 and set in New

England during the Civil War. On Christmas, the four sisters were asked by their mother to give up their presents in recognition of the war and to take their holiday breakfast to a poor family, a type of charitable offering, which became increasingly popular in the new society. They did, in fact, each receive a gift of a small Bible tucked under their pillows, the colored covers carefully selected by their mother (beloved "Marmee") to correspond to their tastes, with a few inscribed personal words. The girls gave no gifts to each other but took their bit of money to buy or make some small tokens for their mother, which they planned to put in a basket on the table in the parlor.

Thus melds the sacred and the secular in our path to the modern day Christmas, and we

Engraved illustration from an American Tract Society publication, 1820s. *Author's collection.*

MORAVIAN CHRISTMAS TRADITIONS

Frolicks and Other Christmas Temptations

Succumbing to the exhilaration of hunting and other such temptations was a continual problem in Wachovia through the years. On 21 May 1806, the Elders in Salem recorded, "A public warning shall be given in all our congregations, reminding our Brethren not to go to horse races, musters, shooting matches, or frolics, with notice that failure to observe our rules will not pass unnoticed."[iv] "Frolick" (a period spelling) was a commonly used word during this period. An 1828 dictionary with a provenance from Salem described it as a wild prank, a flight of whim or gayety.[v] Frolicks took place during Christmas, as well as other times, and the mere fact that the Moravians were warning against them meant that they were being held by the outsiders all around. Examples of local frolicks included harvest corn huskings and other such farm-related activities, as well as country weddings, planned during the winter months when more leisure existed. Putting up Christmas decorations at church could even be construed as such an occasion, especially if accomplished by a group of young people of both sexes not properly chaperoned.[vi]

Consequences of participating in a frolick could be momentous for a Moravian. The Bethania Committee reported in 1816, "that the single Anton Hauser here in the village, on the second Christmas Day of the past year, took part in a Negro-frolick in this neighborhood. Hauser was excluded from the community."[vii]

MESDA's Cherry Grove Parlor.

can begin to see why a Charleston woman in 1912 called the holiday the "great domestic festival."[45] Back in Salem in the 1920s, Winifred Kirkland's book *Where the Star Still Shines*, sponsored by the Woman's Auxiliary of Home Moravian Church, invited adults to drop the "crippling pack of maturity and become once again a little child stepping along a Christmas road."[46] As a writer in the *Wachovia Moravian* stated in December 1895, "The Moravians know how to keep Christmos [sic]", but "the simple secret" of such a Christmas is "that the Lord Jesus Christ must have the first place in it."[47] Now, let us, too, step on the path to discover even more of the Christmas roots of the Moravian past, particularly in the South, but also to some extent in America and even Europe. During the journey we will explore some of the most loved and recognized traditions, which bring to us all "the mysterious quickening to life of...[our] buried childhood."[48]

Salem's Home Moravian Church.

Chapter 2

The Christmas Tree and the Pyramid

"a treat for our young ones with a little decorated tree"

— John and Anna Rosina Gambold,
Springplace, Georgia, Moravian Indian Mission, 24 December 1814

Moravian sister Anna Rosina Gambold recorded the first written documentation of the Christmas tree in the South on 21 December 1805, at the Moravian Indian Mission in Springplace, Georgia. She wrote: "Soon after breakfast we drove with our pupils in our cart to the Connasaga River, about 3 miles from here, to fetch a small green tree for Christmas... ." [*grune Baumchen fur Weynachten*].[1] That same year, at the beginning of Advent on December 1, Missionary Gambold remarked that the children had been asking for a long time how many Sundays there would be until Christmas and smilingly rejoiced that the number was dwindling. On Sunday the 8th there was a *Singstunde*, a song service, at the conclusion of the regular service. Then, on the 24th, "a happy lovefeast" was held at which "burning wax candles were distributed" and selected verses were sung. Spruce branches had been strewn on the floor[2] and a wreath hung in the window. Soon after breakfast on Christmas Day the children received small presents and "verses with colorful borders." On the 26th they presented to the Cherokee chief's wife, Mrs. Vann,[3] "a little painted wreath" with a text inside that read, "Unto You is born a Saviour!" During the week after Christmas "many Indians" came to look at the "Christmas decorations."[4]

The next year, again on 21 December, Sister Gambold wrote, "In the afternoon Brother Byhan went with our children on horse to fetch shrubs and little trees for the Christmas decorations. This

was a delight to the children... ."[5] These shrubs would have been part of the frequently erected Moravian *Putz*[6] decoration, which included assorted greenery and the Nativity at Christmas; "the little trees" were probably intended as Christmas trees.

One wonders about the appearance of those early Christmas trees. To enhance our imagination we may consider one of the earliest pictorial depictions of an American Christmas tree created by Lewis Miller (1796-1882). Miller, a German carpenter and chronicler of people and events by his folk drawings in York, Pennsylvania, sketched a picture of Seifert, a blue dyer, with his family, and in the background was a Christmas tree, which appears to be decorated with springerle cookies and fruit, perhaps apples.[7] The date on the drawing is 1809, which would make Miller sixteen years old when he made the picture. However, he was a neighbor of Seifert at that time, and the curator of the collection of the Historical Society in York believes it to be an accurate date, although the possibility exists that Miller may have drawn the picture later, as part of his reminiscing collection of "a looking glass for the mind."[8]

Another source sets the date for the Miller drawing between 1819 and 1821.[9] Regardless of the exact date, it does afford a visual rendering of an early American Christmas tree, such as the Gambolds might have put up at Springplace.

There is a lapse of some years before the mention by Gambold of the next reference to a decorated tree in Georgia, which appeared on 24 December 1814. The translation from the old German script of this document reads as follows: "Soon after the service [which was held in the evening] the party left Brother and Sister Gambold's to go to our Brother's house where Gonstadi had prepared a treat for our young ones with a little decorated tree, [*mit einem gepuzten Baumchen*] and we sang as if with one heart and mouth, 'I will rejoice in God my Saviour!'"[10] Gonstadi was a young boy of about five who had been brought by his father to be educated at the mission. A child of this age would probably have been guided in such a decorating project by his teacher. The "Brother" was probably John Gambold's brother Joseph, and the reason that they went to his house was to keep the tree a complete surprise in order to heighten the drama until the moment of revelation. The dramatic unveiling of Christmas trees was common behavior at that time.

One may well ask why the Gambolds instituted the use of Christmas trees at the Georgia Moravian mission. The Reverend John Gambold (1760-1827) and his wife Anna Rosina Kliest (1762-1821) were the couple in charge of the mission at Springplace beginning in 1805 and were devoted to service in God's kingdom. They had both been part of the Moravian community of Bethlehem, and he maintained close connections as well in Nazareth, Lititz, Salem, and Wachovia. The founders of these communities had ties to Germany where the birth and death of Jesus had long been honored with visual images. The upper Rhineland is thought to be the source of the first European Christmas trees.[11] The Moravians in Bethlehem may have had the first Christmas tree in America. For a synod in 1748 the church minutes described a lovefeast for the children in October, which included what appeared to be a Christmas-like tree. At that church meeting in the Saal (meeting hall and chapel) of the Single Brothers' House there was a green tree from which hung gifts of apples and Bible verses for the boys and girls of the congregation.[12] If such decorations were used for a synod lovefeast in October, then they were undoubtedly used for Christmas as well. The Gambolds were simply following such beloved traditions for festive occasions at Springplace.

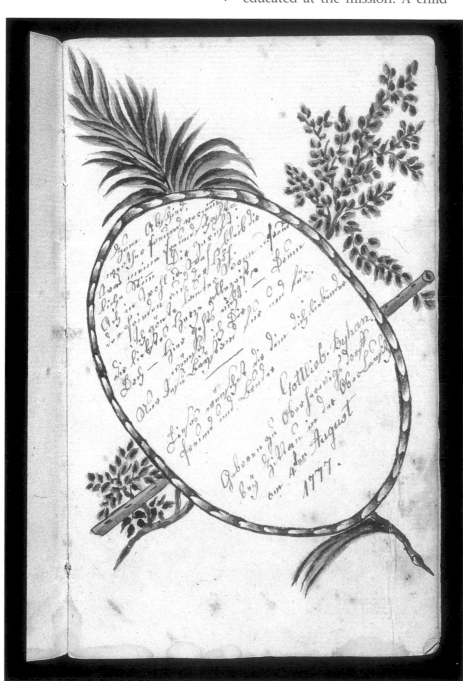

Embellished wreath from Springplace Moravian Indian Mission, 1807-13. *OSMG.*

The Gambolds of Springplace

To better understand the undertaking of the Gambolds at the Springplace Moravian Indian Mission, one may read the comments of distinguished scholar Henry Steinhauer who was head of the Fulneck school in England to train the ministry and was then principal of the Young Ladies' Seminary in Bethlehem. Steinhauer wrote:

The indefatigable exertions of Brother Gambold and his wife are almost beyond credit. Besides providing food, raiment, shelter and fuel for themselves and their scholars, attending to the school daily, acting as advisers and physicians to the whole neighborhood, entertaining every visitor—and they are numerous who draw on their hospitality—writing letters, and on Sundays teaching, admonishing, etc., they find time, even, to oblige their friends in various ways.[i]

Steinhauer went on to marvel at the ability of Sister Gambold to reply to his request for "botanical products" by sending "between twelve and fourteen hundred specimens of dried plants, besides near a hundred packets of seeds, several minerals, specimens of all the Indian manufactures of cane, etc. and a number of other curiosities," with apologies for not having done more.[ii] His opinion was that it represented at least a half year's work "for one person's undivided attention, under the most favorable circumstances. And yet this person, banished as she is from civilized society, cheerfully laboring year after year with scarcely any promise of success, yet undauntedly persevering was the first teacher in the Bethlehem Young Ladies' Seminary, and seemed its main support... ."[iii]

Anna Rosina took her study of natural history seriously and valued her collection. After her death, Reverend J. R. Schmidt wrote to Salem from Springplace to say that "Anna Rosel" (an endearing moniker) had given him her botanical collection, and he intended to apportion it along with some of his own additions to three people: Von Schweiniz (a noted botanist) and Van Vleck in Salem and Huffel in Bethlehem.[iv]

In a similar testimonial, Correa de Serra, Portuguese minister to the United States and a "distinguished naturalist and linguist" himself, spent a day and night in Springplace and wrote in a letter:

Judge of my surprise, in the midst of the wilderness, to find a botanic garden, not indeed like that at Paris, or yours at Kew; but a botanic garden, containing many exotic and medicinal plants, the professor, Mrs. Gambold, describing them by their Linnean[v] *names... . I there saw the*

Embellished wreath from Springplace Moravian Indian Mission, 1807-13. *OSMG.*

sons of a Cherokee Regulus learning their lesson, and reading their New Testament in the morning and drawing and painting in the afternoon, though to be sure, in a very Cherokee style; and assisting Mrs. Gambold in her household work or Mr. Gambold in planting corn.[vi]

John Gambold had written after his wife's death, "We could hardly do without her and a Sister will never be found again who works with such engagement for the salvation of the poor Indians. I love the Indians sincerely. She too."[vii] He was never able to write her *Lebenslauf* (Memoir),[viii] although former pupils like John Ridge wrote from Connecticut to ask about a published testimonial of her life.[ix]

Watercolor of girls and teachers at the Bethlehem Girls' School presenting a program, 1801. *Courtesy of the Moravian Archives, Bethlehem, Pennsylvania.*

Anna Rosina Gambold, a rare person for any era and truly a woman for all seasons, was a gifted teacher who enjoyed using imaginative, inventive tools in her roles as innovative leader, linguist, naturalist, and botanist, so it is not surprising that she would choose the Christmas tree for the pleasure of her students in Georgia. While "principal tutoress" at the girls' boarding school in Bethlehem, Sister Gambold was "willing at all times to vary the monotony of its routine by the offerings of her fertile inventions."[13] She was described as having a "superior facility in oral instruction,"[14] and was "sprightly...in fancy and imagination."[15] Leaving the comforts of Bethlehem for the wilderness, she married late in life, at the age of 43, greatly attracted by the idea of being a missionary to the Cherokees with her new husband.

Sister Gambold brought considerable talent to the mission all year long but most particularly at Christmas. One of her specialities was the creation of little painted flower wreaths into which she printed verses from the Bible, a task in which her husband sometimes assisted. Indeed, they were unique, as Brother Gambold referred once in a letter to the "verses with the Springplace borders."[16] However, the idea of creating small paintings as gifts and tokens of remembrance was not unique to Springplace. Old Salem Museums & Gardens' Paula Locklair wrote that there was "a distinctive body of work...produced in Salem in the eighteenth and nineteenth centuries."[17] Such paintings also existed in Pennsylvania. Did Anna Gambold teach the children to create these little wreath-encircled verses as gifts to their parents and friends? Certainly, drawing and writing were part of a child's education. Henry Steinhauer from Bethlehem remarked once after a visit to

Springplace that he saw the Cherokee boys studying and reading the New Testament in the morning, and "drawing and painting in the afternoon, though to be sure, in a very Cherokee style."[18] That the wreaths were produced with certain identifiable characteristics such as distinctive borders is testified by Anna's husband John in 1813 when he remarked on the gifts to the children of "the Christmas wreaths painted by a well-known hand with verses written on them... ."[19] The little paintings were given as gifts and as reminders of the Savior's love for His children, and they were treasured by the recipients, old and young, who kept them from one year to the next, often bringing them back to the Christmas service and reciting them from memory. As incentive, the wreaths were withheld from those who showed apathy to God's word.[20] Thus, rewards for good behavior helped in producing tangible results.

Christmas at the mission at this time included "a public examination in Bible and Christian Doctrine"[21] and awards, which probably included these

delicate paper treasures. Whether the children executed wreaths or other designs of their own imagination, some were obviously well done, as the Gambolds sent samples of artwork of a boy named Darcheechy to the Superintendent of Indian Trade, in Washington, D.C. in 1817.[22] To their gratification, Superintendent Thomas McKenney responded with a gift to the mission of $100 and to the boy "a box of crayons [pastels] and brushes and a very elegant penknife."[23]

Such wreaths could have been used to decorate the Springplace Christmas trees. This speculation is based on a letter from the Gambolds to Christian Benzien in Salem about a birthday party at the mission on 15 August 1810, where water-colored wreaths were fastened on a white cloth on a wall as part of the festive decoration, along with greens and flowers. The honoree had received the painted wreaths "for her Christmas and birthdays since our being here... ."[24] Although we do not know exactly how the Springplace Christmas trees were decorated, Anna Gambold's mention of flowers as decorations on 25 December 1807 provides another possibility. She wrote that in the children's house they had "made a putz from pine branches and had tied little flowers onto it."[25] As a botanist, Anna had collected hundreds of specimens from the area, so even if nothing was blooming in December she may have had dried specimens. Flowers were often used as Christmas decorations.[26] See Chapter Three for other related references to their use.

The beautifully executed wreaths combined the words of the Gospel with small flowers and apples from God's own hands along with perhaps a few candles to represent Christ as the light of the world—what better decorations could the devout sister have desired for the little trees!

After Anna's death of dropsy of the chest (heart edema) in 1821, the new mission leader, the Reverend J. R. Schmidt, wrote to Salem to reiterate the importance of the little decorated wreaths. He emphasized this pressing matter well ahead of time in anticipation of Christmas that year.

I almost forgot an important request. It is customary here [illegible]...Christmas Eve for the people [illegible]...are distributed. Now dear Anna Rosel, who made the [wreaths] is not here any more. Perhaps our dear Brother Van Vleck would be so good as to make a request for us in the boarding school. Perhaps the pupils will feel moved and make us about 150 wreaths for here and Oochgelogee [a nearby newly created mission where widower John Gambold had moved]. The Savior will bless them for this, and it brings great joy to our dear ones here.[27]

There is a possibility that a Christmas tree existed in Salem as early as 1786, nineteen years before Anna Rosina Gambold erected the Springplace Mission Christmas tree. A brotherly dispute reported in the church records in Salem on 27 December 1786, reads: "Br. Schnepff complained that last Sunday, during preaching, John Tesch, the apprentice of Charles Holder, cut a small pine tree in his field which he [Schnepff] had been taking special care of. John Tesch shall be asked whether he was told to cut this particular tree, for Holder has said he had sent for one from the woods."[28] This complaint was registered on a Wednesday, two days after Christmas, and referred to an incident taking place on Sunday (Christmas Eve), which was when Christmas trees were generally put up at that time. Dr. Adelaide Fries, editor of the Moravian *Records* and a church archivist who translated more material from Wachovia church records than any other person, append-

ed a footnote to this quote, stating that the cutting of a tree on Christmas Eve produced the assumption that it was a Christmas tree, and therefore "the first mentioned in the Salem records."[29] The statement is hard to dispute, because with all the trees available at the time, it is peculiarly relevant that this one was of such great importance to these two men on that particular day, unless they both recognized it as a perfect specimen for a Christmas tree. Unfortunately, nowhere does anyone refer to the tree specifically as a Christmas tree.

Strongly related to Christmas trees were conical-shaped decorations known as pyramids. Some scholars have cited pyramids erected on 25 December 1747 and 1748, by the Bethlehem, Pennsylvania, Moravians as the "first Christmas trees" in America.[30] However, those pyra-

mids were not actual trees, but triangular structures probably created with sticks of wood and greenery. Nevertheless, their appearance was quite similar to a Christmas tree. A more detailed discussion of the pyramid is given later in this chapter.

In contrast to the Moravian pyramid citations by some scholars and the circumstantial evidence for southern Christmas trees already presented, noted Christmas historian Alfred Shoemaker established the date of 1821 in Pennsylvania as the earliest mention of a Christmas tree in this country. His reference is from the diary of Lancaster resident Matthew Zahm, who recorded that on 20 December three young people were "out for Christmas trees" on a nearby hill.[31]

Although apparently unaware of the Springplace references, Shoemaker did, nevertheless, acknowledge that there had

been "no greater celebrators of Christmas...than the Moravians" in Pennsylvania...who "were among the very first to put up Christmas trees."[32] He cited an article of 1855 in an Easton newspaper in which "the inhabitants of Bethlehem...are chiefly noted for their great taste they display in arranging Christmas trees."[33] His validation continued with the statement that "The Moravians made more of Christmas than any other religious denomination in this country—from colonial times on."[34] It is important to reiterate that Anna Rosina Gambold, who put up the first Christmas tree in Springplace, Georgia, in 1805, came out of the Bethlehem environment.

Undoubtedly, trees were in some Salem homes as early as they were in Bethlehem. However, to date, the following is the earliest written specific domestic

"Christmas Eve" by John Lewis Krimmel, 1812-13. *Courtesy of The Winterthur Library: Joseph Downs Collection of Manuscripts and Printed Ephemera.*

"Christmas Tree, 1809," from the Journal of Lewis Miller, vol. I, p. 16. *Collection of the York County Heritage Trust, York, PA.*

reference so far found to a Christmas tree in Wachovia. In Salem in 1861, Caroline "Carrie" Fries noted in her diary on 24 December: "We fitted the tree tonight."[35] The next day Carrie wrote: "Loula [her two-year-old sister Louise Sarah] went down stairs for the first time to see the tree...Mother and I went to the Christmas dialogue and were quite well pleased."[36] This is a very matter-of-fact reference alluding to what appears to be a commonplace custom in Salem by 1861, which is as one would expect, given the close connection to Pennsylvania where trees were widely used in the 1840s.

Caroline noted on 24 December 1862: "Mary John and I went to church, and afterwards we filled the tree."[37] The choice of the word "filling" the tree indicates placement of the gifts on the tree in the German manner. "Filling" is synonymous with other commonly used period terms of "dressing," "fitting," or "fixing" the tree.[38]

Another lengthy reference to a Christmas tree in the Fries family was in 1864 in a letter from Mary Fries Patterson at Palmyra Plantation on the Yadkin River to her sister Carrie in Salem.

We moved the little bed away from the window, in Mother's room, & put the tree in its place... . A large white pine stands in front of the window, which tips over at the ceiling 'in German style' & extends to the bureaus on either side.—At its base is a large hill with a spring & pond & covered with most beautiful mountain moss... . You know I gave out no presents when I came up, but hung them all on the tree. It is quite loaded for wartimes & looks very pretty.[39]

The implication here appears to be that before "wartimes" the tree was decorated more extravagently. As to the "tipping over at the ceiling," there is a colored ink drawing of Zinzendorf's coffin in the salon of the Herrnhut manor house in 1760 in which two evergreen trees droop gracefully from the top to form almost an arch as the background.[40] The landscape "decoration" at the base of the Patterson tree is the *Putz*, so frequently mentioned in Moravian descriptions of Christmas and one that usually includes the Nativity. In an article on "Moravian Customs," written in 1936 by Adelaide Fries,[41] she noted that the *Putz*, sometimes called "a Christmas garden," was arranged around the bottom or beside the Christmas tree in Moravian homes, thus uniting two binding symbols of the holy day. This concept of a "garden" may explain the frequent placement of a fence around the tree, as depicted in John Lewis Krimmel's drawings and elsewhere.[42]

Other historians have recognized the lavishness of German settlers in "providing Christmas trees for the amusement of the young folks."[43] In so doing, the celebration gradually moved from public to private and by the mid-nineteenth century focused on the children in the home as the primary theme within the family.[44]

European Roots of the Christmas Tree

The European roots of the Christmas tree are not easy to identify, but most certainly the trails lead to the Germans. Folk legends intermingle with the facts, and there are many conflicting speculations. An eighth-century legend of the Christmas tree's origins concerns St. Boniface, who was an English missionary to the Germans. The story, which in different sources varies in the details, tells of his coming upon a group of pagans ready to make a human sacrifice in front of an oak tree. He struck the huge tree with such force that it fell with one blow, impressing and instantly converting the pagans to Christianity. Then pointing to a small evergreen fir tree, the saint suggested it as a fitting symbol of their new faith.[45]

According to another source the use of fir trees supposedly helped make the custom more acceptable for Christianity. The story is set in the Garden of Eden when Eve bit into the apple, at which time the leaves of Christmas trees became sharp needles and the fruit hard cones. On the night of Christ's birth, however, fir trees bloomed and produced fruit and flowers together—clearly a miraculous event.[46]

In the tenth century other stories were told of trees miraculously blooming at Christmas. One was the Glastonbury hawthorn, which was said to have been brought to England in the first century by Joseph of Arimathea.[47]

The custom of cutting branches of flower- and fruit-bearing trees to bring indoors and force into bloom for Christmas became widespread in Europe by the late Middle Ages. Some people brought into the house cherry tree branches on St. Barbara's Day (4 December) to force blooms by Christmas. These were then sometimes decorated. The cherry thus connected to this saint's day is still one of the folk symbols used to decorate springerle cookies.[48] These anise-flavored cakes were impressed with motifs from a mold or a carved rolling pin and then enhanced with colored icings. They made excellent Christmas tree decorations. The reader will find further mention of cookies in Chapter Five.

A related German legend about the Christmas tree was that of a poor, ill-clothed child

Rolling pin for springerle cookies by John Vogler, nineteenth century. *OSMG.*

appearing at the door of a wood-cutter and his wife to ask for help one bone-chilling night. The next morning their little guest revealed himself as the Christ child and presented them with a twig from a fir tree to plant and blossom yearly thereafter. To their amazement it took root and grew into a splendid fir tree adorned with gold and silver apples and nuts. Each year thereafter it miraculously bloomed at Christmas.[49]

A mid-nineteenth-century legend, particularly popular with Lutherans, concerned Martin Luther. This story was fostered by a fictional painting depicting the Luther family with a Christmas tree in the sixteenth century. Luther was said to have been walking out under the stars on Christmas Eve when he had the idea of affixing candles to a little fir tree that he brought into the parlor to provide a symbol to his children of Christ as the light of the world.[50]

The most plausible explanation of the origin of the early Christmas tree dates from the late Middle Ages (fourteenth and fifteenth centuries) when the Catholic Church used enactments called miracle plays or "Moralities" to teach the mostly illiterate parishioners certain Bible stories.[51] A popular scene depicted the Garden of Eden in which a fir tree hung with apples as a symbol of human sin was used to present the story of Adam and Eve driven from paradise, but always with the promise of redemption at the end. On the Church calendar, 24 December was the special saints' day for Adam and Eve. Thus, long after the plays ceased to be performed, the symbolism of the paradise tree and eternal life remained in the minds of certain people at this time of year, and they began to erect similar trees in their homes. As late as the nineteenth century in some sections of Germany "figures

of Adam and Eve and the serpent" were sometimes placed under the "Tree of Life," or *Christbaum* (Christ Tree), as it often came to be called.[52]

An ancient Celtic custom of tree worship manifested in the custom of maypoles as the forerunner of a Christmas "May Pole," was used particularly by Germans from the Palatinate and Alsace. Many American Moravians came from the Palatinate. This Christmas maypole evolved into a limb set in a tub and decorated with such items as apples, wafers, honey cakes, and perhaps marzipan or other sugary treats.[53]

Many scholars believe that the lavish use of greenery by the Romans in the celebrations of Saturnalia, Kalends, and such rites as the winter solstice at the end of the year established a precedent for the Christmas tree. Greenery represented eternal life and the promise of rebirth in the midst of a seemingly endless, cold, and lifeless season. Thus, magical properties were attributed to the greens, and they also helped to dispel the gloom of winter when days were short and sunshine minimal. Branches and then trees were hung upside down from the ceiling beams. This centuries-old folk custom of hang-

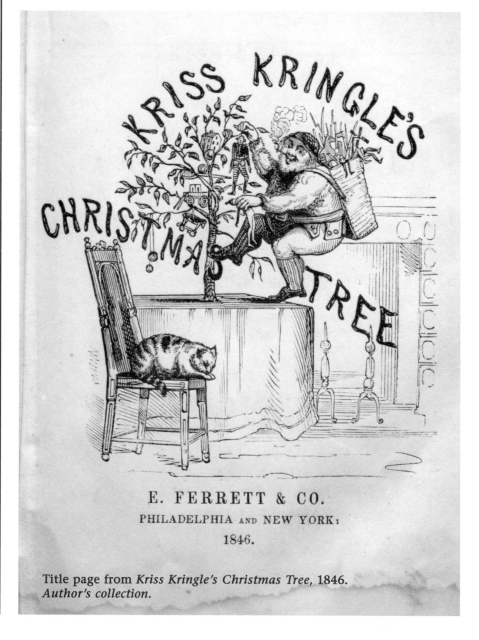

Title page from *Kriss Kringle's Christmas Tree*, 1846. *Author's collection.*

THE CHRISTMAS TREE AND THE PYRAMID

ing decorated trees upside down continued in Germany into the nineteenth century.

Christmas scholars do not agree on what is the first documented reference to a Christmas tree. Phillip Snyder notes that the earliest historical references to Christmas trees appeared in Latvia and Estonia where in two different towns, one in 1510 and the other in 1514, it was recorded "on Christmas Eve, after a festive dinner, black-hatted...merchants carried an evergreen tree decorated with artificial roses to the marketplace" where they danced around it and then set fire to it.[54] Whether this scene describes a pagan rite or a celebration with the revered tree burned as a sign of respect, we will never know.

Whatever its exact origin, the tree is widely accepted as a German-developed tradition. In 1531 in Alsace, Christmas trees were purchased at the market in Strasbourg to be set up in homes undecorated. Curiously, in the same area in 1561, an ordinance was passed that no individual "shall have for Christmas more than one bush of more than eight shoe lengths."[55] Whether this was to encourage conservation or limit iconic representations for the solemn holy day is unknown.

There is a citation of a decorated tree (*Dattelbaumchen*) in a guild hall in Protestant Germany in 1570. The custom may have spread and become popular from such municipal celebrations. The decorations on that tree consisted of dates (*datteln*), apples, pretzels, nuts, and paper flowers. The tree was shaken by children on Christmas Day or Twelfth Night in order to obtain the goodies.[56] Twelfth Night, also called Epiphany, celebrated the coming of the Magi to Bethlehem.

An English visitor to Strasbourg in 1605 spoke of "fir trees set up and hung with paper roses of many different colors and with apples, flat wafers, gilded candies, and sugar."[57] The flat wafers were related to the communion host, a symbol of the body of Christ, and so a wafer-decorated tree was termed a *Christbaum,* or Christ Tree. A tree with edible ornaments, such as cookies and candies, was sometimes also called a "sugartree."[58] The rose was a symbol of beauty and love and in Christian art represented the Virgin Mary.[59] Gilded decorations, including fruit, nuts, cakes, and even on one occasion potatoes, were popular for centuries.[60]

As Christianity replaced pagan religions, people, especially in northern Europe, continued to use evergreens for special occasions, although the Catholic

Twentieth-century Thanksgiving postcard. *Author's collection.*

Church in particular sought to discourage this carryover practice before finally embracing it by reinterpreting it as a Christian custom. Eventually the tree, so ensconced in German culture, became transformed into a Christian symbol, but not with the approval of everyone. In about the middle of the seventeenth century, a Strasbourg theologian spoke of "the Christmas- or fir-tree, which people set up in their houses, hang with dolls and sweets, and afterwards shake and deflower." He did not approve and thought they were "far better...to point the children to the spiritual cedar-tree, Jesus Christ."[61]

At about the same time the English Puritans who came to America did not approve of Christmas pageantry either. They were reacting to the carnival-like atmosphere of sometimes sinful and lewd behavior, a significant degeneracy that had developed at Christmas in England, which was represented by the verse, "Let's dance and sing, and make good chear, For Christmas comes but once a year."[62] An English almanac publication called *Poor Robin* in 1702 wrote of the change there in Christmas celebrations during the Reformation, which ultimately limited the festivities and decorations in New England for a longer period than in the rest of the country.

Although Prince Albert, the German husband of Queen Victoria, is credited with bringing the Christmas tree to England and making it fashionable, a member of the court recalled a tree in 1800 in the lodge of Queen Charlotte, who was also German.[64] He wrote, "In the middle of the room stood an immense tub with a yew tree placed in it, from the branches of which hung bunches of sweetmeats, almonds, and raisins in papers, fruits, and toys, most tastefully arranged, and the whole illuminated by small wax candles."[65]

But now landlords and tenants too
In making feasts are very slow;
One in an age, or near so far,
Or one perhaps each blazing star;
The cook now and the butler too,
Have little or nothing for to do;
And fiddlers who used to get scraps,
Now cannot fill their hungry chaps;
Yet some true English blood
*   still lives,*
Who gifts to the poor at
*   Christmas gives,*
And to their neighbors make a feast,
I wish their number were increast,
And that their stock may never
*   decay,*
Christmas may come again in play,
And poor man keep it holyday.[63]

Prince Albert's trees were decorated with small containers of expensive sweets of all kinds, including gilded gingerbread and sugared fruits. In 1848 an engraving appeared in the *Illustrated London News* of the royal family around the tree. Two years later the same engraving, but without the royal trappings, appeared in America in *Godey's Lady's Book*. Its influence was unmistakable. Sarah Josepha Hale, the publication's energetic editor, had long campaigned for the recognition of Thanksgiving as a national holiday, and a Christmas holiday was another of her top priorities for American families. Using her influence she published stories on the Christmas tree in 1853, 1855, and 1860.[66] In the latter, for the first time in print, "a floor tree in a domestic setting" appeared.[67]

The redemptive story of Scrooge and Tiny Tim in *A Christmas Carol* (1843), created by the popular English writer Charles Dickens, had a profound effect on the development of Christmas. Some years later in 1850, Dickens described a laden tree, which he called a "pretty German toy," for a magazine article:

I have been looking on, this evening, at a merry company of children assembled round that pretty German toy, a Christmas tree. The tree was planted in the middle of a great round table, and towered high above their heads. It was brilliantly lighted by a multitude of little tapers; and everywhere sparkled and glittered with bright objects. There were rosy-cheeked dolls, hiding behind green leaves; and there were real watches (with movable hands, at least, and an endless capacity of being wound up) dangling from innumerable twigs; there were French polished tables, chairs, bedsteads, wardrobes, eight-day clocks and various other articles of domestic furniture (wonderfully made in tin) perched among the boughs, as if in preparation for some fairy housekeeping; there were jolly, broad- faced little men, much more agreeable in appearance than many real men—and no wonder, for their heads took off, and showed them to be full of sugarplums; there were fiddles and drums; there were tambourines, books, work boxes, paint boxes; there were trinkets for the elder girls, far brighter than any grown-up gold and jewels; there were baskets and pin cushions in all devices; there were guns, swords and banners; there were witches standing in enchanted rings of pasteboard, to tell fortunes; there were teetotums [a child's toy similar to a top but spun by the fingers instead of string], humming tops, needle cases, pen wipers, smelling bottles, conversation cards, bouquet holders, real fruit, made artificially dazzling with gold leaf; imitation apples, pears, walnuts, crammed with surprises; in short...everything, and more.[68]

Although Dickens's stories attracted much attention to the spirit of Christmas and to the Christmas tree, the Moravians, as we have already observed, made use of Christmas symbolism much earlier. Former Salem schoolteacher Peter Wolle, living in Lititz, Pennsylvania in 1828, wrote: "Our little Christmas tree

Cover of *The Christmas Tree* by Hans Christian Andersen, nineteenth century. *Author's collection.*

The Christmas Tree In Early America

The novelty of a "famous Christmas tree"[70] attracted attention, as Peter Wolle observed, and some enterprising people began to exhibit one to raise money for charity. One such group was the Dorcas Society of York, Pennsylvania, in 1830. This association of charity-minded women, also organized later in Salem, may have displayed the first public tree in this country. The profits from the sale of a ticket for six and 1/4 cents would provide clothing for "the poor widow and the friendless orphan."[71] Similarly, later in Salem in 1885, the Reverend Edward Rondthaler made an observation on "...the poor children's Christmas tree, for which as an experiment very poor children were gathered from far and near."[72]

Christmas scholar, Dr. Alfred Shoemaker, portrayed Pennsylvania as richly decorated with trees by the 1840s:

In the 1840s the Christmas tree began to become more or less commonplace. Literary pieces, alluding to the custom of putting up trees at Christmas, began to appear with some regularity each returning Christmas season. The very popular, and widely advertised children's book, Kriss Kringle's Christmas Tree, *published in 1845 in Philadelphia, brought a pictorial representation and knowledge of the Christ-*

mas tree and Kriss Kringle to children all over the nation. Trees started going up everywhere in the state, from Philadelphia to Pittsburgh.[73]

The editor of the *Kriss Kringle* book prefaced the 1846 edition with what is curiously called an "Advertisement," which it certainly was! He wrote:

Fashions change, and of late Christmas Trees are becoming more common than in former times. The practice of hanging up stockings in the chimney corner for Kriss Kringle to fill with toys, pretty books, bon-bons, &c., for good children, and rods for naughty children, is being superseded by that of placing a Christmas tree on the table to await the annual visit of the worthy Santa Klaus. He has, with his usual good nature, accommodated himself to this change in the popular taste; and having desired a literary gentleman to prepare his favourite Christmas present in accordance with this state of things, the following volume is the result of the new arrangement, and all parents, guardians, uncles, aunts, and cousins, who are desirous to conform to the most approved fashion, will take care to hang one, two, or a dozen copies of the book on their Christmas Tree for 1846.[74]

Most people, particularly in rural areas cut their own trees. It is interesting to note for those who did not cut their own, Christmas trees were on sale in Philadelphia markets as early as 1848.[75] In 1851, entrepreneur Mark Carr from the Catskill Mountains brought the first trees to Washington Market in New York City and thus created instant success and the beginning of that city's ongoing holiday tradition.[76]

In Charleston, South Carolina, in 1850, a lighted tree was arranged for Jenny Lind, the famous singer called the "Swedish Nightingale," who toured the country sponsored by P. T. Barnum.[77] Some ladies of the city saw to it that the tree under her window was illuminated on Christmas Eve.[78] One of Jenny Lind's friends was Hans Christian Andersen, a Dane who became known as the father of the modern fairy tale. Five years before Lind was in South Carolina, Andersen had produced a story, translated variously as "The Christmas Tree," or "The Little Fir Tree," which became very popular in the moralistic literature of the times and was included in numerous children's publications, along with another of his poignant Christmas tales, "The Little Match Girl." Andersen's fairy tales often depicted characters who find happiness in life (or at the end of it) only after adversity. In "The Christmas Tree," the little fir tree longs for recognition and fame reaching far beyond its tranquil forest home. Sadly, the moment of glory and adornment for which it had yearned soon passes, and its final humiliation is to be burned to ashes, leaving only the overlooked gold star that crowned its peak on the happiest day of its life.[79]

Along with stories like Andersen's, American newspapers and magazines such as *Harper's Weekly, Godey's Lady's Book, Good Housekeeping, Ladies Home Journal*, and *Peterson's National Ladies Magazine* all helped to spread knowledge of the custom of erecting and decorating a Christmas tree. As a telling example, Mahala Eggleston, a niece of Jefferson Davis who had married James Roach and lived in the Vicksburg, Mississippi, area, wrote in her diary of Christmas in 1851: "The children had such a number of gifts that I made a Christmas tree for them; Mother, Aunt and Liz came down to see it; all said it was something new to them. I never saw one *but learned from some of the German stories I had been reading*" [author's emphasis].[80]

Many other Americans learned from newspaper and magazine articles about important citizens' Christmas celebrations. Former

Although decorations called the Putz *along with green trees had long been used in the Moravians' Springplace Indian Mission, in Bethlehem, and in Wachovia, the official Moravian Records first began to mention Christmas trees at church in Wachovia in the 1870s.*

President Andrew Jackson, who is said to have loved Christmas, had a pine tree frosted and encircled with little flavored ice animals in 1835.[81] In 1856, President Franklin Pierce (1853-57) from New Hampshire had the first Christmas tree set up in the White House.[82] During his presidency, Teddy Roosevelt (1858-1919) banned a tree at the White House for reasons of ecological conservation, but his determined son Archie revealed to the family a little Christmas tree secreted in a closet on one Christmas, thus embarrassing his father and prompting a lecture, but not changing the presidential mind.[83] Woodrow Wilson (1856-1924) was the first president to preside over a "national Christmas tree ceremony" on 24 December 1913, and Calvin Coolidge (1872-1933) initiated the first official lighting of such a tree in 1923.[84] During the Second World War from 1942 to 1945 there were no official trees

in Washington. A "Pageant of Peace" was attached to the ceremony "after the Korean War"[85] and has since then been introduced sometime each year well before the traditional Christmas Eve. In recent years, Old Salem Museum & Gardens has joined in the national celebration by contributing handmade ornaments to be placed on one of the outdoor trees for this pageant.

A Christian newsletter speculates that American culture was so influenced by the Puritans' negativity towards the desecration of the holy day of Christmas that there were only eighteen states that officially recognized Christmas by the 1860s.[86] When that happened, the first states to legally acknowledge the day were southern—Alabama in 1836, followed by Arkansas and Louisiana in 1838. Surprisingly, Pennsylvania waited until 1848, perhaps due to its many Quaker citizens. North Carolina adopted the official holiday in 1881.

It was sometimes at a Sunday School gathering that American children had their first introduction to the Christmas tree. Although Sunday Schools, a nineteenth-century phenomena in America, embraced the Christmas tree, it was not without heated opposition. The earliest schools to adopt the custom in the 1840s and 1850s usually charged admission to the festivals and used the money for supplies. In 1840, a newspaper reported at a German Protestant Church in Rochester, New York, that on Christmas evening the children celebrated "according to the custom of the Old Country"[87] with a religious exercise and an evergreen tree of ten to twelve feet high, "brilliantly illuminated and adorned with a great variety of toys and sweetmeats suspended from the branches."[88] However, in Puritan-influenced New England, as a carry-over from the Reformation, Christmas was still a workday for the common man in

Young people sledding in Salem's God's Acre, c. 1885. *OSHPC*.

1855, and in Boston in 1870 school children were in class on December 25.[89]

Although decorations called the *Putz* along with green trees had long been used in the Moravians' Springplace Indian Mission, in Bethlehem, and in Wachovia, the official Moravian *Records* first began to mention Christmas trees at church in Wachovia in the 1870s. This does not necessarily mean that there were no local Christmas trees earlier. It could be that either certain diarists did not consider such decorations worthy of mention in the records or that perhaps they were so commonplace as to need no mention. In Salem in 1871, there was a Christmas concert given by the Sunday School, and Albert Oerter described the sanctuary: "A large Christmas tree had been erected on the platform, the pulpit

having been removed. It reached up to the keystone of the arch behind the pulpit, and was decorated and hung with numerous ornaments and beautifully illuminated with wax candles."[90] In 1874, the Bethania decoration included "finely proportioned" pine trees decorated "with bright gilt and other coloured paper and illuminated with wax tapers as Christmas trees."[91]

In Salem at the African American Church, St. Philips, a tree was noted on 25 December 1874: "A Christmas tree occupied the platform before the pulpit."[92] Trees were also mentioned in 1872, 1873, 1875, and 1876; on the fourth occasion "it was lit up."[93] On Christmas Day in 1879, "the church had a large [illegible: tree?] which was [illegible: laden?] with gifts for the children."[94]

By the 1870s, many American Sunday Schools had joined the Moravians in celebrating Christmas with gifts and trees as the centerpiece of the event. Mississippian Mahala Roach noted as early as 1860 that her family went "to the Episcopal Church to see the Christmas tree for the Sunday School (both white and black)."[95]

By the late 1800s, descriptions proliferated of trees for the children at Moravian churches. In 1897, in Friedland near Salem at the close of the Sunday School exercises, "the Christmas tree was made bare of its contents."[96] In other years, trees were mentioned in Bethania, at Mt. Bethel, and at Carmel where "a beautiful Christmas tree graced the occasion heavily laden with candies, apples and many other presents which were distributed."[97] In 1898 at Wachovia's

Christ Church for the Sunday School entertainment, volunteers created a vignette of a room in readiness for Christmas. Curtains were drawn from across the platform at the front where was revealed the "interior of an old fashioned room on Christmas night. Over the fireplace hung the filled stockings; near by was a cradle with its sleeping dolls; and in the opposite corner stood a lighted Christmas tree."[98]

The students at the Salem Girls' School were not overlooked at Christmas, as the following description attests:

On Christmas morning we girls, usually so sleepy, needed no second warning to make us quit our comfortable beds, but were up and dressed in a twinkling. We made our way down stairs in the grey dawn of the early morning, to find our rooms resplendent. The Christmas trees, which had been placed in every room, were brilliantly illuminated, and on all of our desks were lighted tapers and curious looking bundles. [99]

By 1885, for those who remained at school, there were sleigh rides while covered with buffalo robes, and "richly filled boxes, Christmas trees, surprises given and received".[100] In 1886, there was a Christmas tree flanked by "two pyramidal transparencies" in the church for the Sunday School cantata.[101] "Most of the dwelling-rooms had trees, and evergreens wreathed around the pictures, nothing more."[102]

A Salem resident spent Christmas Eve of 1936 in Herrnhut, Germany, and described the evening service at the church with "two large fir trees... adorned with lights" flanking the pulpit. Afterwards the minister's family celebrated with "a large tree all alight with candles." They sang Christmas carols, opened their presents, and had refreshments.[103] In Germany the typical pattern was, and to some extent still is, to gather on the night of Christmas Eve for the opening of presents around a candlelit tree.[104]

The Pyramid

Earlier in this chapter the pyramid, described in both 1747 and 1748 in Bethlehem, Pennsylvania, was mentioned as

Salem Girls' School students riding in a sleigh, c. 1894. *OSHPC.*

THE CHRISTMAS TREE AND THE PYRAMID

Four-tiered pyramid from Erzgebirge, Germany, 1910-20. *Collection of the Old Salem Toy Museum (hereafter OSTM).*

a brushwood creation used by the Moravians as a decoration at Christmas and was even called a Christmas tree by some scholars.

A 1747 quote from Bethlehem reports:

For this occasion several small pyramids and one large pyramid of green brushwood had been prepared, all decorated with candles and the large one with apples and pretty verses. On either side were pictures drawn in perspective and, also, illuminated with candles. One represented the angels and their care of the children. The other represented the Child Jesus in the arms of his mother. Close by were to be seen the Bethlehem stable, with the oxen and the asses, as also, the shepherds, to whom, first, the joyous tidings of the Savior's birth had been brought. Below all of this the word Children!" [105]

In a similar vein, it was recorded in the Bethlehem Diary on 25 December 1748:

Quite early, the little children enjoyed a delightful festal occasion. Their brethren had decorated various pyramids with candles, apples, and hymn stanzas and, also, drawn a picture in which the children were represented as presenting their Ave to the Christ-child all of which Brother Johannes [von Watteville] explained to them in a child-like manner, so that the love-feast conducted for them at the same time had a very blessed effect upon them as well as upon all the brethren and sisters present. [106]

The candles as ornaments are thought by some to be the most important element of the pyramid, and one German name for it is the *Lichtstock*, or light stick. Traditionally the nativity was placed on the broadest shelf along with other adornments such as apples, gingerbread cakes, greenery, and illuminated Bible verses. If the decoration was in the church, the items on it would later be distributed to the children in the congregation. By the seventeenth century, the pyramid was a popular tradition at Christmas in Germany. Sometimes it was garnished and suspended from the ceiling. [107]

Although not a Christmas reference, the following quote contributes to the lavishness of celebratory Moravian decorations. In an eighteenth-century description of a use of a pyramid by the Moravians in Germany for the consecration of the dormitory of the Brethrens' House in Herrnhut on 31 October 1745 included what was remarked as "an incomparable sight," as the entire house "resembled a sea of flames from top to bottom. Pyramids and individual candles turned... . These lights and the illumination of the other two Brethrens' Houses were probably the most beautiful thing we have had in Herrnhut... ." [108]

A variation of the pyramid held a propeller at the top, which by heat of the lighted candles turned the revolving shelves on an axis. This type is still made today, sometimes by Germans in the same area of Saxony where building pyramids became a thriving cottage industry by the mid-nineteenth century. The specialized craft was an outgrowth of the construction of full-size wooden structures like ventilating windmills in the local salt mines. [109] Saxony continues to be known for its diminutive, wooden Christmas folk items, such as pyramids, nutcrackers, "smokers," [110] and ornaments. One scholar believes that a tree and a pyramid, the first unlighted, the second lighted, stood side by side in many German homes by the late-eighteenth century. [111] Another scholar believes that the pyramid became a "common substitute" [112] for the tree in Saxony and other country places during the nineteenth century, and that a gradual shift of the candles from the pyramid to the Christmas tree took place.

A paucity of quotes concerning pyramids in Salem exists, although they were almost certainly there at an early date, since they were mentioned in Pennsylvania in 1747. In describing the Jubilee Festival of 19 February 1816, Peter Wolle wrote that there was an elaborate pyramid with fifty burning tapers along with twenty-five other candlesticks. [113] On 1 January 1818, Wolle wrote, "This afternoon Herman took apart and put away his beautiful pyramidal Christmas Putz with 8 inscriptions." [114] After his move to Lititz, Pennsylvania, Wolle recorded fixing a frame for a pyramid and purchasing greens on 23 December 1829. [115] Susanna Kramsch wrote of decorating a pyramid on 22 December 1822 in Salem. [116] Also in Salem, on Epiphany (6 January) in 1872 at the church, "A pyramid had been made and placed on the upper platform of the pulpit... ." The text "Go ye into all the world...appeared on the pyramid in illuminated letters." Four long festoons of greenery and artificial flowers were draped with the number fifty at the top in white. [117] In 1874 at the Bethania church "a pyramidal four-sided transparent inscription with three representative scenes occupied a place before the pulpit, and on each side of this a finely proportioned pine tree was placed, decorated with bright gilt and other coloured paper and illuminated with wax tapers as Christmas trees." [118] Cedar garlands in festoons completed the display.

No early Christmas pyramid structures exist locally, understandably so, since if they were constructed from brushwood they were simply discarded or burned for kindling after the intended use. However, as Wolle observed, Brother Herman's structure was special enough to be packed away, at least for some period of time.

Christmas feather tree, nineteenth-century. OSTM.

Twentieth-century Christmas postcard. *Author's collection.*

Other Types of Trees

One type of artificial Christmas tree from Germany that became very popular in the last third of the nineteenth century was the feather tree. These were patterned after the widely spaced limbs of the German fir tree or white pine tree and provided ideal display space for ornaments. Again, the industry was a German cottage-based one with some basic parts factory made, such as wire, wood, and berries. Feathers most commonly used were from turkeys and geese and sometimes swans. They were dyed and stripped from the quills and attached to the trunk with wire. Red berries on the tips of the branches and a sturdy wooden base completed the ensemble. A variety of sizes and colors was made. The trees were easily collapsed for storage and brought out year after year, thus making them convenient and economical.[119]

Another somewhat unique regional tree was created by wrapping the branches of a bare tree with cotton batting to simulate a snow-covering and was documented in Lancaster, Pennsylvania, in 1897. Shoemaker calls it "a not uncommon practice in Berks County since at least 1900."[120] Snyder ascribes the custom to "thrifty German farmers in Pennsylvania [who] stripped Christmas trees of their needles after they were dried out and placed the skeleton in the attic. The following year the tree was brought down again and wrapped in cotton, so that it resembled a tree in the forest after a snow storm, and then it was decorated. After Christmas the tree was returned to the attic, where it was covered with old newspapers to keep the cotton clean."[121]

Early-twentieth-century photograph of a Christmas tree in the home of the Petersens of Salem. *OSHPC.*

A cotton-covered Christmas tree was reported to be the cause of a domestic fire in Indiana.[122] Fires have long been a hazard for Christmas trees, but few who used candles seemed deterred by that fact. Some took precautions, such as having on hand a wet sponge tied on a long stick, or several buckets or cups of water in readiness,[123] but whatever the case, Christmas trees continued to escalate in popularity.

By 1900, one family in five had a Christmas tree in America,[124] although most children knew about them from Sunday School, school, or a neighbor's house. The custom continued to spread, and by 1910 in most parts of the country "nearly all children had a tree at home.... . By 1930 the tree had become nearly a universal part of the American Christmas."[125] Harkening back to those Cherokee pupils at the Moravian Springplace Indian Mission, on Christmas Eve of 1805, countless children in the last two centuries have experienced the same awe of the magical tree that those few must have felt in that simple room in the Georgia wilderness so long ago.

THE CHRISTMAS TREE AND THE PYRAMID

The sanctuary of Salem's Home Moravian Church decorated for Christmas.
Courtesy of Home Moravian Church.

Chapter 3

The *Putz* and Other Decorations

"There is scarcely a family . . . that has not, at least, some attempt at decoration."

— *The Wachovia Moravian, December 1900*

The Putz

From the earliest days the Moravians enjoyed embellishing and adorning their churches with added beauty for special occasions, and that beloved custom was also brought into the homes. "Ornament or added beauty" is the definition of "decoration" in an 1828 dictionary.[1] The verb is defined as "to adorn, to embellish." At no event did the Moravians embellish more than at Christmas. Their decoration was called a *Putz,* from the sixteenth-century Saxon-dialectal word *putzen,* meaning "to decorate." At Christmas the nativity, or the *Krippen,* was a focus of the *Putz* (pronounced like the third person singular of the English verb "puts"). The *Krippen* may have begun as a substitute for human figures in church miracle plays of the Middle Ages.[2] They were at first carved, especially in Northern Italy and the mountains of Germany, particularly in the Reisen-gebirge and Erzebirge regions, not far from Herrnhut, where the Moravians may have learned the art.[3] The figures surrounded by embellishments including moss, rocks, and greenery provided "a bit of poetry" for the holy day, according to one Moravian minister.[4] Although developed pri-marily for the young people of the congregation to understand the true meaning of Christmas, the decoration could "sway the heart of an adult."[5]

Greenery was an essential part of the *Putz,* certainly because it dispelled the gloom of winter, but also because it repre-sented everlasting life and the Creator of mankind. In 1881 the Reverend Edward Rondthaler made reference to this important connection in his assessment of the Christmas decorating at Home Moravian Church in Salem:

"It is indeed a graceful service thus to make God's house beau-tiful with the works of His own creative hand."[6]

A young student at the Moravian girls' school in Bethelehem expressed the impact of the *Putz* on 24 December 1788: "Some of us had never seen the like or heard much of this impor-tant matter. The children said they would not be at home for ever so much; they only wished their parents could share their joy."[7]

Eliza Vierling Kremer, youngest daughter of Salem's Doctor Vierling, remarked on the *Putz* of her memory from the early 1800s:

The beautiful custom of Christmas decorations was no doubt inherited from our German ancestors so that in almost every house in town children were made happy by having a Putz. Some were on a very extensive plan representing land-scape scenery with hills and rocks and fountains. Then there was the well-known shepherd dressed in Oriental costume with his flock and faithful watchdog before him and familiar Noah's Ark from which animals known and unknown issued in pairs. There was also sometimes a cave or little house representing the place of the Nativity with the moth-er and child, a manger, etc. It was a happy time for children to go from house to house, to see and admire the various decorations, and every door was thrown open for them.[8]

By the time Eliza Vierling was a child, admiring the neighbor's *Putz* may have been an established tradition. It was, however, a new experience for some English children on Christmas Eve 1760, when it was recorded that they came to see the Moravian decoration in Bethabara. It was, of course, a *Putz*,[9] believed to be the first in North Carolina.[10]

Far from Wachovia, in the midst of the backcountry at the Moravian Indian Mission in Springplace, Georgia, it was recorded with pleasure on the day before Christmas, 1806: "For this celebration Brother and Sister Gambold's house was as beautifully decorated with greenery, flowers and writings as it is possible to do in this country, and it was lit with wax candles."[11]

Exactly a year earlier the Gambolds had decorated in a somewhat different way. That occasion may be the first mention of a wreath at an indoor window in America. It was written that "the floor of the room was covered with green branches of the spruce tree and one window was decorated with a wreath of the same."[12]

Greenery, embellished Bible verses, and candles were all part of the Moravian *Putz*. Another popular element of a *Putz* was flowers, although probably not as many fresh ones were used as artificial, or perhaps dried, until the Victorian period when hot houses became more common. In 1859 James Henry spoke of "chaste flowers" amongst the hemlock, moss, and laurel in Bethlehem, and he, too, emphasized the creation of "the poetical picture" in arranging the *Putz*.[13] On Christmas Day 1874, the meeting house at Spanish Grove in Wachovia was decorated "with cedar wreaths and the altar trimmed with evergreens and flowers."[14] In the latter part of the nineteenth century and continuing to contemporary times, there are Christmas pictures of Home Moravian Church decorated with pots of forced flower bulbs.

During the Christmas of 1815, an Americn Indian woman came to visit the Springplace mission, and the Gambolds described another decoration of the *Putz*, one that included both the birth and the death of Jesus. Powerful reminders of His sacrifice were important to the meaning of Christmas for Moravians, especially in the eighteenth century.[15] The Gambolds wrote: "our decoration and especially the small pictures of Jesus' birth and crucifixion gave occasion for pleasant conversation."[16] The images were a source of enlightened discussions for family and visitors alike. However, twenty years later, in 1835, Bethania minister George

Twentieth-century Christmas postcard. *Author's collection.*

Bahnson addressed this "manger to the cross" aspect of Christmas somewhat critically after attending a Christmas dialogue with his wife at the Salem Girls' School. He remarked that it was made up of "rather...strange contents, being a kind of dogmatical exposition of the whole Christian doctrine, from the manger to the cross—It could not be called a Christmas dialogue." He did concede that the minister who created it was attempting to work into the play many aspects of the Christian religion for those girls who might not spend more than one Christmas in Salem and thus would have no other opportunity of hearing the important message.[17]

The Moravians were just one of many groups that used evergreens at Christmas. A visiting botanist from Sweden in Philadelphia in 1749, Peter Kalm remarked on branches of laurel decorating church pews and altars at Christmas.[18] A young boarding student at the Salem Girls' School wrote of her youth with nostalgia in 1882, "From earliest childhood we have associated the scent of evergreens with Christmas, and it would hardly seem to be Christmas without them." She continued with a description of the preparations in Salem:

Often during the early days of December we see upon the street wagons laden with pine and cedar trees, trailing-pine and holly boughs, recalling to our minds the Christmas tree with many eager children's faces gathered around it... . The laurel is also a favorite Christmas evergreen.

We do not often get the rhododendron from the mountains, but are content with its humble step-sister, the kalmia,[19] which answers the purpose just as well.[20]

An entire greenery-decorated room or the sanctuary of the church could essentially become a *Putz.* As an example, in 1887 the church decorations in Salem were described by one student as being extensive and handsome:

With the usual festoons from the pulpit and galleries to the center of the ceiling. There were small trees in each window, with the unique feature of an inscription on the two opposite galleries,—on the one, 'Unto us a child is born,'—on the other, 'Unto us a son is given,' the large letters being made of brightly colored and varnished autumn leaves. The recess behind the pulpit was a large

Illumination of Nativity by Grunewald, c. 1839. *OSMG.*

THE *PUTZ* AND OTHER DECORATIONS

Postcard of Salem's Home Moravian Church, c. 1932. *Private collection.*

cavern of artificial rock-work in which was the picture of the Nativity,— the child Jesus on his mother's knee. The picture...is a copy by Mr. Daniel Welfare, a painter of some local note years ago, from Correggio's 'La Notte,' the third great treasure of the Dresden gallery.[21]

The student continued her description to include the school rooms and personal spaces of her fellow students:

There was no large decoration in the Academy like those of years ago, but all the study parlors, the dwelling-rooms were decorated according to the taste of inmates. The younger girls had trees, and otherwise beautified their surroundings; the Seniors left trees for the Juniors, and made their respective rooms as handsome as mistletoe with its berries of seed pearl, holly with its blood-red drops, laurel and cedar could make them.[22]

Mistletoe, a semi-parasitic plant once believed to have powers of magic and healing as well as averting misfortune in certain European countries, had been incorporated into an English tradition associated with kissing a chosen one under a sprig which could then lead to marriage. An 1816 geography book described it as common in North Carolina and remarked, "It is a shrub different from all others never growing out of the earth, but on the tops of trees; the roots run under the bark of the tree, and incorporate with it."[23] It is therefore interesting that Salemite Birdie Goslen noted in her diary 16 December 1891: "Mama bought a lovely large bundle of mistletoe today and Emma brought me over just as much as she could carry, so I am bountifully supplied." Three days earlier her beau Henry "had been out to Old Town hunting mistletoe."[24] It was obviously no easy task to obtain it. By then, various cultures were incorporating each other's traditions into their American celebrations.

The Salem student's description of "the picture of the Nativity" in Home Church reveals another important element of the *Putz*: illuminations. These painted pictures were lighted from behind by a candle, which caused the scene of the birth of Jesus or a similar Bible story to come to life. An oil-on-paper transparent illumination painted by the artist Gustavus Grunewald is one of Old Salem Museums & Gardens' oldest Christmas decorations, dated and signed 1839, Nazareth (Pennsylvania).[25]

The illumination painted by Daniel Welfare for Home Moravian Church was later replaced by another copy of Correggio's *Nativity*. Moravian archivist Dr. Adelaide Fries said that according to tradition, in the summer of 1889, James T. Lineback, while attending the General Synod of the Moravian Church in Europe, ordered a reproduction of Corregio's *Nativity*, which took four or five years to be sent.[26] Reichstein of

Saxony was said to have been the artist.[27] The Home Church record of 23 December 1894 concerning the "illumination of the nativity" almost certainly means this copy, which was worked in silk (one can understand why it took four or five years to be sent) and used until it deteriorated, in spite of efforts to preserve it by encase-

ment. A newspaper article from sometime in the 1960s (there is no attribution) noted that Home Church had the silk transparency copied by local artist Ralph A. Herring Jr., who specially prepared a plexiglass panel onto which he painted the reproduction in oils.[28] It is that copy which is used in Home Church today.

While a student at Salem in 1819, Louisa Lenoir wrote a letter to her mother about the Christmas celebration and the decorations, which included two illuminations:

The Chapel was beautifully decorated with evergreens & artificial flowers; also two large transparent pieces of painting, one represented Jesus in the manger with Mary & Joseph & the Shepherd who had come to see him, the other his presentation in the Temple, Simeon holds Jesus in his arms & Zacharias, the Priest, Anna the

Salem's Home Moravian Church sanctuary, 1939. *OSHPC.*

Unto you is born a Saviour which is Christ the Lord.

Interior of Salem's St. Philips Church.

Prophetess, & Mary & Joseph stand by. In fixing the decoration gurlains [sic] were hung up at one end of the room with a space behind large enough to contain a piano & several persons.[29]

Salem student Miranda Miller Scarborough described in October 1890 the setting of the Christmas dialogues held in the chapel when she was a girl in 1835:

The eastern end of the hall was partitioned off by white drapery from floor to ceiling. Along the ceiling heavy festoons of evergreen reached from end to end, dropping to the floor on either side, while a bank of evergreens along the floor met the festoons, thus forming an evergreen frame whose enclosed space was divided into panels wrapped with festoons of cedar, laurel and spruce. In these panels were placed transparent paintings of the Nativity and other Bible scenes, among them portraits of the prophets and the temple scenes, with aged Simeon holding the Babe in his arms, the devout Anna standing by.[30]

Illuminations incorporated by Moravians into the *Putz* were not always pictorial. Harkening back to embellished manuscripts of the Middle Ages, some Moravian illuminations took the form of written words. Sometimes Bible text and verses were nicely printed, perhaps in colored inks, and hung in windows for the light to shine through. In St. Philips Church in Salem in a Sunday School window upstairs (before the restoration) there was a tattered shade left from years ago with a printed Bible text through which the sun could shine to illuminate the words.[31]

At the Moravian Springplace Indian Mission on 24 December 1805, above the wreath-decorated window "was the writing, 'Christ is born!' illuminated with golden letters, which were beautifully lighted by three burning wax candles."[32]

Cut-out letters to create phrases were also very popular, and var-

The pleasure of creating the Putz *started with the excursion to the woods to gather the greens and moss. Children were lovingly included in this experience in order to more fully integrate them into the entire Christmas celebration.*

ious materials were used for this purpose. The decoration for South Bethlehem Moravian Church in Lancaster, Pennsylvania, in 1863, included the letters "Glory to God in the highest" made out of ivy leaves.[33] In 1866 at the African American church in Salem the evergreens were tastefully used to create "an arch rising in front of the pulpit having in its apex the inscription, "Unto you is born a Saviour which is Christ the Lord."[34]

The power of the *Putz* was not only evident in the church, it began to manifest itself in the domestic scene as well. George Bahnson recognized the impact of the decorations when he recorded his own daughter's reaction to their simple household embellishments in 1835: "[o]ur sweet Angelica sat, as happy as an angel, looking at some lighted waxtapers placed before the houses brought along from Bethlehem."[35]

The Bahnsons' "houses" before which Angelica sat may have been part of an extended *Putz*, including a Nativity scene, which they

had had in Pennsylvania. The family used those houses on more than one occasion, as a *Putz* could be created all during the year for any special occasion.[36]

Then, as now, parents enjoyed vicariously the pleasure of their children in the decorations of Christmas and were disappointed when joy was not forthcoming. In 1837 the newly widowed Bahnson wrote, "My darling Angelica did not enjoy her 'Putz' nor any thing to day as much as I had fondly anticipated she would." He did allow, however, that the child had been sick with a cough and was crying and "hollow"[ing] most "pitifully."[37]

Careful planning was made for the Christmas decorating, both at church and at home. Birdie Goslen's diary survives from the 1890s, in which she spoke of "clearing" the parlor and cleaning up the house just before Christmas.[38] "Clearing" refers to the readying for the tree, the *Putz*, and other decorations. In Germany, a separate room in the house called the *Weinachtsstube* (Christmas room) was employed "to intensify expectation" by concealing the readied *Putz* and the *Krippe* (Nativity). The candlelit tree and the presents, perhaps in a separate room, were all part of the German Christmas Eve celebration.[39]

A letter from Mary Fries Patterson at Palmyra Plantation on the Yadkin River to her sister in Salem in 1864 addressed the thought and anticipation of decorations:

Are you going to have a large decoration in the new-room this year? I should like to see it, but as I can't do that, you must give me a graphic word painting of the whole.—I have made a kind of plan for ours, but it will have to be in the parlor & therefore not very expensive & I fear not very pretty. Are you going to have Tableaux, or something so?[40]

The *Putz* and Other Decorations

"Tableau" was a term used later in the century as a more generic word for the *Putz*. Indeed, a local newspaper writer in 1911 called the Christmas *Putz* a "tableau with the Child as the heart and soul."[41]

The pleasure of creating the *Putz* started with the excursion to the woods to gather the greens and moss. Children were lovingly included in this experience in order to more fully integrate them into the entire Christmas celebration. One can almost feel an added lilt to the step and a skipping of the heart in reading of the preparations. Anna Gambold wrote from Georgia: "drove with our dear pupils to the Connasaga to fetch greenery for the Christmas putz, and we arrived home with it towards evening."[42] On Christmas Eve 1807, the Gambolds's house was decorated "with greenery, flowers and writings."[43] The children in their little house had made "a putz from pine branches and had tied little flowers onto it."[44] The decorative "writings" within watercolor wreaths, popularized by Anna Rosina were essential to any Christmas at Springplace during the Gambolds's leadership. Another year in Georgia, lest the adults had by some small chance forgotten, the boys "asked for permission to fetch the cedar branches...for the Christmas decorations."[45]

Peter Wolle recorded a greenery excursion in 1814, "In the afternoon young Wohlfahrt [Daniel Welfare] and I went with the children to the great mill to get boxwood."[46] George Bahnson, ever more descriptive, noted in 1834:

In the afternoon I went out to Shorstown, with Edward Butner, Herman's son, in order to get greens for our decoration. I rode on horseback & Edward followed with a wagon... .We passed on to Werners where we were assisted in getting a whole load of cedar boughs, the only greens to be had here beside box; spruce is not to be got. Ephraim Strub had gone out in another direction to look for greens, & brought home a whole load, all of which was deposited on the sister's choir which is never used, & in the cabinet.[47]

Several years later, Bahnson remarked on 23 December 1837, "Fetched a little moss for an intended decoration."[48] Much later, R. P. Leinbach wrote in early December 1863 of gathering moss and then later laurel to work "at the decoration."[49]

With an ample supply of greenery and moss on hand, the decorating could begin, often with the help of the young people. While in Bethania on 22 December 1834, Bahnson wrote, "I found a great many people busy in decorating the church, & they seem to come on very well indeed, in the evening all the young people came & something got done by the joint exertions. We spent the evening there too. It looks right nice."[50] It was Bahnson that year who mentioned the use of apples on a Christmas *Putz*, which would have added texture and color to the decoration.[51] In addition, apples served as gifts to the children and as an important food source, as explored in Chapter Five.

Working on the *Putz* could be a lengthy and often secretive labor of love to produce the added element of dramatic surprise, just as was the decorating of the Christmas tree. Wolle, as a beginning teacher at Nazareth Hall, in Nazareth, Pennsylvania, described the project for the year 1809. He stated that he and another brother were "constantly busy with preparations for the Putz" in the large *Saal* (worship hall) even canceling some classes. As they completed sections, they concealed them with bed sheets "for fear that the strangers who always appear in great numbers might see some of it and come back next year in even larger numbers."[52] Space was often a problem for the Moravians at Christmas. Some years they resorted to admittance tickets in order to control the crowds.[53]

The buildup of anticipation continued until the dramatic revelation of the completed decoration. After his move to Salem, Wolle again exhibited zeal in the *Putz* preparations. He began on 11 December 1814, continued all day on the 17th, got boxwood on the 20th, and worked all morning and part of the afternoon on the 24th, before showing it to the children that evening. Of course, they were "most pleased," and "many Brothers and Sisters gave us a reward... ."[54] The "reward" may have been a lovefeast in honor of the workers, which was a frequent occurrence.

Wolle did not describe the 1814 decoration, but he did elaborate on another, which was much more lavish, for a 19 February Jubilee Festival in 1816. Although this was not a Christmas decoration, it is valuable in the detailed description of a similar decoration. This particular *Putz* consisted of a "painted urn and wreaths of spruce adorned with twenty-five roses. "At the back wall, behind the table, was the number '50' [commemorating the beginning of the permanent occupation of Salem in 1766] bordered by a wreath of spruce, and provided on the upper part with a red silken bow." Painted flowers were "fastened skillfully in a convex manner to a strip of white paper" and then festooned. The Sisters' Choir had leather garlands with small bouquets of flowers and "1816" surrounded by a wreath of spruce. The Brothers' Choir had in the center of the festoons the number 1755. There was a pyramid with "50 burning tapers." Twenty-five candlesticks had been brought of the same size. "The lights in the two other chandeliers were decorated with beautifully cut out paper."[55] Wolle jokingly remarked once about the church candles that "the mice in the church were accused of theft, since they gnaw so much on the candles."[56]

Using lights for special occasions was often employed and symbolically represented the glory of Christ as the light of the world. There are many metaphorical references to that symbolic light and how brightly or dimly it burned in people's lives. An example on 2 January 1817, from the Springplace Indian Mission reads, "with deep shame for the weak burning and flickering light of our little candle, which He has set up in this dark land."[57] Light was a focus of a decoration for the Brothers' House on 1 January 1819. Wolle described it as being "beautifully illuminated in front—on the front door was a sign 'Hope for better Times.'"[58]

Presenting lighted candles to children and later to adults during the Christmas lovefeast was certainly a decorative aspect

Early-twentieth-century photograph of a *Putz* in the home of the Petersons of Salem. *OSHPC.*

of the service, but most importantly was a symbol of accepting Jesus into one's life. In 1907, the Reverend Edward Rondthaler noted a new custom of giving the candles to everyone in the Salem Congregation: "Sunday evening, December 22nd, the Morning Star Anthem was sung in the beautifully decorated church, so ushering in the happy Christmas season... . The evening service was particularly pretty this year because the lighted tapers were given to all, instead of only the children."[59]

James Henry noted in 1859 that for the Moravians tapers were "important articles of merchandise" during the week of Christmas. He referred to "the wax-candles—yellow, red and blue"—for which there was "unlimited" demand.[60] There is a Moravian tradition that beeswax candles represent the "sinless purity of Christ."[61] Beeswax was also preferred for use at church because it was less messy and did not drip as much as tallow candles.

Simply putting candles in windows or on other items like fence posts and steps was another use of illumination. Note the remarks by schoolteacher Peter Wolle on 1 January 1819:

What a lovely sight as we left the church for the congregation. The front of the Choirhouse had been illuminated most beautifully, six wax candles in each window, except for one (the room for the sick), in which the date of the year 1818 was affixed, but which did not have the desired effect;—above the door was affixed an arch of lights, lights also on the steps, as well as on the posts and the trees.[62]

A Moravian writer in Bethlehem, Pennsylvania, reports that the city's twentieth-century tradition of "a candle in every window" dates to the eighteenth century when Zinzendorf's house in Herrnhaag (called Lichtenburg, or "Castle of Light") had a candle in every window "to welcome

Socially in homes there were "Putzing" parties in Bethlehem and in Salem, which were popular during the last of the nineteenth century and the early part of the twentieth century.

the Christ child" during the season of Advent.[63] Many from that congregation immigrated to Bethlehem and undoubtedly brought the memory of the custom with them. Today the far-reaching appeal of candles lighted in windows represents warm hospitality to visitors in a city known as the "Christmas City USA."[64] Countless individuals from other areas have adopted the custom, even extending it beyond the Christmas season.

The pleasure in and importance of the effect of the lighting was expressed by Bahnson in 1837 at Bethabara where it was still broad daylight for the meeting on Christmas Eve: "[T]owards the close of it lighted candles were brought in, in spite of the broadest daylight a bright sunshine upon snow could produce. But no matter such things must be enjoyed in a childlike spirit & simplicity."[65] On Christmas Day Bahnson was back in Bethania for the evening meeting, with the weather uncomfortably cold and slippery. He admitted, "I felt a little out of humor that not even the decoration had been lighted up."[66]

With the enthusiasm of creating a *Putz* might arise the element of rivalry amongst households and some businesses. On 27 December 1838, Bahnson, then

in Bethlehem, wrote with an understanding of how competition in decorating could get out of hand: "After supper some of our party looked at the decorations at Brunners, Webers Knauss & Gutter, it is indeed astonishing what trouble they are willing to give themselves for the gratification of I hardly know whom or what. It would even appear to me as though they had not felt very kindly towards one another, but jealous of the respective beauty of their decorations."[67] Bahnson may have been referring to merchants' decorations of their shops, but it is possible he was referring to individual homes.

Socially in homes there were "*Putzing*" parties in Bethlehem and in Salem, which were popular during the last of the nineteenth century and the early part of the twentieth century.[68] They took place between Christmas and New Year's in the evenings between seven and nine o'clock. Afterwards, cookies including the beloved Christmas cakes would be served with fruit punch or cider. The *Putz*-makers who were confined to their homes as hosts of these events made it a point to go out in the afternoons to see their competitors' work, as it was somewhat of a friendly competition.[69]

Besides competition, the decorating of the *Putz* also posed the problem of the risk of the "frolicking" aspect of decorating committees, particularly if they consisted of both sexes working closely together. In 1859 in Salem, it was noted: "Several young brethren have applied for permission to decorate the church at Christmas. Pleasing as it is to have the church decorated on the occasion, the Board nevertheless hesitated to give its consent. When in former years the church was decorated, it gave rise to protracted evening gatherings of young people of both sexes in the chapel, and caused various complaints at the time. The originators are well meaning persons, but cannot exercise a controlling influence. At all events the warden is to be consulted, and even if there should be no objection from that side, the superintendence of the preparations by married persons of weight must be secured."[70]

Contrasting the Moravian concerns with frolics, in Pennsylvania in 1859 *The Pottsville Miners' Journal* on 24 December wrote of the flurry of exciting activity where the sexes did work together:

We will go out with the boys into the woods and get the "greens" for Christmas wreaths, and dig in the snow for the beautiful pine, and will ride to the church on top of the loads of pines, and hemlocks, and Kalmia, and will help the girls to weave them into festoons, and wind the pillars and hang the galleries, and make the star and work the green letters for "glory to God."[71]

Later in the nineteenth century decorations moved out of the realm of church and home and into the workplace. Employees began to be treated to Christmas celebrations with decorations. In 1882, the Reverend Rondthaler remarked on the "unique and happy festival which occurred on Saturday evening, Dec. 23rd, in the Arista Cotton Mills, where amid evergreen splendors from bottom to top of the spacious building, employers, employees and friends rejoiced together with genuine Christmas pleasure."[72] By 1902, he noted, "business, if not entirely suspended...[was] at least meeting with a welcome pause."[73]

Secularization of Christmas decorations continued when new technological creations and modern themes were meshed with traditional literature and incorporated into the Christmas

programs, even in Sunday Schools. In Bethlehem, the Christmas Eve Sunday School concert in 1871 used parts of Bunyan's allegory of *Pilgrim's Progress* and interspersed the extracts with magic lantern illustrations.[74] In 1895 in Bethania, the Sunday School Christmas cantata was called "Santa Claus on Time," which must have used the image of the jolly gift bringer as decoration.[75]

The Salem Girls' Boarding School was often the scene for much more traditional decorations including elaborate *Putzes*.[76] These decorations were created by the teachers for the students, some of whom could not go home for Christmas. In 1866, the academy decoration was especially lavish to entertain the girls during an epidemic of smallpox when fifty or sixty were confined to their beds.[77]

Early-twentieth-century photograph of Josephine Peterson in front of the *Putz* in her Salem home. *OSHPC*.

THE *PUTZ* AND OTHER DECORATIONS

Lula, formerly a student at the Girls' School, wrote in the correspondence column from Webster, North Carolina, on 25 December 1878: "I can see, with my mind's eye, the decorations of last Christmas, and three previous ones, and remember with what joyful hearts we lent a helping hand to those who were preparing them for our enjoyment."[78]

In December 1884, at the Girls' School there was a large decoration "representing mountain crags with castles perching upon them, caves, streams of running water, fountains, and the like."[79] This was just one of numerous descriptions of the elaborate *Putzes* that began to be built. As one century folded into another, the *Putz* continued to expand and develop its own social significance.

In the book *Where the Star Still Shines*, Winifred Kirkland wrote in the 1920s about Salem: "Everyone, no matter how aged, has a Christmas tree and every Christmas tree has its 'putz.'"[80] She described some of them in detail on their tables or platforms, often anchored in moss and laid out in valleys, mountains, and caves, with sometimes working mills, or tiny fountains, and incorporating many activities as well as animals, especially sheep, and a variety of diminutive people.

Moravian archivist Dr. Adelaide Fries wrote of the importance of "the white sheep" in the *Putz* when they appeared "on the hills of moss [to] hint of the angels' message while shepherds watch their flocks by night."[81] Fries wrote that in Wachovia the simulated outdoor landscape included at least a cave, "with its reminder of the cave-stable of the Nativity."[82] She remarked also that it usually was arranged around the bottom or beside the Christmas tree. People sometimes called these arrangements gardens, which accounts for the fences often placed around them. Embellishments might include thick moss with berries, lichens, twigs, trunks, branches, pebbles, sand, a fence, and even sometimes running water, as well as extra villagers, the essential sheep, various other animals, poultry, birds, angels, stars, and a card-

Nativity figures (above) and a *Putz* (below) made in Germany, c. 1850. *OSTM.*

Paper foldout
Nativity scene,
Germany,
nineteenth
century.
*Author's
collection.*

board sky, to name a few. Fries noted that the fancy of the maker controlled the size of the *Putz*, some being small enough to place on the dinner table and others so large as to fill a whole side of a room.[83]

The private room of the principal of the Girls' School in Bethlehem in December 1864 included in its *Putz* "a nice little pond with living fishes."[84] In 1859, James Henry wrote that a large part of a room in a house might be used for the *Putz* and "incongruous elements" were sometimes brought in to please the visitors, especially the children. Thus, the "living fishes" in Bethlehem would indeed have created such an appeal. Henry remarked that the ingenuous designer was usually the "Pater Familias" (father of the family).[85]

As the *Putz* became more elaborate, some felt the need to justify the embellishments, as did Edmund de Schweinitz, an editor of *The Moravian*, who in 1864 mused thoughtfully on what had come to be a distinguishing Moravian characteristic. He wrote: "Though there is nothing of a specially religious character in those displays otherwise than that the great object of our Christmas adoration, the newly-born Savior, is generally brought prominently to mind in some illuminated picture or inscription, or by a representation...we cannot help admitting that these peculiar Moravian observances help to foster that charming simplicity of faith, brotherly-love and social equality which continue in a considerable degree to distinguish our people, and deserve for these reasons to be encouraged."[86] A church pamphlet on the construction of a *Putz* keynoted an essential Christmas aspect: "A good putz evokes a hush of silent contemplation... ."[87]

While the nativity aspect of the *Putz* was the essential element of the eighteenth- and nineteenth-century Moravian Christmas, the depiction of scenes from the Bible goes back at least to the Middle Ages. St. Francis of Assisi is credited with arranging a display of the nativity with live people and animals to highlight his sermon on the subject in 1224.[88] Onlookers enjoyed this novel reenactment so much that it spread through Italy and Europe. Many countries depicted the birth of Christ and called the scene by different names, such as *Krippe* (German), *crèche* (French), *presepio* (Italian), *nacimiento* (Spanish). Some Americans called it the "Christmas crib."[89] The Italians, Germans, and French were particularly active in creating figurines to expand the Biblical scene. The French included ordinary people from the village, such as the farmer, the housewife, the baker, the potter, etc., that they called

Salem *Putz* at Home Moravian Church's Candle Tea.
Courtesy of Women's Fellowship, Home Moravian Church.

santons ("little saints"). These figures seem to have been "stock
characters in folk Nativity plays"
popular in the Middle Ages.[90]
Today Marseille in France is
known for its *santon* markets
held before Noël, and Munich in
Germany is known for a museum
collection of *Krippe* figures "gathered from many old churches"[91] as
well as new ones sold at the annual *Christkindles-markt* in that city.

The folk figures of the Nativity
scene included various materials
in their construction. Paper was
the most popular and the least
expensive. By the second half of
the eighteenth century, Moravia
was the foremost center for
printing the paper *Krippe*, which
was then hand painted in watercolors. These sets had many
figures.[92] *Krippelbilder* or Nativity
pictures made of paper were
mentioned beginning in the seventeenth century. They were used
as replacements for or additions
to the dimensional figures. The
Krippelbilder "was cheaper than the
carved wooden or wax dressed
figures, it took up less space, could
be quickly reproduced, and was
capable of depicting countless
details which could be arranged
to create astonishing effects of
depth."[93]

A contemporary *Putz* in
Salem includes a large Nativity
used to tell the story of the birth
of Christ. Part of the "decoration"
organized by members of Home
Moravian Church in two separate
rooms, this Nativity is paired
with a depiction of Salem set up
in the cellar of the historic Single
Brothers' House during their
Candle Tea. This special event
is organized annually by the
church as a fundraiser, but most
importantly, as a loving gift to the
community and a reminder to the
members of their heritage, atten-
dance at which many people
consider to be essential to the
celebration of Christmas. (The
Candle Tea is discussed further in
Chapter Six.) A newly created
miniature replication of a Salem

Folded paper Moravian stars. *Author's collection.*

THE *PUTZ* AND OTHER DECORATIONS

building or other landscape embellishment is added to the display every Christmas. One source has remarked that the religious and secular are separated in different rooms in this way in Germany.[94]

The Moravian Star

The many-pointed star, sometimes called the Advent star or the Christmas star, was introduced to Salem in the early 1900s, according to Archivist Adelaide Fries.[95] It had been developed either as a handicraft or as part of a geometry exercise in several boys' schools in Niesky and Kleinwelka, Germany, in about 1850 (reports vary somewhat). Pieter Verbeek, who had been a student in Niesky in the 1880s, later began to make the stars.[96] His son continued the tradition by opening a small star factory in Herrnhut, Germany, and began to export them to America and other countries. By then the father and son were running the Herrnhut bookstore, and the orders were processed from there with directions printed in four languages,[97] but because of World War II the factory closed. During that period, in Wachovia, Julius Lineback found two wooden star molds and made stars for more than twenty years; his son continued the operation.[98]

Now one can again purchase the stars from Herrnhut and also from many local sources. Colors vary in Germany from red and yellow to white; in Wachovia they are usually white. The points of the original Verbeek stars were attached to a metal base; today they are held together with clips.[99] Materials vary from paper to parchment, plastic, metal, and glass. The traditional star has twenty-six points, but some have more or less, up to one hundred ten points. Some are lighted and some are not—and sizes vary. A popular modern variation of the larger star is a small origami-type star (folded paper strips in white

and colors) used for tree and gift decorations, and even jewelry.

Many people in Winston-Salem who are not Moravians hang their stars at Christmas, starting at the first Sunday of Advent to Epiphany, 6 January, the traditional time of the coming of the Magi. However, those who consider it a Christmas star hang it just before Christmas. Often the larger stars are hung outside on a porch; in Germany where porches are few, they are hung in an entry hall. Churches also use them during this season. The star was begun to be used in Moravian churches in Germany about the time of the First World War or a little later. "The rays of the star symbolize (1) the greatness of God who made the universe, (2) the star which led the wise men to the Christ Child, and (3) the Divine Star, Christ Himself."[100]

In 1959, the city of Winston-Salem began to use the star as part of the Christmas street decorations. Sixty-four were distributed on light poles, thus representing the early heritage of the city.[101]

In a nostalgic look back at Salem in the early-twentieth century, Winifred Kirkland wrote of "the star faith of Salem."[102] The memorable hymn "Morning Star," with music composed by Salem native Francis Hagen, is believed to have been performed for the first time on Christmas Eve 1836 in Salem. No one who has ever attended a Christmas lovefeast service can forget the beautiful antiphonal rendering of a child soloist and the choir and congregation. "Morning Star" is a name for Jesus, and the song was dedicated to "the children of the Moravian Church" as well as to "the child in each of us that Christmas sentiment evokes."[103] Chapter Six will further discuss this Christmas hymn.

Stars of a different nature were being used by others in their decorating of the Christmas tree. A gilded star was atop the first

Christmas tree documented in Williamsburg, Virginia. The tree was put up by a German immigrant teaching the classics at the College of William and Mary in 1842. For the pleasure of his friends, the Nathaniel Beverley Tuckers, Charles Minnigerode placed on the tree with the star, "candles adhered with twisted pieces of wire" and "bits of brightly colored paper."[104]

Other Decorations

Along with the Advent or Christmas star, another Moravian decoration also used by other denominations is the Advent wreath.[105] It is a circular wreath of greenery topped with four candles, one lighted each Sunday in Advent. Sometimes there is a center candle representing Christ, which is the last to be lit with the other four on 25 December. In Wachovia the wreath may also contain certain symbolic items: red ribbons, a small star, miniature Moravian figures, a tiny Bible, and other remembrances that are meaningful to a particular family. Mrs. Evelyn Spach is credited with first adding these little items to Advent wreaths in Winston-Salem in the 1950s.[106] The candles on the wreath "symbolize (1st Sunday)...preparing for the Messiah's birth, (2nd Sunday) the coming of [the] Lord in glory, (3rd Sunday) the sharing of Christ's love with all the world, and (4th Sunday) the glad tidings of great joy that are now at hand."[107] The circle of greenery denotes the unending love and care of Christ.

The decorations hanging below the often-used crowning star on a tree varied greatly. The Follen family in Boston in 1832 hung several dozen homemade gilded eggshell baskets to hold sweets.[108] Girls, women, children, and even men and boys spent long hours creating such adornments. A doctor in Pennsylvania in 1876 decorated over sixty blown eggshells.[109] Cotton, netting, lace,

Window of Salem's Winkler Bakery with cookie decorations.

colorfully lithographed paper scraps, carved wood, and cardboard were just some of the materials employed. Favorites were all manner of sweets and edibles, such as cookies, candies, pretzels, *schnitz* (dried apple slices), peanuts and other nuts, cranberries, apples, oranges, plums, figs, raisins, lemons, and popcorn.[110]

The little painted paper wreaths encircling religious verses so loved by Anna Gambold and her pupils at Springplace,

Georgia, may have been used as tree decorations there and perhaps elsewhere, especially in Moravian communities.

German cottage industries utilized wax, soft tin, glass, wood, and cotton batting to produce a myriad of imaginative ornaments, including the handsomely embossed and painted cardboard figures called Dresdens, and literally thousands of blown and mold-formed glass shapes.[111] From such abundance most fru-

gal families might choose one or two selections each year to add to their own homemade creations. Anything that could be suspended or balanced was used. Toys and small items perched on the branches as gifts served as multipurpose decorations.

Cookies were a popular tree decoration from the beginning. Another aspect of their use was highlighted by a Pennsylvania Christmas historian who stated that some of that state's German population enjoyed hanging cookies in the windows in the very early twentieth century. An article in the Lebanon Historical Society Proceedings of 1905 refers to "the custom of children to display them [Christmas cakes] in rows in the windows of the living room" on Christmas morning.[112] Historian Alfred Shoemaker likened this custom to "a sort of Christmas greeting to passersby."[113] Certainly bakeries would have practiced this custom much earlier for advertising purposes. Whether it was done by other individuals and in other areas before 1905 is so far not documented.

An advertisement from the Bethlehem store of Timothy Luckenbach in *The Moravian* of 1870 was headed "SANTA CLAUS 'AT HOME!'" and along with "TOYS IN ENDLESS VARIETY... Christmas Tree Decorations" were mentioned in smaller print, as well as "trimming goods as usual."[114] Historian Shoemaker claimed that the oldest advertisement for Christmas tree ornaments was dated 1867 from Easton, Pennsylvania.[115]

An article in *The Moravian* of 1871 described elaborate decorations including balls on Christmas trees at the New Dorp Moravian Church of Staten Island, New York. "Besides four stately cedars, there were two balsam-fir-trees *par excellence*—beautifully overhung with strings of popcorn, red berries, spangles, reflectors, silver, red and

Glass Ornaments

Glass-ornament makers used imagination in creating elaborate forms and embellishing them with additional materials, such as "wire tinsel, cotton batting, or silk-thread tassels. One of the most beautiful—and difficult—variations was hand wrapping the crinkled silver or gold wire that was always done for balloons and airships... ."[i] This pristine early example from the Old Salem Toy Museum dates from the 1850s.

Making glass ornaments had begun in Lauscha, Germany, about sixty miles from the toy center of Nuremberg, in the 1590s.[ii] By the 1820s large thick-walled glass balls called *kugels* were being made and silvered on the interiors with a newly invented silver nitrate solution to make them shiny and mirror-like.[iii] In the 1840s Christmas ornaments were being blown;[iv] the first documented orders were taken in 1848. By 1870 molded glass ornaments were produced, the first being the pine cone and later the universally popular bird with the spun glass tail. Lauscha was on its way to becoming the world center for glass ornaments for Christmas trees and remained so until World War II.[v]

Hand-blown hot air balloon ornament, unknown manufacturer, 1850s. *OSTM.*

golden balls, richly gilt and flowered cornu-copias filled with candies and bonbons, and wax candles red, white, and blue."[116] The candle colors reflect post-war patriotism.

If the "silver, red and golden balls" on the Staten Island tree were glass, they may have been from Germany or were some of the first American glass ornaments, advertised in New York in 1871.[117] Five-and-ten-cent store merchant F. W. Woolworth popularized the German ornament market, although his beginning was inauspicious. Woolworth was looking for toys for his very first store in Lancaster, Pennsylvania, before Christmas of 1880 when he was persuaded by the importer to take risk-free an order of twenty-five dollars worth of colored glass ornaments. When they arrived, he indifferently put them on the counters, only to realize two days later that they were all gone and that he had totally miscalculated their immense and instant appeal.[118] Ten years later he sailed for Europe to place his own orders amounting to more than two hundred thousand ornaments at the cottages of the often poverty-stricken workers, who made the process a family business, each member contributing some part of the work.[119] The two World Wars destroyed the German Christmas ornament market, but America's love of those ornaments has never abated.[120]

Although nationally the "glow of the Christmas season"[121] continued to expand, nothing exceeded the simple beauty of the meaningful decorations of the Moravian Christmas. As a writer in *The Wachovia Moravian* stated in 1894, "If, therefore, in homes and Sunday Schools we make the children happy, we are doing what Jesus did in his birth at Bethlehem."[122] By 1900, the paper remarked with confidence, "There is scarcely a family...that has not, at least, some attempt at decoration."[123]

Decorated entrance to Salem's Single Brothers' House.

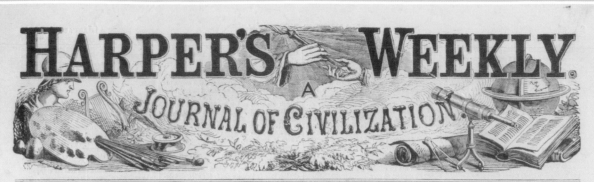

HARPER'S WEEKLY.

A JOURNAL OF CIVILIZATION.

Vol. XIII.—No. 627.]   NEW YORK, SATURDAY, JANUARY 2, 1869.   [SINGLE COPIES, TEN CENTS.
[$4.00 PER YEAR IN ADVANCE.

Entered according to Act of Congress, in the Year 1868, by Harper & Brothers, in the Clerk's Office of the District Court of the United States, for the Southern District of New York.

Image of Santa Claus from the cover of an 1869 *Harper's Weekly. Author's collection*

Chapter 4

The Evolution of the Gift Bringer and Gifts

"A little stocking pinned to the chimney-shelf. . .
A spray of evergreen stood in a box, blossoming with toys. . .
Whatever it is, it makes Christmas real, as the Christ-child
or Kris Kringle and Santa Claus are real."

— *The Moravian, 30 December 1869*

The Gift Bringer and Its Evolution

The tradition of Santa Claus is an American one, but the benevolent, generous, and paternal figure of today is really an amalgamation of centuries-old customs from many Old World sources. Some of them began in religious contexts and gradually spread to the secular to produce the large, jolly, red-clothed resident of the North Pole. The spirit of the gift giver was captured for all time by an editor of the New York *Sun* newspaper in 1897 when he wrote in response to a query from a little girl named Virginia O'Hanlon, "Yes, Virginia, there is a Santa Claus." Editor Francis Church went on to say "He exists as certainly as love and generosity and devotion exist... . Nobody sees Santa Claus, but that is no sign that there is no Santa Claus. The most real things in the world are those that neither children nor men can see... . Nobody can conceive or imagine all the wonders that are unseen or unseeable in the world... . No Santa Claus! Thank God he lives, and he lives forever."[1]

In essence Church's editorial was a tribute to the most elevating quality at the core of human existence, love. Being a religious man, he may have considered the Apostle Paul's New Testament letter to the Christian community of Corinth, Greece, in the creation of his response, "And now abideth faith, hope, love, these three; but the greatest of these is love."[2] Paul's message was that no gift of God means anything without love. In nineteenth-century America the home gradually became the proverbial hearthstone with one's family and children representing this love at its noblest. This essence was real, said *The Moravian* in 1869, and "it makes Christmas real, as the Christ Child or Kris Kringle and Santa Claus are real."[3]

The cozy familial scene at Christmas had not always been the case, however, as has been discussed earlier. Religion was the central focus for the eighteenth-century Moravian Christmas. And while faith remained central, by the mid-nineteenth century an emphasis on family during the holiday was growing in Moravian societies, as well as in American homes in general. Thus, by the 1850s the time was ripe for the beloved gift-giving Christmas figure of the American childhood to blossom into full-blown existence. "Mr. Moravian," writing in the Youth Department column of the weekly *Moravian* publication spoke positively of Santa Claus in 1856,[4] and in 1857,[5] and wrote specifically in 1869: "A little stocking pinned to the chimney-shelf... . A spray of evergreen stood in a box, blossoming with toys... ."[6]

Although no documented evidence for the Moravians' predilection for any one of the gift bringers before the mid-nineteenth century has been found, it is intriguing to speculate that along with their love of Christmas and children, perhaps some of them embraced aspects of the gift-bringer customs wherever they lived before that period. What is true is that Santa Claus gradually became a household word in the Moravian publications by the mid-nineteenth century. For that reason the long evolution of the gift bringer is here explored up to and after that point as a major element in the history of the American Christmas.

Certainly, St. Nicholas was one of the key figures in the evolution of the gift bringer, although there is speculation that an even earlier ancestor may have been a mixture of the mythological Teutonic (Germanic) gods Woden[7] and Thor,[8] as well as other Saturnalian[9] figures.[10] St. Nicholas is a somewhat shadowy figure who has attained such mythic proportions that researchers have become unsure of where the myth stops and the real person begins. In fact, there is no historical document attesting to his existence.[11] Whatever the case, he has become "a bridge between myth and history."[12]

What is generally stated about Nicholas is that he was born in what is now Turkey in about 270 or 280 A. D. and died perhaps on 6 December, about 343. He is said to have had a privileged Greek upbringing and early in life became an archbishop of Myra. Stories of his benevolence extended from Spain to Russia. Up until the Protestant Reformation Nicholas "was the foremost saint in Christendom," and early on became known as a patron of children.[13] One of the most widely known Nicholas stories concerns the rescue of three motherless daughters of an impoverished nobleman, who was planning to sell them into slavery or a worse fate because he had no money for their dowries. Nicholas saved them by throwing bags of gold through the window (or down the chimney) on successive nights. The detail that the money landed in stockings hung from the mantel to dry or shoes resting on the hearth may have been the foundation for the legend of hanging stockings or putting out shoes to receive gifts at Christmas.[14]

Some scholars believe that the association with Nicholas and the giving of gifts to children at Christmas occurred in the Middle Ages as early as the twelfth century[15] in France where Catholic nuns started the tradition of giving presents to poor children on the eve of the Saint's feast day.[16] Other researchers believe that the custom of gift giving to children began with St. Martin and passed on to Nicholas (see sidebar). Nevertheless, the custom became widespread. In Holland, the Bishop Nicholas was depicted riding on a white horse to deliver the gifts. Coincidentally, a folk belief was that St. Martin also rode a white horse in Belgium to deliver sweets on the eve of his Saint's Day, 11 November, or Martinmas, a festival especially popular in Belgium, Germany, Austria, and Denmark.[17]

As the Protestant Reformation intensified, Catholic saints were no longer in favor, and so the benevolent qualities attributed to Nicholas, for example, had to be transferred to a more suitable gift bearer. Sometime, probably in the 1600s, German Protestants chose the Christ Child (*Christkind, Christkindl, Christkindel,* or *Christkindlein*) as the surrogate of St. Nicholas. *Christkindel* was often portrayed pictorially as an angelic girl with wings who flew from house to house and rang a tiny silver bell when the presents and sometimes even the tree were delivered. Most children and adults found the angel more credible as a gift bringer than a tiny baby. The name eventually became Americanized as "Kriss Kringle," which finally melded into "Santa Claus." The name "Santa Claus" itself may have evolved from the Dutch *Sinterklass.*[18] The Christ Child was used as a gift bringer in other countries as well, such as in France as *Le Petit Noël* and in Spanish America as *El Nino.*[19]

Somewhere along the way shrewd parents saw the gift bringer as a way to induce good behavior from their children at Christmas, and thus the threat of the "rod," as earlier mentioned in Chapter One, was employed in a unique way. Synonymous with the "rod" were the switches and the black lumps of coal sometimes

St. Martin

Saint Martin, who died in the late fourth century, was an early pope and a martyr for whom there developed a Christian festival of partial fasting before Christmas. This period came to be known as Martinmas and later developed into Advent. It probably grew out of harvest celebrations, for in Germany St. Martin became known as the "patron saint of the harvest and a champion of the poor." The sixteenth-century Protestant Reformation altered the reference of "St. Martin" to Martin Luther, and the holiday became "Martin's Festival" or "Martin's Day," at which there were lantern parades and feasting (including the traditional goose usually associated with the celebration).[i] In some countries in Europe, St. Martin was a gift bringer to children. In Germany today, children may present rhymes and songs to neighbors in return for goodies and coins on 10 November, the eve of Martinmas.

left in the shoes, stockings, on the plates, or in the caps of the most recalcitrant children. Some nineteenth-century authors in America sought to discourage such demeaning methods of discipline. In 1848, a writer in Philadelphia's *Saturday Courier* cautioned that no stocking should "hang empty in the chimney corner; and even if Harry and Natty haven't been quite as good children as they ought to have been, don't disappoint them with a whip or an old rusty jews harp by way of punishment."[20] Author Marion Harland never forgot a rod in her stocking placed there by a visiting jokester.[21] Grown adults remembered with chagrin instances in their childhood of misplaced disciplinary cruelty at Christmas. One such occasion was recalled when the three brothers in a family excitedly hung up their stockings to await their treats. One received an abundance of gifts; the second received an orange and a book; the third received a rod. He did admit he had been a truant from school the day before and wondered how Santa knew that![22] The adults in this youth's family undoubtedly adhered firmly to a popular nineteenth-century maxim for children: "Prizes are the reward of labour. It is not sufficient to carry off the prize, but we should merit it."[23]

The actions of naughty children were addressed by various means in the gift-giving process. In order not to defile either the good Saint Nicholas or the Christ Child, these two personalities often brought helpers as servants to wield the punishment, exact the discipline, and produce the switches. The helpers were known by various names, such as *Krampus, Knecht*

Early-twentieth-century postcard featuring an angelic *Christkindel. Author's collection.*

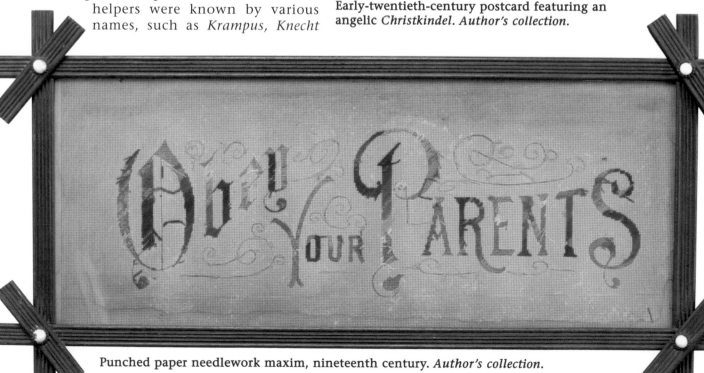

Punched paper needlework maxim, nineteenth century. *Author's collection.*

The Dark Side of the Gift Bringer

Magazines like *Godey's Lady's Book* and *Harper's New Monthly Magazine* presented various images of the gift bringer and his helpers to the American reader. In July and August 1863, in *Harper's* in two parts appeared a richly detailed account of an American family's extended stay in Germany. The *nouveau riche* John Brown from California (with seven children) experienced a German Christmas complete with the visit of Nicholas on his day, but this was a Nicholas like no other they had experienced! Mr. Brown wrote the following account, which began with the opening of his door to a spectacle that he said he could not have thought possible to happen in the nineteenth century!

It was a live goblin of the most ferocious aspect, full six feet high, with a tremendous long nose, and a chin to correspond, both fearfully red, and almost meeting at the points. His great goggle eyes absolutely glared; and when he snapped his nose and chin together it was terrible to behold him. His dress was of the most outlandish description: a great fur coat, hanging in folds to his feet, and fantastically decorated. Around his waist was a belt, from which hung three great bags filled with nuts, apples, and cakes. I assure you it was enough to startle a man of the strongest nerves. Without a word of explanation this gigantic monster marched into the middle of the room, bowing and scraping in the most absurd manner, to the profound astonishment and terror of the young ones. "SHOW ME ALL THE BAD CHILDREN!" said he, in a deep, sepulchral voice. This he said in German... munching nuts and flourishing his bunch of switches as he waited for a reply. Mr. Brown answered: "Ich glaube dieses Kinder sind alles gut! [I believe that the children here are good.]" to which the monster responded "Das is schon! Das is recht! Kommen sie hier, Kinder! [That is splendid! That is right. Come here, children.]" All were silent; and some of the little ones tried hard to get under the sofa. When the monster saw what a serious panic he had created he assumed a friendly and congenial aspect, and by dint of coaxing succeeded in drawing them out again, and forming them in a circle around him. Then he catechized them about their conduct and studies at school, and having satisfied his mind on this point, began to cast out whole handfuls of nuts and apples and cakes over the floor. They could not resist this display of munificence, as may well be supposed, but straightway, with merry shouts, fell to scrambling after the good things. The monster roared laughing at the fun, which set all the youngsters to laughing, partly in fear, and partly because they couldn't help it; whereupon, affecting to be highly enraged at being laughed at, the monster began to switch them up and down the room, hopping, skipping, jumping, rearing, and tearing like a madman let loose... I well-nigh burst my sides at his antics; and as for Mrs. Brown, she has been troubled with stitches ever since. Where he came from, or who sent him, or what his usual occupation is, I haven't the least idea. I only know he cost me two gulden [undoubtedly the tip]; and all this happened on St. Nicholas's day. The Germans call him Nicholas."[ii]

To further complicate matters, in describing the preparations for Christmas Day, Mr. Brown referred to "the genial spirit of Kris Kringle."[iii] Curiously, Brown's Nicholas acted and looked like the disciplinary helper, rather than the saint. In fact, he fit perfectly a description of the Pennsylvania German Belsnickle.

"Show me all the bad children!" from *Harper's Weekly*, 1863. *Author's collection.*

Ruprecht, Hans Trapp, *Swarte Piet, Pelznickel,* or *Peltz-nickel* (Nicholas dressed in fur). "Belsnickle," or "Bellschnickel," was an American derivative of the *Peltznickel* in "Pennsylvania Dutch" country. The Belsnickle in that area, in fact, sometimes took the place of Santa Claus.[24] Since these characters did the "dirty work," so to speak, their fur costumes and hair reflected it, and often they were soot-smeared (particularly if they had negotiated the length of a chimney) ragged, and wild. They were also terrifying, the degree of their fright, of course, determined by the parents, relatives, neighbors, or friends, who crafted the impersonations. They entered with a roar and a whip, catechized the frightened children, and threw edible goodies on the floor, occasionally stinging a bolder hand or a backside with the tip of the whip. Sometimes the names and attributes of these characters became scrambled in transmission and in tradition, but by whatever name, they had impressive power.

Another Christmas figure with no strong religious ties that gradually became popular in secular Germany in the nineteenth century was the *Weihnachts- mann,* ("Watch Night Man"), somewhat akin to the English Father Christmas.[25] Traveling alone, he carried both toys and switches and brought Christmas trees as well, as did the little Christ Child, also frequently depicted with decorated trees. However, it was mainly the Christ Child, or *Christkindlein,* that immigrated to America and often rode a donkey in making the rounds. Sometimes said to slip through the keyhole, the invisible *Christ- kindlein* deposited the gifts on a plate or in a basket. A candle might be placed in a window by the family to light the way. Children left hay or straw as a treat for the donkey, just as they would later leave cookies and milk for Santa.

A candle might be placed in a window by the family to light the way. Children left hay or straw as a treat for the donkey, just as they would later leave cookies and milk for Santa.

Christkindlein gradually became "Kriss Kringle," and two widely sold books[26] published in the 1840s with this name in the titles made the transformed elfin man an instant success. He hung the presents on the tabletop tree in the German manner and continued in popularity until his melding into Santa Claus. Kriss Kringle, however, was not above being a disciplinarian, either. Note the introductory warning in an 1852 book: "If there should chance to be any idle, disobedient, bad-tempered boy or girl in the house, who neglects lessons, beats brothers and sisters, scratches faces, tells lies, breaks things, &c. &c.," that child could expect a rod and would feel disappointed on Christmas Day when the others were enjoying their gifts.[27]

In America, the disciplinarian St. Nicholas as described by John Brown (see sidebar) would have been the Belsnickle (derived from *Peltznickel,* or Nicholas dressed in furs), who performed much like the German servant-helper. This figure had immigrated to America, but was now an amalgamated personage created by either single men, often neigh- bors and friends in rural areas, or groups of young carousers in urban areas out for a rousing good time at Christmas. Sometimes the intent was positive, sometimes not. Often from the lower classes, these figures emanated intimidation by their outlandish dress and their bold manner. In England, a related custom the "Lord of Misrule, or comptroller of the revels," also called the "Christmas Prince," may have had as its source the European custom of the Boy- Bishop, which had its origin in Roman times. This tradition went back to 867 in England and originally was intended "to control or superintend the festivities at court."[28] The novel idea was a total reversal of class and power in which a boy was allowed to be a bishop for the day or even longer. The concept made the voyage across the Atlantic and was known by the Moravians in Salem at least in theory during the nineteenth century, as a student at the girls' school wrote that there were "still those to whom the senseless excesses, the drunkenness even of an Abbott of Misrule, or a Lord of Unreason, are dearer pleasures than the Holy joy of a sanctified season of remembrance, of home love, of charity, of good-will to men... ."[29] Certainly the Belsnickle fit into this stereotype.

The African Americans in the coastal area of Wilmington, North Carolina, had their carousing and begging "John Cooner" at Christmas, a custom with roots in Jamaica and the West Indies. The English had another somewhat similar tradition called mumming, a custom that was practiced in Philadelphia in the nineteenth century. A newspaper of that city recorded one of the speeches used by the Christmas mummers, a word described in the 1828 Walker's *Dictionary* as "maskers" who frolicked.[30] The speech began with the following:

SANCTE CLAUS goed heilig Man!
Trek uwe beste Tabaert aen,
Reis daer me'e na Amsterdam,
Van Amsterdam na 'Spanje,
Daer Appelen van Oranje,
Daer Appelen van granaten,
Die rollen door de Straaten.
SANCTE CLAUS, myn goede Vriend!
Ik heb U allen tyd gedient,
Wille U my nu wat geven,
Ik zal U dienen alle myn Leven.

Saint Nicholas, good holy man!
Put on the Tabard,* best you can,
Go, clad therewith, to Amsterdam,
From Amsterdam to Hispanje,
Where apples bright † of Oranje,
And likewise those *granate* ‡ surnam'd,
Roll through the streets, all free unclaim'd.
Saint Nicholas, my dear good friend!
To serve you ever was my end,
If you will, now, me something give,
I'll serve you ever while I live.

* Kind of jacket.   † Oranges.   ‡ Pomegranates.

St. Nicholas broadside by Alexander Anderson commissioned by John Pintard, 1810.
Collection of The New-York Historical Society, negative #28883.

Room, room, brave gallants,
    give us room to sport,
For in this room we wish for
    to resort.
And to repeat to you our merry
    rhyme,
For remember, good sirs, this
    is Christmas time.
The time to cut up goose pies
    now doth appear.
So we are come to act our
    merry Christmas here... .[31]

Mumming came out of an Episcopalian custom brought from England in which performers and singers presented a short folk act as they went from house to house where they expected refreshments and/or small coins as gifts on Christmas Eve. Eventually it evolved into gangs of young men who sometimes became obnoxious in their daring and intrusive entrances into households. The custom was described in *The Moravian* of 1 January 1863 as one no longer practiced, but there are other reports of its much longer existence in various forms, such as the Belsnickle. Though no reference has been found to this custom in Wachovia, the North Carolina Archives contains a little book belonging to the Samuel Patterson children (whose mother was Mary E. Fries of Salem) in the mid-nineteenth century in which a picture labeled "Belsnickel" appears. However, the little man going down the chimney looks much more like Kriss Kringle and was probably meant to be a genial gift bringer, proving once again that much confusion existed in just who these various personages really were.

One author attempts to explain all the confusion in the following way:

Like a river winding its way to the sea fed by countless tributaries, the festival we call "Christmas" has rolled down to us over the course of two millennia. It has taken many

COVER OF AN EARLY COPY OF *THE NIGHT BEFORE CHRISTMAS.* AUTHOR'S COLLECTION.

twists and turns on its journey across the rugged landscape of the ages, thereby gaining and losing a range of meanings, legends, customs, and symbols. It has been fed along the way by such tributary sources as the Bible, pre-Christian calendar customs, Christian lore and tradition, and a wide range of folk practices, beliefs, and symbols. The interventions and innovations of many individuals, be they saints, kings, queens, musicians, writers, business men and women, manufacturers, scholars, clergy, or politicians, have also swelled the flow. Today, standing at the mouth of the river, the yearly phenomena we call "Christmas" roars past us each December, a joyous tumult composed of all these influences.[32]

St. Nicholas came to America with the Dutch in the fifteenth century, but gradually faded away until revived in the nineteenth century by the writer Washington Irving, who wrote a book that made

Nicholas widely known. The book was *Diedrich Knickerbocker's History of New-York*, and it became a best seller, helped along with some very clever advertising and an appropriate release date of 6 December 1809. Some of Irving's significant details that later led to the grounding of the American Santa Claus were:

[L]o, the good St. Nicholas came riding over the tops of the trees, in that selfsame wagon wherein he brings his yearly presents to children... . And he lit his pipe by the fire...and as he smoked the smoke from his pipe ascended into the air and spread like a cloud over-head... . And when St. Nicholas had smoked his pipe, he twisted it in his hat-band, and laying his finger beside his nose, gave the astonished Van Kortlands a very significant look, then mounting his wagon, he returned over the tree-tops and disappeared.[33]

Irving's literary friends, caught up in the Nicholas story, helped to make it more American. His brother-in-law changed the visit to New Year's Eve, making it somewhat English in custom. So, depending on where one lived and one's culture, the gifts for the children might be brought on the eve of 6 December, of 25 December, or of 1 January. Irving promoted long-forgotten English Christmas traditions in 1819 in his stories of Squire Bracebridge in *The Sketch Book*, another influential book of nostalgic holiday customs, which also included "The Legend of Sleepy Hollow" and "Rip Van Winkle."

In 1810, John Pintard, also a New Yorker and friend of Irving, created a celebratory broadside of Nicholas as a present to the members of the New York Historical Society for their annual meeting

A Merry Christmas

on 6 December. Nicholas in a long robe with bare feet, stands with his scepter surrounded by a saintly halo, above which are inscribed his name and dates, and at his side are a beehive with bees (symbols of industry and hard work) and a small bulldog (symbol of fidelity). On the other side are a fireplace with a boiling teapot, sausages, and a plate of waffles (probably dripping with honey, and altogether symbolizing the comfort of good food and fellowship), along with a cat (sign of domesticity), a warm fire (sign of togetherness at the hearthstone of home), and two stockings hanging from the mantel. One is bulging with toys; the other holds a bunch of switches. A smiling little girl with an apron full of toys and fruits stands above the filled stocking;

a crying boy is shown above the empty stocking. Thus, goodness is rewarded; naughtiness is not. Clearly, many symbols of the American Christmas surrounding St. Nicholas have been put into place in this one early picture, which was by Pintard's calculated design. He was seeking to establish positive American traditions suitable for the republic, rather than the pointless, noisy, drunken, and destructive behavior that had become accepted Christmas behavior all over the country. For example, to show his predilection for suitable official holidays, Pintard had lobbied for the birthday of George Washington and the Fourth of July.[34]

More Christmas symbols were introduced in 1821 in a poem entitled "Santeclaus" (see Chapter

One) in which a judgmental gift bringer arrived by reindeer on Christmas Eve to leave presents for good boys and girls and the dreaded rod for naughty ones. Thus appearing within a short period of time in the first two decades of the nineteenth century were a number of invented traditions that set the stage for the ultimate American gift giver in a poem that one commentator called "the greatest piece of genre word-painting in the English language."[35]

In 1822, just before Christmas, Clement Clark Moore, an Episcopalian of Dutch ancestry who was teaching Oriental and Greek literature as well as Hebrew at a theological seminary he had helped to found in New York, created for his children a long poem, "An Account of a Visit from St. Nicholas."[36] Moore described the saint as a "right jolly old elf," who arrived on the roof in a miniature sleigh pulled by eight reindeer all with distinctive names. After filling all of the stockings of the children, he laid "his finger aside of his nose" and rose up the chimney to depart while calling out, "Happy Christmas to all and to all a good night." (The first printing of this line was "Happy Christmas"; "Merry Christmas" appeared in 1862.[37] An early alternate opening line sometimes used into the 1840s was "'Twas the night before New Year's."[38]) It is interesting to note that Salemite Charles Bahnson, in a letter home to his family during the Civil War, wrote, "Happy Christmas & a Merry New Year."[39]

Moore was not immediately known as the author of the poem, probably viewing it as a frivolous flight of whimsy for his children, but in 1823 the poem appeared in the *Troy Sentinel* of New York two days before Christmas. It was not signed, but the story of how it was published gives credit to a female visitor in the Moore home who copied it and sent it to the paper. Moore acknowledged the poem by its inclusion in a publication of his verses in 1844 as "A Visit." In an 1862 interview, he said he patterned St. Nick after "a portly rubicund Dutchman" who lived in New York near the house of his father.[40]

Since Moore read widely and moved in the same circles as the other previously mentioned authors of influence, he undoubtedly borrowed images from them as well as others. Whatever the case, Moore "wove a subtle reinterpretation of the gift-bringer into a memorable vignette that balanced magic with reality."[41] St. Nicholas, good-natured, believable, and physically solid, was appearing in an authentic American home setting with the father of the household as witness and narrator. As told, the astonishing event seemed quite plausible.

There were various artistic attempts at depiction of St. Nick that varied considerably through the next decades, but it was a German immigrant who encapsulated the image. Noted political cartoonist Thomas Nast, beginning in 1863, spent years refining the presentation of Santa Claus, which we essentially still use today. The toys and other gifts this Santa made came from his own hands; in essence he was the household producer, as well as the distributor, with the elves helping in the workshop. He had the characteristics of an admirable citizen: punctuality (Nast drew him with a watch), generosity, affability, dependability, and industry in handmaking his products, in opposition to what some considered rampant capitalism. Nast's thirty-year project depicted a portly Santa dressed in a red outfit at his workshop at the North Pole with his list of behavior of all the good children, countless toys, and last but not least, the letters "US" on a strap. Thus, the toys and the abbreviation for the United States indicated the importance of the nation's children.[42] Nast himself created this image with his own children by decorating his house and lavishing presents on the family. His most original touch, according to one historian, was the North Pole. Nast's grandson claimed that his grandfather chose this location because "it was equidistant from most countries in the Northern Hemisphere,"[43] a place to work without disturbance, and one that "no country could claim as its own."[44]

Adults, of course, were ultimately the ones to provide continuity and embellishments to the Santa Claus myth, and they did so through stories, pictures, and household traditions such as letters written at the kitchen table by Santa and tell-tale crumbs left from the "cookies and milk" put out by the children for the global traveler. *The Moravian* validated this practice in 1869 by writing, "And then the letter from Santa Claus him-

Christmas ornament top featuring Uncle Sam and Santa Claus, twentieth century. *Author's collection.*

The Evolution of the Gift Bringer and Gifts

The Gift of the Magi

Briefly exploring the history of gift giving will lay the foundation for how American children began to be encouraged by the delightful reception of Christmas treats, a situation that had already existed for several centuries in the Moravian Church. The custom of gift giving had spread all over Europe by the Middle Ages. The association of gifts and Christmas began over two thousand years ago with the presentation of gold, frankincense, and myrrh brought by the Three Wise Men to the baby Jesus.[iv] Gift giving had been in existence for centuries practiced by the Romans who exchanged with family and friends goodwill tokens such as special deity-related twigs, cakes, honey, candles, wax fruit, clay dolls, and coins at midwinter during the festivals of Saturnalia and Kalends.[v] Gifts were also presented to the Roman emperors by their subjects. These gifts were New Year's tokens, and it took centuries in early Christian times for the practice to be transferred gradually to Christmas.

Fraktur with the magi drawn in the upper right corner, by Johann Carl Scheibeler, Frederick County, Maryland, c. 1790. *MESDA*.

self, telling us to be good children always... ."[45] One writer has suggested that grownups needed Santa and the Christmas tree to counteract the materialism that was becoming an increasing concern in the country.[46]

It was inevitable that Santa Claus would be drafted into the commercialism of the country. By the mid-1820s he appeared as a purveyor of goods in some advertisements. By the 1840s he was being used as an attraction by many merchants. In Salem, although the *People's Press* began operation in 1851, the ads for Christmas did not proliferate until the 1870s and 1880s. In 1879 F. W. Meller began his ad for November 27 with the headline, "HEADQUARTERS OF SANTA CLAUS." Elsewhere in the country such headlines as this were beginning to appear in the 1850s. The earliest known was in Philadelphia in 1841 when a live impersonator appeared in a local store as "Criscringle."[47] Schouler's New Store in Salem, as advertised in December 1889, started its ad with "HURRAH FOR SANTA CLAUS!" and claimed that year to have for sale "1,000 dolls from 1 cent to $5." A student wrote in the publication *The Academy: A Monthly Journal of Salem Academy* in December 1880, "We were occupied with the pleasant duty of visits to the gay and glittering stores, where Santa Claus is annually at hand to help us in our Christmas joys."[48]

By 1903, there was recognition of the new technology of the twentieth century in providing unique modern transportation for Santa. Calvary Moravian Church reported in *The Wachovia Moravian*: "[E]ach member received a picture of some scene in the life of Christ, with a cornucopeia [*sic*] of confectionary on the back, whilst the smaller children were the recipients of an 'up-to-date,' Santa Claus in his automobile loaded with nicely assorted candies."[49]

Gifts

Children in the nineteenth century American home were not always given the Christmas of treats and toys they were beginning to hear about in books, in Sunday School, and in the classroom. In addition, as we have seen, parents sometimes struggled to maintain authority through withdrawn, often rigid, dignity that they had been shown in their own childhoods. They felt uncomfortable and uncertain as to how to proceed with or whether to indulge in these new Christmas customs. However, it was beginning to be realized that the mind of a child was not that of a miniature adult as had been thought from the Middle Ages to the Enlightenment.[50] Charlestonian William Gilmore Simms, in an 1840s southern plantation Christmas story called "Maize in Milk: A Christmas Story of the South,"[51] explained the main character, benevolent gentleman farmer and parent Colonel Openheart, in this way: obviously deviating somewhat from the everyday social norm of the time, "He had a queer notion that children were only children, and that play was as necessary to their hearts, their growth, nay, their morals, as *birch, logic and religion* [emphasis added]."[52]

Giving children time to play and not making them solely "machines for work"[53] was a subject about which parents and other adults were having to come to terms. A Moravian missionary in Springplace, Georgia, wisely undertook this subject, writing in a letter to Salem on one occasion, "pupils must certainly have time for pleasure."[54] At another time he said, "With love and kindness one can achieve anything... ."[55] Brother

Handwritten text decoration in the window of Salem's Single Brothers' House

Jacob Van Vleck from Salem wrote the next year, that with youth "encouragement is often more effective than an order."[56]

In England, people presented presents "to those... above and below them in the social hierarchy...which did not necessarily express affection but rather acknowledged one's place in a system of social rank."[57] The "presents" might be farm produce from the peasants to their lord and a Christmas feast from him in return. The New Year's offerings to royalty by the nobility could be extravagantly lavish. Little English Princess Mary in the early 1500s received as New Year's gifts such diverse items as a cup of gold, a pomander, some wrought smocks, handkerchiefs, a little chain, hose in gold and silk, a gown of carnation satin, a silver-gilt pepper box, a diamond ring, a fair steel glass, a pair of

silver snuffers, a pen and inkhorn, silver gilt, a fuming box of silver, and a marchpane.[58]

In certain European countries the eve of St. Nicholas Day, 5 December, became a time for the giving of gifts to children. There was a thirteenth-century French song that began:

Nicholas patron of good children,
I kneel for you to intercede.
Hear my voice through the clouds
And this night give me some toys.[59]

In Germany there were "Christ-bundles" for children as early as the sixteenth century.[60] One researcher states that, "In Germany in 1531 Martin Luther noted that children put out their stockings in hope that St. Nicholas would fill them with good things." A sixteenth-century list of Christmas presents for German children included[61] apples, nuts, sweetmeats,[62] coins, dolls, clothing, religious books, and paper for writing, as well as the ominous small stick.[63] At this time the well-known "Nurnberg Christmas Fair" (famous for its toys) was appropriately called "the Children's Market."[64] It is now known as the *Christkindlesmarkt.*[65]

Early gifts in America were most often given to the poor by the rich. Masters gave to their apprentices and journeymen; gentlemen gave to their servants; adults gave to children. Presbyterian Philip Fithian, tutor to the wealthy Robert Carter children in Virginia, groused somewhat in 1773 about the custom of responding with an endless round of money to the morning greetings of "Joyful Christmas" by all the servants.[66]

Active buying for Christmas as well as money being given for presents was recorded by the Moravian Brethren Steiner and Von Schweinitz on a 1,300-mile trip from the North that ended in Salem on 28 December 1799. They wrote: "The 23rd. In Abingdon (Va.) it was very lively, as many from the neighborhood had come to buy something for Christmas... . In Austinville we spent the night at the inn of the widow Jenkins. Mrs. Jenkins complained that it had been wild in her house that day, for Mr. Austin had given a dollar to each person connected with his lead workers and they had been enjoying themselves. Now, however, the money was all spent, they had gone home, and the house was quiet... ."[67] Proffering money as gifts, dating at least from the Romans, continued to be practiced and became quite popular by 1890 when new bills and shiny gold pieces were obtained from the banks for this purpose.[68]

A descriptive example of money for gifts in an upper-class American family was documented by Robert Gilmor in 1826.[69] He wrote that as it was "the annual festival of peace and joy,

The Moravians started very early in giving gifts as symbols of their religious beliefs and as affectionate tokens to children at church on Christmas Eve. Lighted candles, beautifully printed Bible verses, and tasty treats such as ginger cakes or honey cakes (lebkuchen) and apples were all popular eighteenth-century gifts.

especially in families," his family of eighteen without children dined with him at 4 o'clock on Christmas Day. The children were promised to come the next day, but most came after breakfast to get "the usual Christmas gifts." He called on his infirm mother after church, "and the females were well rewarded by a handsome gift of money, cash. My wife received one hundred dollars, being the same my father used to give her." As promised, the next day Gilmor reported that the "younger children of the family dined with my wife and me and amused us much with their humours and playfulness."[70]

A decade later Moravian minister G. F. Bahnson wrote touchingly while in Salem on 2 January 1835 of "a small package enveloped in paper" for his wife as a "New

year present." It was fifty cents from "quite a poor girl who has to earn every cent by her own hands & whom my H[ortensia, his wife] had seen but one single time." She took it "with a view of making some present or other in return."[71]

The Moravians started very early in giving gifts as symbols of their religious beliefs and as affectionate tokens to children at church on Christmas Eve. Lighted candles, beautifully printed Bible verses, and tasty treats such as ginger cakes or honey cakes (*Lebkuchen*) and apples were all popular eighteenth-century gifts. One researcher believes such gifts given by the Moravians in Bethlehem in 1745 to their children to be the earliest on record in America.[72] Sometimes other items were added. In Bethlehem on 24 December 1756, the children received candles, and in addition the girls, to their great joy, got "new red ribbons for their caps."[73] The next year the children got "little English salt-books" (possibly *psalters,* or books of the Psalms.)[74] The Nazareth, Pennsylvania, store account of 1795-1806 noted on 18 December 1799 that Jacob Van Vleck paid 10 shillings for "100 Christmas gifts," probably for the children.[75] From the same store there is also an entry from 31 December 1796 of "cakes at Christmas 4. 5."[76]

"A piece of cake" as a gift was recorded in 1760 in Bethabara, an outlying community in Wachovia. "On Christmas Day the English children from the mill came to see our Christmas decoration, they were so poorly clad that it would have moved a stone to pity. We told them why we rejoiced like children and gave to each a piece of cake."[77] In the nearby farm community of Bethania that same year, the Moravian records noted that each of the twenty-four children from the neighborhood attending a lovefeast were given "a pretty Christmas verse and a ginger cake, the first they had ever seen."[78]

Embellished wreath with a Christmas verse, unknown maker, Salem, NC, 1805. *OSMG.*

Ever thoughtful of education, the Moravians in Salem in 1784 noted that particular Christmas that they decided not to write the verses in colored ink and gave the reason that "[I]t is better to give them an opportunity to write their own verses, each according to his or her ability."[79]

The power of little painted wreaths with Bible texts and verses inside was attested to on 22 December 1806, when Anna Gambold at the Springplace Moravian Indian Mission wrote of

such gifts frequently given by the Gambolds as a visual reminder for both children and adults of letting Jesus into their lives. She recorded:

In the evening a traveler named Thomas Lewis came to spend the night with us... He was very friendly, and when he saw the colorful little wreaths which we painted as Christmas presents for the children, he asked us for one of them. This pleased us very much, and we told him that he could choose one. Then he took a little wreath in the shape of a heart, and asked for it, and also

asked that we write something inside it for him. Brother Gambold wrote the text, "Only give my Son your heart and let my ways be pleasing to your eyes." This provided an opportunity to explain to him to whom the heart belonged, and how happy one is when he has really given his heart to the Savior, during which he listened quite attentively. He is still a young man.[80]

Using these embellished verses as attractive reminders of Jesus's love was common at the mission, and withholding them from

Painting of Jesus, Mary, and John the Baptist by John Valentine Haidt, 1755-65. *OSMG.*

Certain images of the "poor and mean" child produced powerful results. On 30 December 1807, an American Indian named "the Flea" came to see the Springplace *Putz*, which included a picture of the Baby Jesus wrapped in rags on one side and a picture of the young John the Baptist in colorful garments on the other side. Anna Gambold made note of the fact that the colorful nature of the latter was totally lost on the man who saw only the humble baby and wanted a picture for himself, but not under glass, as this obviously was, but just a copy on paper.[84] Did Anna Rosina then make a gift of a watercolor or pen and ink sketch of the original for this man? One would think so.

Testifying to the labor and care involved in the creation of the little verses within painted wreaths, school items, goodies, and clothes given to the children, is a letter from John Gambold at the mission to Christian Benzien, 29 November 1808: "[j]ust now before Christmas there are many school items to be written with which I cannot refrain from helping my dear little mother."[85] In a letter written on 30 January 1808, the items were detailed. For each of the children "who had learned and recited the answers" [to the "Catechisation"] was given..."a copy of the same bound in beautiful colored paper. . .and in place of a title page provided with a short Bibleverse [sic] framed in a little flower-wreath." All of the four children received a new cotton shirt; for those learning arithmetic "the multiplication tables [were] written out in full and pasted on a little board." Also, treats included "some honey cakes, sweet potatoes, dried peaches, walnuts, hazelnuts, peanuts and chestnuts." In addition, they received a scarf (or neckerchief) and "cotton for a frock." The fabric, if not purchased readymade, could have started with sowing, tending, hoeing, weeding,[86] and

oncs who strayed was also practiced. Reward and punishment was a recurrent theme at this time. On 29 December 1807, a young man named Caesar came to the house to show the verses he and his relatives had received the previous year. He was told that the reason he did not receive one this year was because of his "apathy towards God's word."[81]

In a letter to Christian Benzien from John Gambold on 7 December 1806, Gambold mentioned, "The verses with the Springplace borders," which may make those from Anna's brush unique to that area and particularly desirable to people like Caesar and his family.[82]

An early painted wreath in the Old Salem Museums & Gardens collection may very well be from the hand of Anna Rosina Gambold and judging from the content was undoubtedly made as a Christmas gift. It is dated 1805 and contains the following Christmas verse, which with the exception of one word, is verbatim from verse 2 of hymn 66, tune 22, in the *Moravian Liturgy and Hymns*. The hymn is attributed to Martin Luther:

Awake my heart; my Soul
    rejoice [arise].
Look, who in yonder manger lies.
Who is that child, so poor
    and mean?
'Tis he, who all things doth
    sustain.[83]

growing the cotton, then picking, carding, and spinning it before dying the thread, weaving the cloth, and finally cutting out and sewing the garments by hand.[87] Although not as intensive, much labor would also be required to harvest, prepare, and dry the peaches, as well as mix and bake the honey cakes, and grow the sweet potatoes and peanuts. Since candles were always part of the Christmas lovefeast, a cold day would have to be found to dip those. Byhan wrote that year, "Dorel [his wife] was just then making wax candles for Christmas Eve... ."[88] It was a prodigious task, indeed, to create such loving gifts in the wilderness—although it should be noted that the American Indian children did help with the chores.

In 1812, in Springplace on 25 December, it was written: "Then those children who can already read each received a Bible as a gift from the honorable members of the Philadelphia Bible Society in Salem. Numerous useful books, little Primers and other spiritual little tracts increased their joy, some from the congregational Brothers and Sisters, some sent by the honorable Female Cent. Society in Newark."[89]

Along with the books and tracts, the children also received "ginger cakes, dried blueberries, chestnuts, hickory nuts and other things of the kind, also some of the dried apple slices... also sugar candies," as well as the green wax candles (sent by the Kramsches from Salem).[90] On 25 December 1817, two American Indian families were sent on their way from Springplace with presents of "apple biscuits."[91]

On Christmas Day in 1819 after the children's hour, the Gambolds "handed out small children's cookies, apple chips (*Schnize*), chestnuts, etc., also the sugar candy sent for them by dear Sister V. Schweiniz... . They also received tracts and little

Then those children who can already read each received a Bible as a gift from the honorable members of the Philadelphia Bible Society in Salem.

wreaths with Christmas Eve verses to those who had not been here the evening before."[92]

A gift book frequently used by the Moravians and other religious groups was the moralistic tale or the religious tract, published by such groups as the Sunday School Union and the American Tract Society. As the latter emphasized on the title page of one of its volumes of the 1830s: "The benefits to be derived from Education may be greatly assisted by the dispersion of small cheap Tracts on religious and moral duties."[93] There is in the Old Salem Museums & Gardens collection a small book published by the American Sunday School Union in 1832. It is much like the little tracts given out at Springplace, at St. Philips, and many other places. The title is *Julia Changed, or, The True Secret of a Happy Christmas.*[94] This was meant to be a special gift, as the spine and corners are leather, and it is illustrated with engravings. It belonged to "Adelaide," according to the ink signature, and she carefully colored some of the pictures. The message is that after much thought Julia gives her heart to Christ on Christmas Day and writes Him a letter to that effect, thus becoming even more of a model child than she is already.

The importance of these books in spreading the gospel is

testified by John Gambold in a letter to Salem, "The tracts distributed at Christmas and since then continue to preach in silence, of which we receive encouraging reports from time to time."[95] Johann Leinbach on a buying trip to Fayetteville in 1830 deplored the bad breakfast and the dirty surroundings at a place near "Ashborough" but he was so taken by the owner's children that he gave sixpence to one and tracts to the others.[96] Leinbach, while not a missionary, as a lay person obviously still had tracts on hand for such occasions.

The effect on the children of the missionaries and their little gifts of tracts was evidenced by Salem lay missionary Van Zevely along the Blue Ridge in the 1830s. He arrived at a mountain house where no one seemed to be at home, but when he looked through a crack he saw "huddled together on a bed...a number of children" who would not open the door until he identified himself as "the man who gave little books to children." Then they scrambled to the door and cried cheerfully, "Oh! is it you, Granddaddy?"[97] Zevely was often called this affectionate name by the children and universally referred to by most inhabitants as "the good old man."[98] Along with a small pig that was lying on the hearth they then all shared the warmth of the fire and chatted agreeably. Zevely learned that their father was attending a shooting match, which he called "the bane of this neighborhood," and their mother was gathering chestnuts. He, of course, gave a tract to each child and described them as "greatly delighted" with their gifts.[99]

Along with passing out tracts it was a given matter that adults in positions of responsibility in the church and in the school organized and participated in the creation of Christmas gifts and decorations. As a mature woman, Eliza Vierling, daughter of Dr.

THE EVOLUTION OF THE GIFT BRINGER AND GIFTS

Samuel Benjamin Vierling, reminisced about her youthful days as a teacher at the Salem Girls' School in the 1820s. She wrote:

The girls all wore caps instead of hats outside the house. These caps were made of bobbinet [a kind of netted gauze or lace made by machine]—a round crown, & all about it a very full double ruching [a trim made by pleating, fluting, or gathering a strip of fabric]. In the edges of the ruchings strands of floss were run & the more threads of floss were used the fuller & prettier the caps were. For one Christmas I had to make 21 of those caps one for each girl in my room, & often stayed up until twelve o'clock working at them, but did not receive a cent of pay for the extra work."[100]

Like the useful caps, presents in Wachovia during this period were probably few in number and generally simple, handmade items or edible goods. Although they were sometimes mentioned, they were seldom described, perhaps indicating that the thought rather than the gift itself was the important aspect. Schoolteacher Peter Wolle spoke in 1816 of small gifts like sugarthings purchased at the store for his godchildren.[101] He mentioned receiving a Christmas gift of "a waxcandle with three wicks and 2 apples."[102] Susannah Kramsch wrote of receiving an orange from Mr. Bagge on 13 December 1821. The next year she recorded on 19 December 1822, "got some oranges from Mr Bagge."[103]

Oranges and sugar things notwithstanding, German toys, sophisticated for the time, had begun to enter North American markets by the end of the eighteenth century. In 1784, orders were placed by importers from Philadelphia. The large markets in Germany were in Nuremberg, Leipzig, and Dresden. Fueled by the wishes and demands of the public, sellers were requesting quantities. John Jacob Astor (1763-1848), a native of Germany who became an emulated financier, began

Oranges and sugar things notwithstanding, German toys, sophisticated for the time, had begun to enter North American markets by the end of the eighteenth century.

his career by ordering toys; one year he ordered an astounding 17,000 dolls, 6,000 noisemakers, and 17,622 musical instruments.[104] The first mention of toys in Salem came in 1785 when "one green tin box with playthings" was recorded.[105]

Brother Biwighausen in his "small ware stall" in Salem had "Nurnberg toys" in 1804, along with a miscellany of brushes of all kinds, ribbons and ropes, raisins, almonds, sweetmeats, salted fish, and cow-feed.[106] In 1810, when Brother and Sister Kramsch were running a "small-goods" store in Salem where they sold some toys, she recorded playthings bought by out-of-town visitors, but not at Christmas.

The first mention of the word "toy" in the Salem congregation's pottery inventory was in 1822, although in 1806 the inventory for the Girls' School listed "'Potters Toy ware' at 37 cents under the heading 'Merchandise.'"[107] It was noted that animal molds, perhaps counted as toys, appeared in 1804. By 1822, toy dogs and sheep were listed and dolls appeared the next year.[108]

In 1830 what is possibly the earliest documented Christmas gift toy in Salem was a peep show, or optical toy, given to five-year-old Antoinette Schulz, daughter

of the shoemaker Samuel.[109] Optical toys such as this, which the viewer could enjoy by peering through a small hole, were later developed into toy theaters.[110] Naturally, the monetary value of the toys children received was based on the economic status of their families. Affluent people could spend more money for costlier and fancier goods; people of few means might make some items for their children.

The unusual placement of a faraway Baltimore merchant's advertisement of toys in the *Raleigh Register* (North Carolina) appeared in October 1818 and included: "A few boxes of Toys, suitable for Christmas gifts. Which, together with a great variety of other Staple and Fancy Articles (too numerous to specify) will be sold on accommodating terms." In Washington, D.C., in 1818, a notice highlighted "a variety of German and French TOYS, suitable for presents for Christmas and New Year" which was proclaimed along with all sorts of nuts, fruits, and sweets.[111]

With guns and rifles a common sight in early America, boys received toy replicas for Christmas or New Year's, as Rosalie Calvert reported in 1815 in Maryland. "[Charles and Henry] fired them twenty times in one minute, until they had used up all the flints that made them fire, and we had to get more. Right now they are marching like soldiers with their muskets on their shoulders."[112] Salem gunsmith, silversmith, and clock and watch repairer John Vogler made a small rifle for his ten-year-old son Elias in about 1835; the boy's name was engraved on the patch-box lid, assuredly a source of pride to the owner.[113] Although hunting at Christmas was common throughout the southern back-country, in Wachovia hunting as well as fishing at Christmas and on the Sabbath were forbidden. Brother Van Zeveley related a conversation with a mountain youth who asked about the harm of enjoying these two sports on the Lord's Day. Zeveley's reply was that the Bible forbade it, citing the commandment "Remember the Sabbath and keep it holy."[114]

A 1798 hunting expedition yielded a Christmas gift of sorts: a reunion with a loved one for a little girl in Bethlehem. On Christmas Eve a receipt signed by principal Jacob Van Vleck of the girls' school for Mr. Nathan Beach acknowledged the payment of "Twenty Five Pounds in Deer Skins." Hannah Beach, a student at the school during this period, must have enjoyed her father's carefully calculated visit at this particular time of year, not only to pay her school fees with an unusual commodity but also to see her and perhaps enjoy together the Moravian Christmas traditions.[115]

Another doting father, G. F. Bahnson, wrote in December 1836 about a gift for his little daughter received in a letter from his aunt, "containing a very nice little ring for our darling Angelica."[116] Later that month he noted, "Our good Sr Nancy Bagge made her appearance to day, having come quite alone in the stage. She presented us with a whole load of good things, for ourselves & child. The nicest cooking apparatus for little children to play with cakes, wine &ct oh she is kindness personified."[117]

Louisa Hagen (Sussdorff) wrote on 24 December 1837 that she made Mr. S. (who turned out to be her future husband) "a gift of a [unintelligible]." Even though we do not know exactly what this gift was, it must have been handmade. The next day she recorded, "Christmas gifts are the order of the day, I received a number of them!"[118] Bahnson mentioned in his 1838 diary that on Christmas Day in Bethlehem the family "bestowed

nice presents upon our darling Angel. Aunt was much pleased with her wreath, it looks indeed beautiful."[119] In Lisette Vogler's account book of expenditures she mentioned "candy for the baby" on 19 December 1840 in Salem. On 20 December she recorded "8 sleigh bells (for Elias)—.80" and "a small Britannia mug (for Alfred)—.25."[120]

Eliza Vierling Kremer recalled gifts for Christmas at the Salem Girls' School in the second decade of the nineteenth century: "When the call [to get up] came, there was a rush to the rooms to view

A Christingle with gum drops and red ruff. *Author's collection.*

the tables where on the previous evening the principal and teachers had distributed for each girl a package of cakes, nuts and confectionery with a lighted taper at each desk. There was scarce time to enjoy breakfast so eager were they to return to their rooms. Then there was an exchange of presents from one to another."[121] Eliza's description is only one of many similar mentions of Christmas gifts by various girls at the school all through the nineteenth century. The unforgettable experiences with the lingering memories were best expressed by Sarah H. Rand, who wrote from Banks, Wake County, North Carolina, on 29 December 1879: "I well remember the only Christmas I spent at Salem. It was seven years ago, but I have carefully preserved the little wax candles that remind me of that Christmas morning."[122] This sentiment was echoed by Annie L. Ogburn who enthusiastically described the Christmas cakes received in brown paper bags and proclaimed "what girl" could "forget to remember them forever after!"[123]

A candle-related custom called Christingle appeared sometime in the nineteenth century in British Moravian services. As in Salem, candles were given as a meaningful gift at the climax of a service for children, such as a Christmas lovefeast. A Moravian minister described the Christingle thusly:

Each child receives a candle, trimmed with red and white paper, stuck in the top of an orange and surrounded by "sweetmeats," candies and raisins. The candle is the Symbol of Christ as the light of the world; the red and white paper, a reminder of the "blood of the Lamb" which 'washes us and makes us whiter than snow.' The orange represents the globe, and the 'sweetmeats' represent the sweetness of belonging to the Savior. Goosequills or toothpicks may be used to hold the sweets. If goosequills are used,

Tiles with biblical scenes on the fireplace surround of MESDA's Edenton bedchamber; below, detail of a tile featuring the David and Goliath story.

they represent the fowl of the air and the Gospel of Christ, which have flown all over the world. In Labrador, turnips are used instead of oranges, as the latter would be difficult to obtain.[124]

The origin of the word "Christingle" is unknown. It may come from the Saxon word *ingle* meaning "fire," thus "Christ-fire" or "Christ-light." Another derivation may be from the German word *engle* or *kindle* to mean "Christ-angel" or "Christ-child."[125]

Moravian archivist Dr. Adelaide Fries wrote that "the use of red paper frills around the wax tapers distributed in the Christmas Lovefeast" in Wachovia was "of comparatively recent origin." Fries said that when she was a child in the 1870s and 80s red paper frills were not used, although she understood that at some former time they were but were given up because of the expense and danger of fire. She recalled that she and the other children were taught to cut paper at home to then take to the lovefeast to wind around the candles to prevent drips and burns to fingers. Then a generous lady offered to pay for the red tissue paper, and thus the custom was begun for some church members to meet and trim the candles well before the distribution as symbolic gifts.[126]

As a contrast to the simple Moravian gifts of candles, Bible verses, and cakes, commercialization introduced to the general consumer manufactured goods in profusion. With more and more people having the money to purchase gifts, stores made it easier for them to do so. During the 1830s, gifts included Christmas books, which appeared with suggestions for games and puzzles. Lydia Maria Child published *The Girl's Own Book* in 1831, two years after Bostonian

William Clarke's *The Boy's Own Book*. Ready-made games like trangrams, chess, backgammon, dissected maps and puzzles, and numerous cards for increasing knowledge, such as geographical, scriptural, botanical, literary, etc., were all available. By the 1840s, one source states that the number of "games had reached flood proportions."[127] There was even one called "What d'ye Buy," which was a Christmas shopping game.[128]

"A Happy Christmas," a story of charitable goodwill published in the *Moravian* in 1861, described some toys at a Christmas fair. There were "gigantic gingerbread" men, "beautiful picture-books, tin soldiers, wooden horses," and a "cuckoo with real feathers, that cried 'Cuckoo!' when its back was stroked." Displayed also were a "populous farm yard," with lambs and goats, and "a gaily dressed doll with the little gold watch [on] its belt."[129]

As a result of all this available merchandise, the downtown shopping scene changed. By 1831, stores in New York City were open until midnight during the season of Christmas.[130] Gas lights illuminated "whole rows of confectionery stores and toy shops, fancifully, and often splendidly, decorated with festoons of bright silk drapery, interspersed with flowers and evergreens. In the evenings and into the late night, visitors of both sexes and all ages filled the streets, some selecting toys and fruit for holiday presents; others merely lounging from shop to shop to enjoy the varied scene."[131] On the day after Christmas in 1842, Isaac Mickle strolled down Chestnut Street in Philadelphia and remarked: "I never saw so many people turned out to celebrate Christmas. The main streets were literally jammed."[132] Indeed, promenading in one's best clothes was part of the pleasure of seeing and being seen.

The Moravian reported in 1863 that in Philadelphia:

The thoroughfares during the day preceding Christmas are thronged with pedestrians: and as evening advances, a dense mass of humanity is packed almost immovably in the more frequented streets; and a perfect saturnalia is held far into the night, and scenes are enacted which are far from creditable to those engaged in them. All kinds of musical instruments are brought into requisition, from a penny-trumpet to the noisy boatman's horn; numerous Calathumpian[133] Bands vie with each other to make night hideous: the police meanwhile appearing to be quite oblivious until some serious outbreak compels them to interfere.[134]

By 1910 stores began to close earlier with no appreciable decline in sales, and the overworked employees were then able to celebrate Christmas Eve at home.[135]

Collection of items made by students at the Salem Girls' School, c. 1760. *OSMG Photo P59.*

THE EVOLUTION OF THE GIFT BRINGER AND GIFTS

Gift Books

Gift books were literary annuals designed to be given to girls, women, and children. They first appeared in England in the 1820s and caught on in America in the first quarter of the nineteenth century to remain popular until about the Civil War or later. These elegant volumes included in their titles names like gift, token, forget-me-not, keepsake, and offering. They were intended chiefly as Christmas presents and established a precedent of annual gift giving, as subsequent volumes were published each year. The books contained engravings from the top artists of the time, including Thomas Sully, known in Salem through his connection as teacher and friend to local artist Daniel Welfare. They often contained writings by prominent authors of the time. One contemporary collector declares these books to be the beginning of big Christmas shopping and commercialization, as they were recognized by the recipients as status-symbols that they expected to receive yearly from their admirers and relatives.[vi] Autograph books served a similar purpose.

Similar to the example shown here, there exists in the Old Salem collection an autograph book with a gilded, embossed leather cover and inscription to Miss Mary Senseman from her uncle "E.A.V., Salem, N.C., 25 December 1857." (Elias Alexander Vogler was the brother of Mary's mother, Louisa, and the son of John and Christina Vogler.)

Sarah "Sallie" Vogler received an album in 1861 called "Forget Me Not," a gold-embossed gift book, with engravings of women interspersed throughout the pages. It was filled with pious verses written by relatives, fellow students at Salem Female Academy, and friends—the first one by Minister G. F. Bahnson. He wrote, "Thou art bought with a price, therefore glorify God, in thy body & in thy spirit, which are God. . . Be thou faithful unto death & he will give thee a crown of life."[vii]

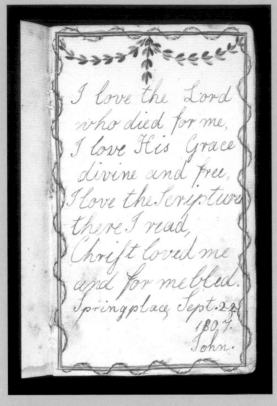

Decorated verse from Karsten Petersen's memory book, 1807. *OSMG*.

Autograph book from the early twentieth century. *Author's collection.*

In Salem, the stores began to advertise for Christmas beginning in the 1850s with an increasing number of ads throughout the remaining decades of the nineteenth century. An advertisement by Hall & Hall (Salem Confectionery and Fancy Store) on 2 December 1859 began, "HO FOR THE HOLIDAYS," and highlighted all manner of goods from "toys, to perfumery, soaps, China Ware, and Fancy Articles," as well as an assortment of "Plain and Fancy CANDIES," and "Fruits and Nuts, Pickles, Sardines, Pep. Sauce, Crackers, Maccaroni, Vermacelli, Cigars, Smoking Tobacco, &c." That same year Francis W. Meller had a very similar ad for his "CONFECTIONERY AND FANCY TOY STORE" in Salem.[136] The store operated by Blum highlighted in 1867 Fireside Books (note the emphasis on the hearth as symbolic of the home) for adults and many specific books for children, including Hans Andersen's Stories, Aesop's Fables,[137] and Old and New Testament Narratives.[138]

Salem stores were advertising autograph books and scrap books throughout the second half of the nineteenth century. Such books made appropriate Christmas presents. In 1880 at Blum's store, twenty-five different styles were highlighted "among which are the new and beautiful shell album, golden floral albums, landscape albums, and embossed pansy albums with a lot of cheap and pretty illuminated albums for children." An autograph book owned by Regina E. Leinbach of Salem contained verses written in English and German and artwork interspersed by some friends, including one of a lyre... with a wreath of roses in color. The lyre was an appropriate motif for Salem where music was "an important element of life."[139] In the book a tiny hair wreath has been laid into the pages with the inscription:

Cover of an 1864 issue of *Harper's Weekly* with children celebrating Christmas. *Author's collection.*

"*Vergiss mein nicht*" (Forget Me Not). Whether this was made as a memorial or as a gift of remembrance perhaps at Christmas from one of Regina's schoolmates is unknown.[140]

In Salem, Moravian housewife Carrie Fries Shaffner noted both homemade and purchased Christmas gifts in a letter in 1864, "All send thanks for your contributions, the three pen-wipers, the primers for the children. Miss Carrie made & gave me a little linen collar, ruffled round, & Mother a pair of mittens, & a very pretty fruit-knife with a silver & pearl handle. I made them each some linen crochet trimming & gave the latter that strawberry emery[141] a thing she has wished for several times. We postponed the Christmas dinner until today. We spent a quiet, happy day, no one here except the family".[142]

There were quantities of stories to encourage children to share with those less fortunate than themselves. In *The Moravian's* Youth Department of 1860, a

Christmas Cards

Along with gifts, cards became more and more popular. Some Christmas historians have traced greeting cards back to eighteenth-century school boys, who composed intricate letters to their parents to display their penmanship. These were created on hand-decorated paper, and the theory is that their parents enjoyed them so much that they began to include decorated letters of their own at Christmas. Without definite proof, this speculation is, nevertheless, interesting. The first commercial card was produced in December 1843, in England by artist John C. Horsley. In America, Richard Pease, an engraver in Connecticut, issued the first commercial card in 1851, and along with the advertisement appended the greeting "A Merry Christmas and A Happy New Year."[viii] Much earlier in 1842 Pease had used a popular woodcut of "Santa-Claus" entering a chimney with an abundance of toys as advertisement for his store. A similar image with a different advertisement was found in a local children's book owned by the Samuel Pattersons. A German lithographer named Louis Prang, who immigrated to the United States, popularized the Christmas greeting card by introducing it in the mid-eighteen-seventies.)[ix]

Christmas cards were sometimes being given to certain acquaintances along with, or in place of, the token gift. Prang's cards were quite popular and could stand on their own as tasteful remembrances. In January of 1881 there appeared a remark about such trends in Salem: "Mr. Blum's cozy little parlor is always the place for lovers of the beautiful in birthday and Christmas cards and other gifts. A very pretty lot of valentines have just been received. Prang's cards are especially fine; some very handsome ones, silk-edged, are lovely specimens of flower paintings on satin."[x] A Salem Girls' School publication reported in 1885 that the long tables prepared by the teachers for the girls included cakes, candies, raisins, and "tables glittering with presents, and cards, formed the most attractive feature of each room".[xi]

Reproduction of an advertisement for Louis Prang's cards. *OSMG.*

poem sought to inspire the efforts of children for distant missions:

Little deeds of kindness,
Little words of love,
Make our earth an Eden,
Like the heaven above.
Little seeds of mercy,
Sown by youthful hands,
Grow to bless the nations
Far in distant lands.[143]

In Louisa May Alcott's popular novel *Little Women*, published in 1868, tomboy Jo grumbled in the opening line of the book: "Christmas won't be Christmas without any presents."[144] On Christmas morning "No stockings hung at the fireplace," for Marmee, the girls' mother, had proposed that they should have no presents when the men in the country, including their father, were suffering in the Civil War.[145] The sisters were not entirely without treats, however, as the eccentric elderly gentleman next door sent over for their supper pink and white ice cream, cake, fruit, French bonbons, and four big bouquets of flowers from the hothouse. Before knowing the name of the giver, Beth suggested that it was Santa Claus.[146]

In a similar vein of charity, the December 1865 edition of *The Moravian* spoke eloquently on gifts to Christ for Christmas "...as a thank-offering to Christ at Christmas, let them bring their gifts-to the doors of poverty, to the bedside of the sick, to the hospitals where our brave soldiers are suffering, to the tents of the defenders of our country, to the homes where their families dwell."[147]

In Wachovia, residents were organized for such efforts as well. In 1872 the Juvenile Missionary Society, formed "among the scholars of the Sunday School," provided "from hearts and hands of the children at home" the needs of

1896 edition of *St. Nicholas Illustrated*. Author's collection.

the poor for clothing and other necessities. There was also "the Poor Fund."[148] Other such benevolent groups were the Female Foreign Missionary Society, the Bible Society, the Home Mission Society, the Young Men's Missionary Society, and the Male Missionary Society (or Society for the Furtherance of the Gospel).[149]

On 26 December 1879, at St. Philips Church for African Americans in Salem, it was recorded that "Gifts of bibles, testaments, clothing, cards and papers, with well filled bags of Christmas cheer were given to the [s]cholars."[150] The Female Missionary Society undoubtedly put together these bags of goodies. The minister in these celebrations was not forgotten, as he wrote on 28 December 1881, "This evening the Colored Sunday School gave its Christmas Entertainment. The recitation and hymns had been very diligently taught by the Northern teachers of the Colored

Day School and succeeded admirably. There was a large tree and there were many presents, among them, a handsome book for me."[151] In 1910, the Helping Hand Circle made its "annual visit to the County Home, carrying its Christmas gifts and cheer to the inmates."[152]

By the 1870s and 80s, "the idea of exchanging gifts in ornate packages first took hold."[153] Previously, the "wrappings" were the stockings, the Christmas tree, which was growing increasingly taller in America, and even the parlor itself where all was secreted. By the 1890s, white and sometimes red and green tissue paper prolonged the surprise, and gradually holly-decorated paper and imprinted boxes became the rage, providing far more color than the plain brown paper used earlier.

By the 1880s, some gifts were becoming more elaborate. The minister at Home Moravian Church received from some members a carpet for his study one year and was "utterly surprised and overwhelmed" in 1887 to be presented a handsome silver service by the members of the Sunday School at the close of the service, while he still stood on the pulpit platform.[154]

A student at Salem's girls' school wrote enthusiastically in 1879 of "the busy visits to the gay and glittering shops, the secrecy, the planning, the last touches to our own handiwork for our loved ones, the bustle and stir... ."[155] Ten years later another student wrote, "Then came the busy visits to the glittering shops, bright with everything that tempts girls; groups of girls gathered apart to consult about this or that gift to be purchased together for a mutual friend; the secrecy and planning, the sudden thrusting of

THE EVOLUTION OF THE GIFT BRINGER AND GIFTS

The Best Christmas Gift for $1.75.

SEE CHRISTMAS OFFER BELOW.

The contents of the 52 issues of the 1904 volume will include

10 SERIAL STORIES, each a book in itself, of American Life in Home, Camp and Field.

50 SPECIAL ARTICLES by Men and Women Famous in every walk of Life.

200 IMPARTIAL AND TIMELY EDITORIAL Articles on Important Public and Domestic Questions.

250 SHORT STORIES of Character, Adventure and Humor, by the best of living writers.

1000 SHORT NOTES ON CURRENT EVENTS and Discoveries in the Field of Science and Industry.

2000 ANECDOTES, Bits of Humor, Items of Strange and Curious Knowledge, Poems and Sketches.

HEALTH IN THE HOUSEHOLD, CHILDREN'S PAGE, ETC.

Announcement for 1904 and Sample Copies of the Paper sent to any one on Request.

The Companion's New Christmas Packet, containing both Gifts 1 and 2, for presentation on Christmas morning; also Subscription Certificate for 1904, will be sent to any address.

Christmas Present Coupon.

If you cut out and send this slip or the name of this paper at once, with name and address and $1.75, we will send

Gift 1 All the issues of The Companion for the remaining weeks of 1903, including the Beautiful Holiday Numbers; also

AND

Gift 2 The Companion's 1904 "Springtime" Calendar, lithographed in twelve colors and gold for Companion subscribers only.

Then the fifty-two issues of The Companion for 1904—a library of the best reading for every member of the family.

THE YOUTH'S COMPANION, BOSTON, MASS.

Advertisement for *The Youth's Companion*, 1903. *Author's collection.*

certain articles out of sight as the prospective recipients chanced to come about, all tend to make a *tout ensemble*, bright and cheery at the time... .[156]

By the mid-1880s when the Salem students were frequently describing shopping in the stores, there was a profusion of items touted, including clothing of all kinds, glassware, writing desks, work boxes, inkstands, albums, scrap books, *portemonnaies* (purses), jewelry boxes, Japanese goods, calling card receivers, watch boxes, gift books, games, dolls, toys, foodstuffs, and Christmas tree ornaments. By 1882, "packages, boxes, and barrels" were being sent to the school girls in such profusion that a "box-room" had been established near the chapel stairs, "which was this year a perfect treasure-house of delights, owing to the unusual abundance...sent the girls from home."[157]

Gifts to well-brought-up children required in turn a polite acknowledgement, albeit sometimes tardy. At the beginning of the year 1887, young Fred Fries Bahnson in Salem wrote to his then out-of-town grandmother Lisetta Vogler Fries, "I am very much obliged to you for subscribing to 'St Nicholas' for me." In typical childish procrastination he explained, "I have thought many a time that I would write to you, but I never got at it somehow." He mentioned her Christmas present of a large photograph album to Carrie and said that his mother had been caring for the entire family during many illnesses and thus "she has not done the first stitch on your Christmas present."[158] Fred's mother wrote to his grandmother in a separate letter, "You could not have given Fred as much pleasure with anything else...as soon as he reads one number of the St Nicholas he looks forward to the time for the next... .[159] Coincidentally a newspaper notice in Salem in 1886 advertised the *St. Nicholas* magazine as "the ideal magazine," with stories by Louisa M. Alcott and others.[160] Fred's grandmother, like most grandmothers, ever mindful of suitable gifts for grandchildren, had perhaps seen such a notice, which then prompted the gift to her grandson.

There has recently come to light a sheaf of papers with a related history to the *St. Nicholas* magazine. A group of Salem children evidently were so inspired by this popular magazine in 1882 that they attempted to emulate it with a journal of their own, suitably entitled "The Holiday Journal." The format consisted of contributions by various boys and girls including eleven-year-old "Addie Fries." (Fries later became Dr. Adelaide Fries, a Moravian archivist who frequently lectured on Moravian Christmas traditions.) There were poems, serialized stories, puzzles, and articles with each edition successively numbered as 10, 11, etc. The content sometimes revealed tidbits of the social history of childhood in their clothing, chores, manner of speech, toys, reading materials, and activities. The following Christmas story was signed "by Addie Fries."[161]

The Toy Shop

There is much amusement in a toy shop during Christmas holidays. Mr. Sparrow [name unclear, could be Starrow] took all his boys and girls to the shop of a German dealer in toys on Christmas Eve to buy them presents. Here were so many fine playthings that the children would not say which they would have. If Harriet selected a doll one moment she saw a basket next moment that she would like to have. Thomas wanted a horse and a drum at the same time, and little George loudly asked for all the pretty things in the shop. At legth [sic] when the shop-keeper began to get somewhat angry, Mr. Sparrow induced his children to say what they would have. Thomas chose a rocking horse; Harriet a doll, and George a drum. Mr. Sparrow paid for these things, and took the children away.

Magazines were a favorite present for adults to give and to receive. On 24 December 1889, Kentuckian Nannie Williams wrote in her diary:

Today I sent Harry a nice box as a home reminder. Have provided each member of the family with something, bought with money that I made selling preserves. For Henry I got "The American Housekeeping"; for Frances "Demorest Monthly"; for John & Teressa "Youth's Companion"; for Robert & Lucy "Babyland." Good solid literature that will come regularly the whole year which I hope will have some good influence on their minds. Books for the others. Tonight we recd a box from Gretta filled with

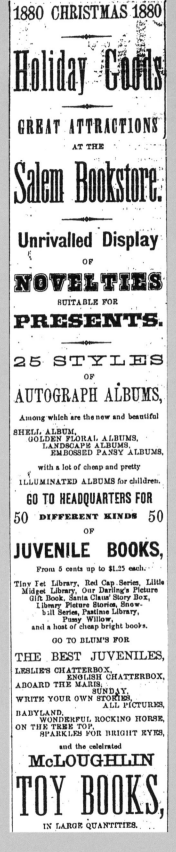

Children's Magazines

St. Nicholas magazine and *The Youth's Companion* were both widely popular with children. *St. Nicholas* was published from 1873 to 1939 and had as its first editor Mary Mapes Dodge, respected author of *Hans Brinker* or *The Silver Skates*. A Salem advertisement for 1886-87 spoke of the magazine as "clean and pure...and helpful."[xii] Some of the best American and English writers contributed to the magazine during Dodge's leadership, including Frances Hodgson Burnett, Mark Twain, Louisa May Alcott, Robert Louis Stevenson, L. Frank Baum, Bret Harte, and Rudyard Kipling. The goal was to inspire and interest children through good literature, and the artwork was equally rich, attracting the leading illustrators of the time, such as Maxfield Parrish, Arthur Rackham, Howard Pyle, and Frederic Remington. With two essential components superbly covered, the magazine with the benevolent saint's name did indeed excite and appeal to its young audience. Ownership problems and a succession of editors contributed to a slow demise of the magazine through the early decades of the twentieth century.[xiii]

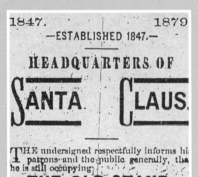

Newspaper advertisements for the Salem Bookstore (left), 1880, and F. W. Meller's Salem store, 1879.

Gingerbread house (modern) with German figures of Hansel and Gretel and the witch. *Author's collection.*

nice things she had collected for the very sweet and thoughtful...I cast an eye to the table and stole a look at the two pretty cups & saucers with my name on cards from my loving Fan & Tress to Mother.[162]

Back in Salem, there is an interesting account of a pre-Christmas children's event of 21 December 1902.[163] It was told by adult Margaret McCuiston about a visit to her aunt's house when she was six years old. All the children of the relatives were invited in the late afternoon to Cedarhyrst (an imposing Gothic Revival castle-like stone house, built in 1894 and located at the entrance to Salem's God's Acre—it is presently used as offices for the Southern Province of the Moravian Church but was then lived in by McCuiston relatives). They gathered in the large, back sitting room where they sat on the floor. The hall doors were

closed by the grownups, who mysteriously disappeared just as it was getting dark. Suddenly there was a loud knock at the door, and the young people all jumped up in consternation. The adults entered, each carrying a tray, which was placed by each child. On the tray was a burning candle stuck in an apple, an orange, some candy, and some Christmas cakes. It was a delightful treat for the children, but years later the adult McCuiston wrote that no one ever explained the reason for this party.[164] Undoubtedly it came out of several traditions that we have mentioned and was unquestionably meant as a special occasion for the children, at least reminiscent of the visit of St. Nicholas and the custom of the Christingle. Perhaps one or more of the adult women had attended school in Bethlehem or had been told of an existing tradition there. A

Pennsylvania writer wrote about that tradition in 1985, explaining that in "Old Bethlehem" St. Thomas Day was "an early Christmas Day," perhaps started as a treat for those girls from the boarding school who would go home a few days later for the actual holiday. This "unique festival" consisted of a house made of *Lebkuchen* (gingerbread) to represent Hansel and Gretel and the witch from the fairy tale. The house was the center of a lighted *Putz* decoration "around the edge of which were placed the wrapped gifts, often exquisite needle work."[165]

In Salem in 1920, Moravian historian Adelaide Fries prepared a little booklet as a gift for her friends and relatives and entitled it "Our Christmas."[166] It contains a poem that she wrote about the beginning of Wachovia and illustrates thoughtful gifts made by the hand and by the heart, requiring hours of work to completion. The second verse, emphasizing the beginning of Wachovia without children, begins:

But once Wachovia had no home,
There were no children here.
At midnight rose the Christmas song
Of Christian pioneer.

The third verse epitomizes "the heart religion"[167] of the Moravians:

Wolves howled around one tiny hut;
Within, on bended knee,
Brave men adored the Infant Christ,
In 1753.

Ultimately, for the Moravians the "best present of all," was the "Gospel" as expressed by Jacob Wohlfahrt (Welfare)—a gift that he wished to be given to all the recipients of the mission efforts, both adults and children.[168] The editor of the children's department of *The Moravian* reiterated Welfare's message in 1856 when he wrote: "Happy Christmas... . I have been looking at your Christmas trees, and handsome toys, and at the cakes and candies, and presents, and good things in general, and they all tell me 'Christmas is here!' But nothing says it more plainly than the sparkle of your eyes, and the sunshine all around them. I dare say you were up bright and early this morning, to see what the famous old gentleman, Mr. Santa Claus had crammed into your stocking, or piled upon your table... Oh! There is no gift for your needy, perishing souls, my dear children, like the blessed Saviour...the best of Christmas gifts,—[is] a sense of his love."[169]

Encouraging Children's Charity Through Puzzles and Riddles and Anagrams

Children were encouraged in their charity by many methods. *St. Nicholas* magazine included in each issue a "Riddle-Box" of puzzles, acrostics, anagrams, and riddles. In the December 1881 issue there appeared the following "Holiday Anagrams." Answers were always given in the succeeding issue. An explanatory note advised that the lines of each couplet rhymed and that the "omitted words may all be formed from the thirteen letters omitted in the last line."[xiv] It may be observed also that the correct number of letters of each word is designated by the number of asterisks.

A fair little maid, with the kindest *****,
Flitted about to bazaar and to ****.

Purchasing gifts, if rightly I guess;
First, 't was a doll, then a board to play *****,

Then, dear Mamma! —'t was surely no ****
To buy for her watch-chain a tiny gold *****.

Hours seemed just little inches of ****; —
They flew till she found she had spent her last ****.

Then, turning homeward, this fair little ****
Saw one whom she pitied and gladly would ***.

"Are you not cold, little girl, with that *****,
And what is your name?" She replied, "It is Bess.

"Yes, I am cold, but," —her eyes they grew ***,
"But I'm only thinking of sick brother ***;

"He's home, and he's lame, and he never was *****,
I wish I could buy him just one little ****."

Her sorrow our fair little maid could not ****
"My purse is quite empty," she whispered *****.

"But here's my gold dollar—; 't is precious! no ******!
Her face is so blue, and her teeth — how they *******."

Then, speaking aloud, — "Little girl, come with **,
For first you need clothing, —that plainly I see.

"A part of my wardrobe and supper I'll spare,
And poor little Tim, too, shall have his full *****.

Very happy that night were those three little ******;
One happy from giving, —two happy with *****.

And our dear little maiden's sweet joy will abide,
And she long will remember that glad ********* ****.

(Lillian Payson)

Answers: 1. heart, mart 2. chess 3. harm, charm 4. time, dime 5. maid, aid 6. dress 7. dim, Tim 8. smart, tart 9. hide, aside 10. matter, chatter 11. me 12. share 13. hearts, tarts 14. Christmas Tide

Chapter 5

Food and Beverages

"For supper I was invited to eat with Br. and Sr. Schweiniz. . . The food was just excellent—a turkey, two kinds of potatoes, cabbage salad, cucumbers, cranberries, tea, and bread and butter—and then also a wonderful pie and wine with it."

— *The Peter Wolle Diaries, 1809-1821, 28 October 1814*

Today when we think of Moravian holiday food, ginger cookies, lovefeast buns, sugarcake, coffee heated with sugar and milk, and chicken pot pie all come to mind. Before these foods became engrained in the traditions of the Moravians, the table was set with what food and drink were available. People with more money could provide a more varied array. Those who had just butchered their hogs might have plenty of pork. Those who had stored, dried, preserved, salted, pickled, or cured would draw from that larder. All things considered, Moravians, like their neighbors, frequently had to "make do" with whatever was at hand.

Although we tend to equate holidays today with certain specific food items such as turkey or ham, dressing, pies, and fruitcake, the general standard in early America was that people who could afford it set out a profusion of whatever was within their power to obtain—this in their culture exemplified "celebration," whether they honored Christmas or not. These items often included foodstuffs that are now familiar and synonymous with holidays, such as roast turkey, pudding, and mince pie mentioned on Christmas Day in 1777 by a Philadelphia Quaker, who did not celebrate the holiday but enjoyed the feast.[1] However, items like "a fat...turkey" and "good mince pies"[2] were not always generally in place on the multicultural national table until the second half of the nineteenth century. At about that time magazines and periodicals began to highlight the recipes and preparation of these foods for Thanksgiving and Christmas, thus widely encouraging their popularity for holidays, which continues today.

Note the following diverse examples of southern holiday foods from two different centuries and three different time periods, each illustrating what was available at that time and place:

A Christmas Day feast in 1778, in what would become Louisville, Kentucky, consisted of venison, bear, wild turkey, rabbit, coon, buffalo, three kinds of cornbread, milk, butter, and cheese with the highlighted favorite being a large whole baked possum.[3]

Mrs. Margaret Hunter Hall, an Englishwoman visiting South Carolina, described a dinner and ball in Columbia to celebrate Washington's birthday in 1828 (this could just as easily have been a Christmas celebration), which included ham, "turkeys, roast and boiled, chickens, roast ducks, corned beef, and fish, together with various dishes of sweet potatoes, Irish potatoes, cabbage, rice, and beetroot." A second course consisted of "*eight pies* down the side of the table, six dishes of glasses of syllabub and as many of jelly, besides one or two 'floating islands,' as they denominate what we call whipped cream, and odd corners filled up by ginger and other preserves." To her surprise, she wrote that tea and coffee were not served after dinner.[4]

Two thirds of a century later (1891), in Savannah, Georgia, a famous local hotel presented its guests with a unique complimentary Christmas dinner. The centerpiece of the offering was "a team of suckling pigs harnessed to a wagon driven by Santa Claus, and loaded with boned turkey garnished with quail… . The second piece was an immense salmon, decorated in green, red, and black and lying upon a bed of green moss made of frozen suet and butter. At the head of the table sat two wild turkeys with their wings and feathers 'on as alive,' and at the foot there rested two proud hams, one figured in sugar representing a vase of flowers, and the other checkered like a chess board."[5]

Food

On 25 December 1846, Lisetta Vogler Fries of Salem entered into her daybook the purchase of a turkey for 25 cents, no doubt meant for the holiday dinner. In certain parts of Pennsylvania one historian recorded that during the period of 1840-1860 turkey and sauerkraut was a favorite combination in public places.[6] Whether or not Lisetta served sauerkraut or cabbage, it was a vegetable that could have still been fresh in December. The Bethania minister George Bahnson described how to prolong the life of such a staple and how, coincidentally, the process looked like a Christmas decoration.

In the afternoon Caty & myself put up the cabbage according to the fashion prevailing here, to put the heads together lightly covering with earth the roots of them, & spreading over the whole concern limbs of pine-trees. We drove out to an old field belonging to Petrus Houser, where pine grows in abundance, loaded our carriage well with them & having visited Jos Werner we returned in full stile green boughs sticking out in every direction, so that people were led to believe that we prepared already for Christmas, whilst they were only destined to screen from the cold our plentiful crop of cabbage.[7]

Sauerkraut has always been an important component of a German meal. The first recipe in the vegetable category in an early-twentieth-century Salem cookbook was for sauerkraut. It was contributed by Moravian archivist Dr. Adelaide Fries, who remarked, "It may be served with pork or sausage." She went on to say that "One of the best known old German menus consisted of sauerkraut and pork, mashed potatoes, gravy, bread, coffee and apple dumplings."[8] Some early Salem residents undoubtedly served such a meal often, and probably at Christmas.

Mary Louise Johnston wrote from the Salem Girls' School, where she was a student, to her father in Monroe, Georgia, on

"Liberty Tree, 1812," with a dog eating sausages, from the Journal of Lewis Miller, vol. I, p. 96. *Collection of the York County Heritage Trust, York, PA.*

14 January 1839, about the preceding Christmas. She told her father to tell "old Aunt Molly" that she would have liked to have had some of her Christmas turkey, but that they also had turkey for dinner at school.[9]

Although not a Christmas dinner, the following Salem meal described by schoolteacher Peter Wolle is the earliest and most complete celebratory meal thus detailed in Wachovia, and it, too, included turkey and cabbage. On 28 October 1814, just a few days after his arrival from Pennsylvania to Salem to be head teacher at the boys' school, Wolle wrote: "For supper I was invited to eat with Br. and Sr. Schweiniz... . The food was just excellent—a turkey, two kinds of potatoes, cabbage salad, cucumbers, cranberries, tea, and bread and butter— and then also a wonderful pie and wine with it. It goes without saying that all of this was very interesting and agreeable... . I did not leave there until ¹/₂ to 10 o'clock."[10]

Serving any meat involved considerable preparations beforehand and sometimes chaos before the cooked animal or bird appeared on the table. Ham, sausage, and bacon were mentioned in local diaries repeatedly. Parts of the animal like the tongue, the brains, the liver, the heart, the stomach (tripe), the kidneys, the head, the ears, the feet (called trotters), and the intestines for sausage casings were all consumed. At the Moravian Indian Mission in Springplace, Georgia, in 1806, the Gambolds were pleased to send on their way two German travelers with "a big thick liver sausage" along with some "welschcorn bread" and pickles.[11]

Postcard of Santa and a turkey, twentieth century. *Author's collection.*

Some adolescents saved pig bladders from the slaughter as toys to be inflated and popped on Christmas, and adults made use of pig bladders as storage containers or crock sealers. To keep meat fresh, it was often kept alive until ready to be prepared. Consider as an example the following tale of three turkeys as recorded by George Bahnson on New Year's Day 1836:

[I] rode alone out to Hr Schulzes in order to fetch 3 turkeys, which the old man could feed no longer. They were very clever fat large fellows, well worth taking along. Having come home I laid them down in the yard beside the carriage to consult where we should keep them for the night—they were as I thought well tied, around their wings & legs but nevertheless when I returned into the yard, all were gone but one. One was sitting on the fence & another way up on the gable end of the horsestable. Levin Grabs was kind enough to get a ladder & catch the runaways.[12]

There was no mistaking the origin of meat for meals, whether it was turkey, chicken, or pork. Bahnson made that clear in 1834 when stopping for breakfast while traveling, he witnessed the inevitable passage of barnyard fowl to the dining table. "Having made known our wish to breakfast, we saw the black women run after a few chickens, strip them of their feathers & so on & after a good while they appeared on the table."[13]

Trying to keep animals fed through the winter was expensive. Allowing them to run free in the woods to forage for themselves exposed them to predators like wildcats, foxes, wolves, bears, and the occasional two-legged thief.[14] The cold weather around Christmas was the best time to process the meat before it could spoil and consequently provided a welcome fresh bounty for the holiday table. With no refrigeration, meats like pork and mutton deteriorated rapidly after slaughtering in warm weather, so they were generally only eaten fresh or dried, salted, or pickled. William Byrd of Virginia remarked after eating roast mutton in July 1709, that he "ate no good dinner because our mutton was spoilt," but added, "however I ate some of it."[15] Spices greatly helped in disguising less-than-fresh meat, as did vinegar. For example, if a cook had birds that were left hanging to ripen too long, several early cookbook writers—Bradley in *The Country Housewife* (1732) and Mrs. Rundell in *Experienced Housekeeper* (1823)—urged relieving the taint by washing the inside well with vinegar and water, which would make them fit for eating, even when kept for a very long time. After drying, one could then scrape away the kidneys, strew pepper inside, and hang for an hour or so.[16]

George Bahnson remarked once that pork and chicken were the backbone of any North Carolina meal. Pork, often salted, was probably the most eaten meat in Wachovia. Minister Bahnson remarked on this when he wrote about Salem on 1 July 1834: "Pork is the principal thing on which people live."[17] It must have long

been so, as an Englishman traveling along the eastern coast of America in 1774 wrote after nineteen days that he had had so much bacon and chicken that he thought he would soon "be grown over with Bristles or Feathers."[18] Captain Charles F. Bahnson, son of George Bahnson, serving in the military during the Civil War wrote on Christmas Day 1863, to his parents that he missed all the pork: "the messes [a southern expression meaning a quantity of food set on the table at one time] of ribs, back bones, souce [souse: pickled, seasoned, and chopped pork trimmings], puddings and sausages."[19] We can only surmise that Captain Bahnson was thinking of Christmas dinners of the past as he wrote on that particular day,

and it is highly likely that pork was part of the traditional Christmas meal in his family.[20]

As the holidays approached, imagine seeing your fresh pork still on the hoof and walking down the road with hundreds of other pigs! Bahnson described such a sight in 1834 (November 21):

After dinner no less than 800 hogs passed through town, under the guidance of 3 white & 3 black men. It was really a show, at least to us from the North. Droves of 4-1,000 hogs pass in our neighborhood toly [tolerably] often about this season, coming from Tenessee [sic] & other western states. Pork has been very scarce a great many pigs about here have died, a natural death, instead of waiting for the

"Butchering, 1802," from the Journal of Lewis Miller, vol. I, p. 20. *Collection of the York County Heritage Trust, York, PA.*

heroic butcher, so that a great many people have to buy from such droves. Some of the 4 legged gentlemen that were sold here weighed above 200 lb & sold 3 ct per pound. Such a drove uses every night 25 bushels of corn & proceeds but about 8 miles per day. What a tedious piece of business. Some of the hog drivers had got the measles coming, so that one had to remain at Sol. Spoenhouers & another here in our tavern; others had immediately gone back home, so that the owner of the drove, who remained sick here, had to hire other hands... ."[21]

Hog butchering often interrupted school in the outlying communities and even in town. Salem schoolteacher Peter Wolle reported on 2 January 1816, "Some of the pupils...were not present [at school] because of business at home. Right at the start of the year the pigs are slaughtered by way of a New Year's present to them!"[22] A few days later he wrote: "The Bagges slaughtered pigs today and for that reason their Charles had to miss school."[23] Thomas Schulz, the "second"[24] boys' school teacher in 1817, deemed it significant enough to mention in his diary, 9 December, "My parents killed hogs today."[25] However, Salem shoemaker Johann Leinbach did not seem fazed by the process, as he noted on 4 December 1831: "Early this morning killed three hogs; by daylight they were hanging; when I took a hunt for Rabbits."[26]

In Bethania on 15 December, 1833, the church records documented, "School was omitted this week on account of baking [Christmas cakes] and butchering among our families."[27] Bahnson remarked on the hectic atmosphere of these events when he wrote on 14 December 1836 that Henrietta, their "help," was trying to give "the house somewhat the appearance of a human habitation, pigs & cakes having caused it to adopt a resemble of the resi-

Men gathered in taverns during December to enjoy Metzelsupp banquets where they consumed "fried sausage, pudding, sauerkraut, pork roast, and pig's feet and tails, all washed down with a steady stream of beer or local wine."

dence of the unclean beasts... ."[28] The baking to which Bahnson referred could also have included the dessert to feed the helpers in butchering. A 1931 Salem cookbook had an entry for "Hog-Killing Pie," so called because "it was used to feed to the hands during hog-killing time." It was a type of cobbler made with dried peaches, butter, brown sugar, and a top and bottom pie crust.[29]

After butchering, families might send a present of some of the meat to a minister or other deserving neighbor, a form of holiday gift as well as a payment of gratitude for the spiritual services provided. Note such mentions by Bahnson on two occasions in 1834: "The inhabitants of our city were engaged in deadly work, killing hogs as fast as they could. A drove had passed through here & many had bought provision for future times. The hogs were principally shot dead & their plaintive cries & lamentations resounded from one end of town to the other. Wherever I went to, to day, I

found old & young engaged in the swinish line, by which we shall probably also be benefited in some degree, for they all send a little something."[30] In the church diary on the same day he added: "Everywhere hog-killing in town, a good time for us, with sausage and spareribs coming in from all around."[31]

The Christmas *Metzel* soup was a rural German custom in Pennsylvania that involved sending to neighbors, friends, the minister, and the poor a portion of *Metzelsupp* (translated literally "butcher's stew," which could be the cut-up pieces of pork, especially sausage meat and puddings). A generous portion of eight or ten pounds might be proffered and expected to be reciprocated when you butchered your own hogs. One historian writes that by the end of the nineteenth century the custom, which had started in Germany as an alcohol-laced pork pudding broth with rye bread,[32] had been forgotten, but suggests that out of that custom may have come the scrapple still common in Pennsylvania and elsewhere, a mixture of variables including cooked heads, livers, hearts, feet, jowls, cornmeal, flour, salt, and pepper, to be cooled, then sliced and fried on a griddle.[33] Another historian asserts scrapple (*Panhas* or *Pannas*) came from the lower Rhineland of Germany, particularly Westphalia, and must include buckwheat flour to achieve the characteristic flavor.[34] Pennsylvania food historian William Woys Weaver remarks that the soup custom continued well into the 1840s when gifts of meat began to be substituted "as a standard feature of the Pennsylvania Dutch Christmas"[35] and rendered butchering an aspect of "social significance." Men gathered in taverns during December to enjoy *Metzelsupp* banquets where they consumed "fried sausage, pudding, sauer-

FOOD AND BEVERAGES

kraut, pork roast, and pig's feet and tails, all washed down with a steady stream of beer or local wine."[36]

One sideline in hog butchering for children in Pennsylvania and perhaps in Wachovia was collecting, cleaning, and selling hog bristles,[37] for which there was an available market at the brushmaker, saddler, or shoemaker. Bartering these bristles for toy candy or other treats was a common practice among children. As already mentioned, saving pig bladders for popping noisemakers on holidays was another enjoyable benefit of hog butchering for the young folks.

A Williamsburg foodways researcher says "there is no doubt that in the eighteenth century...the mostpopular meat" in Williamsburg was beef.[38] Williamsburg was an English town, and Salem was a German settlement, thus reflecting certain cultural preferences in food between the English and the Germans. Consider the meat inventory at the Salem tavern for one day in 1791: 830 pounds of dried hog meat, along with ten hogs, three calves, and twenty-four sheep.[39] By contrast, a Virginia gentleman, Robert Carter, was reported by his children's tutor in the 1770s to estimate an annual consumption for his household and guests of twenty "beeves" in a year, yet Carter's home consumed 27,000 pounds of pork.[40]

As we have seen, the southern holiday table of the gentry might include several dozens of dishes reflecting the bounty of the land, forests, and waters: turkeys, wild ducks, partridges, venison, and other game, as well as various types of pork, saddle of mutton, veal's head, roast beef, fish, shellfish and oysters (where available), and, of course, some vegetables (whatever was still growing or had been protected, buried, stored, or preserved)[41] such as cabbage,

beans, potatoes, cauliflower, beets, carrots, onions, and artichokes. Then there were apples, grapes, raisins, almonds, sweetmeats, jams, jellies, creams, and perhaps gooseberry tarts, fruit pies, and cheesecakes.

As the nineteenth century progressed, the variety and abundance of foodstuffs increased, but still one had to depend upon the seasons. Salem schoolteacher Peter Wolle not only documented but also annotated foods that interested him in his diary. Meats included: "well-prepared" squirrel and "excellent" eels (both of which he claimed to have had for the first time in Salem),[42] hare, chicken (once fried, but also roasted and certainly stewed and boiled), as well as chicken potpie.

He particularly enjoyed the eels with beets. He wrote about pork of many varieties. Wolle mentioned fish, pickled fish, and fish salad followed by the statement that the "meals at Mrs. Eberhard's can in reality not be complained of."[43] (The first time the early Moravian settlers in North Carolina had served fish was on 1 March 1756, when they caught enough in the mill race at Bethabara for each one to have a small portion.)[44]

Wolle enjoyed chicken potpie and potpies with pigeons, doves, and chickens.[45] If the pies were prepared as some period receipts suggest, they might have consisted of a flour and butter dough-lined deep dish into which split chickens or other birds, sometimes par-boiled, were placed, perhaps along with their necks and various organs including gizzards, livers, and hearts. To the meat would be added some gravy or water, salt, pepper, and probably salt pork and/or butter, the whole to be covered with paste (a top crust) and baked for an hour and a half to two and one-half hours.[46] Variations of this receipt are undoubtedly the origin of the potpie that the Moravian's are famous for today. Regional food historians remark that a standard dinner offering at country gatherings was a pot-pie, which was also called "a sea pie" in some countries[47] and may have had as much as four pounds of flour in the paste.[48]

Vegetables included in Peter Wolle's diary descriptions were, of course, cabbage and sauerkraut,

cucumbers alone and as salad, carrots, potatoes, sweet potatoes, beets, and "hommony." He remarked on his love of sweet potatoes in 1816. "Sweetpotatoes taste so delicious, that it requires a considerable share of self command to stop sending them down into the stomach."[49] Spinach and lettuce were also mentioned. Fruits enjoyed were apples, peaches, pears, strawberries, red plums, grapes and raisins, watermelon,[50] cherries, and blackberries. He wrote of taking a glass of wine and some apples together on one occasion.[51] Nuts that Wolle consumed were chestnuts, "chinkapin" ("chinquapin," related to the chestnut), and walnuts. His colleague at the Boys' School, Thomas Schulz, spoke of hunting and gathering with his students such wild treats as hazelnuts, paw-paws ("papaw", the edible,

fleshy, green-skinned fruit of a North American tree), black haws (colorful fruit of the hawthorn), persimmons, and wild grapes. Salem shoemaker Johann Lein-bach once mentioned picking a basket of dew berries.[52]

Oysters were a very popular celebratory food both in the North and the South. One historian believes they were common-place with all social classes in early America.[53] As early as 1608 in Jamestown, Virginia, John Smith and his men made merry at Christmas with "plentie of good Oysters, Fish, Flesh, Wild-foule, and good bread... ."[54]

By 1805 oysters were probably brought into Salem from coastal areas, as Paulina Schober's little handwritten receipt book of that year contains the method for making "Oyster Pye." The receipt reads:

To 100 Oysters, warm'd in their liquor; 4 eggs boiled hard, & as much crumb'd bread as yellow of the Egg cut fine together; season the oysters with 12 cloves, twice the quantity of mace; pepper & salt to your taste, add as much liquor as you think proper.[55]

Two centuries later, the day after Christmas 1836, George Bahnson mentioned his brother's birthday faraway in Philadelphia where he speculated his sibling might celebrate with a good cake and "perhaps oysters crowned the proceedings of the festive day."[56] Bahnson's wife, rapidly deteriorating from tuberculosis, remarked that "oysters would take away a good many of her numberless complaints."[57] About the same period in Cincinnati, Ohio, the English writer Frances Trollope described tea parties which included pickled oysters.[58]

Special occasions required not only special foods but certain acceptable behaviors. During the holidays people often wished each other "the compliments of the season," but not in Wachovia.

According to Bahnson: "The custom...of wishing 'the compliments of the season' as my sweet H[ortensia, his wife] was taught to express herself is entirely unknown here."[59] However, much earlier on 25 December 1773, Philip Fithian, tutor to the Robert Carter children of Virginia, had written in contrast, "At Breakfast, when Mr Carter entered the Room, he gave us the compliments of the Season... ."[60]

In Wachovia simplicity was generally the key in food service, but correctness was nevertheless important to some. It is intriguing to ponder the details of a "fete" that "a fashionable lady" gave on 1 January 1835 for some of the local gentry in town. George Bahnson recorded that it was in turn reciprocated later by a grand "diner [sic]."[61]

Bahnson wrote critically on one occasion of certain people using vesper (an afternoon coffee break, see Chapter Six) as a party to show one's wealth, and he was generally cognizant of etiquette amongst his neighbors and associates.[62] On a visit to Salem with his wife, Bahnson said, "A tablecloth was not used, except at dinner, a fashion which neither of us admired."[63] Just after Christmas in 1836, Bahnson had another comment about the lack of a tablecloth. "Supper was taken in great haste, without cloth, just cold spareribs & bread."[64]

In contrast to the elegant appurtenances of the fashionable gentry, at Henry Schulze's near Bethania, Bahnson remarked in

"David Miller, October 13, 1800," from the Journal of Lewis Miller, vol. I, p. 31. *Collection of the York County Heritage Trust, York, PA.*

November 1835 that they had an excellent dinner "but otherwise entirely in the bush fashion—(pewter plates, tin spoons &ct. to which a person from a civilized country must indeed first become used—)...."[65] Later on that month, Bahnson performed a marriage ceremony, and he and his wife stayed for the supper. He said: "Soon afterwards we sat down to a very sumptuous [sic] but etiquette prevailed to such a degree that there was not much enjoyment at all. About 20 persons had sat down, all of whom were provided with every thing they desired, before any one began to move fork or knife."[66] There were three seatings, "each time less restraint was felt." Turkey, goose, and chicken were cold; cakes not good; and the father of the bride, as well as another outside minister, kept their hats on the whole time. Bahnson remarked about the guests: "[l]adies without bonnets, but gentlemen unable to separate themselves from their hats."[67]

Among the wealthy gentry outside of Wachovia, symmetry and design placement of the main course foods on a finely draped table were of utmost concern and affected one's social standing. Some said the taste of the food was less important than quantity and presentation. Proper utensils were *de rigeuer*, and prominent citizens like George Washington had plateaux and epergnes[68] ordered from Europe to adorn their elegant tables. The correct serving of desserts (without cloth) was just as important as the main course, and creative displays were carefully arranged for the ultimate, fanciful, and dramatic effect. To heighten the drama the supper tables were often concealed from the guests until the moment of unveiling. As discussed in Chapter Two, early Christmas trees were also concealed for the maximum dramatic effect at the moment of presentation.

Liquor, Politics, and Christmas!

"Good liquors" were part of an account of a large Christmas party at the North Carolina Governor's Mansion in 1848 as detailed in a letter from Alexander Campbell McIntosh of Alexander County, who was a member of the North Carolina General Assembly at that time.[i] The affair at the mansion of Governor Graham included three or four hundred ladies and gentlemen invited for eight o'clock. The second room of the "palace," as he described it to his wife, had a sideboard "well furnished with good liquors." The gentlemen in this room "did ample justice to the Governor's French brandy, wine, etc." In the corner of a third large, unfurnished, uncarpeted room were three or four African Americans who were playing a violin and other musical instruments for dancing. McIntosh admired the well-dressed and good-looking ladies, but remarked "there was a little more of the breast and arms naked than would look becoming in the country." The women wore light pale colored dresses with short sleeves and a thin gauze fitted to the arms. He remarked: "Some married ladies engaged in the dance," and that the custom of dancing was very fashionable and on the increase in the area. The abundantly filled supper tables were laid upstairs with one de-voted to meats of all kinds and "the necessary accompaniments." Another was filled with "pound cakes, sweet cakes, syllabub,[ii] ice cream, etc." The third table had oysters "in every style—stewed, boiled, souped, pickled, etc." People stood and helped themselves unceremoniously, and "those who crowded the hardest generally fared the best." He observed that a common goal by all was to "be as social as he can be and enjoy himself to the utmost." Members of both parties of the Whigs and the Democrats were present. McIntosh spent two or three hours and pronounced it "a social party in high life," which at home they would probably call a "frolic." His assessment was that although he satisfied his curiosity, he went "with some reluctance" and enjoyed it "very little," although it served the purpose of soothing the politicians, "who had been engaged in a political fight."[iii]

In summary, one sees at the beginning of the Wachovia venture that the Moravians ate seasonally, depending on the bounty of the harvest, the availability of wild meat, the generosity of their neighbors in selling, bartering, and giving certain items, and the skill with which they were able to grow, gather, preserve, pickle, salt, smoke, cure, bake, distill, brew, dry, and store successfully. Sometimes they had to purchase certain items, such as salt, or meat, and otherwise they simply had to "make do" by eating whatever they had, albeit boring and repetitive. Since detailed descriptions of Christmas-specific meals in Wachovia have not been found, one must surmise that they consisted of what was available in the larder or what they could afford to obtain and enjoy based on their cultural preferences, thus concentrating for the most part on the religious aspect of Christmas Day.

Beverages

Along with food, of course, beverages, mostly alcoholic, were generously imbibed by many people during the holiday season. The Moravian Brethren Steiner

Eggnog and Other Beverages

In 1787 a traveler to North Carolina on Christmas Day wrote that before breakfast they had a drink of eggnog, "according to North Carolina custom."[iv] Receipts for eggnog varied but might include egg yolks, brown or white sugar, beaten egg whites, milk, and brandy or rum.

Eggnog was not mentioned in schoolteacher Peter Wolle's diary from the early 1800s, but he did highlight other beverages that he imbibed in Salem. There were mentions of coffee, cider and bottled cider, whiskey, tea, liquor, brandy, mol (mulled) wine (for Easter Sunday church service), and "milk, fresh from the cow, the first time since I am here."[v] Grog, chocolate (as a drink), wine sangria, beer and "warm beer with ginger," warm punch, tea, Madeira, mint cordial, rum, and French brandy were all referenced by him at one time or the other.

CHRISTMAS IN THE SOUTH—EGG-NOG PARTY.—[Drawn by W. L. Sheppard.]

"A Southern Eggnog Party," from *Harper's Weekly*, 1870. *Author's collection.*

and Von Schweinitz described a thirteen-hundred mile trip from the North, which ended in Salem on 28 December 1799. They observed on 26 December at "the Blue ridge by Ward's Gap... [that] it was rather noisy, for a group of people were closing the holidays with playing the fiddle, dancing, and drinking."[69]

To capture the spirit of the time with food and drink at the center, the *Virginia Almanack* reported a poem from the eighteenth century that reads as follows:

Christmas is come, hang on the pot,
Let spits turn round, and
  ovens be hot;
Beef, pork, and poultry, now provide
To feast thy neighbours at this tide;
Then wash all down with good
  wine and beer
And so with mirth conclude the
  YEAR.[70]

By November of 1756, the first Moravian settlers in Wachovia had raised a log house for a bakery and distillery in Bethabara.[71] The fruits harvested could then be used for alcoholic beverages such as brandy, cider, and wine. However, by 1772 in Salem, concern was expressed by the strong drink being produced, and it was thought that a brewery for beer should be built, as beer would be "more wholesome" and also more marketable to the neighbors.[72] By 1775, the employment of standard measures for the proper dispensing of alcoholic beverages was felt advisable with cider being measured proportionate to beer.[73] Due to high prices of barley in 1777, the strength of the beer had to be made weaker, but the change was delayed until after Christmas.[74]

During the Revolutionary War, alcohol was often demanded by both American and British soldiers passing through Wachovia; in one instance alone, 120 gallons of brandy were confiscated along with leather and iron.[75] In 1780, as Christmas approached,

Apples played an extremely important role in early American life and particularly at Christmas...as decorations on the pyramids and as gifts to children and adults.

Brother Meyer at the Salem tavern "quietly" took down the sign to avoid selling so much brandy to strangers. Certain rules were established to avoid the instance of "too many drunken men" and "quarrels and fights" at the tavern.[76]

Moravians joined others in their enjoyment of eggnog in the nineteenth century. Eggnog or "egg nogg" was a particular favorite in the South and judging from the following references seems to have been savored soon after arising from bed in the morning. Caroline (Carrie) Fries of Salem, granddaughter of the John Voglers, recorded in her diary, Christmas Day 1863: "Miss Mollie Goodloe sent us a eggnog which we enjoyed as soon as we dressed." Mary Fries Patterson, Carrie's sister, on 26 December 1864 wrote to Carrie: "This morning we had egg-nog... ."[77] The custom of drinking alcoholic beverages early in the morning had been in existence for some time as William Attmore remarked in his diary in 1787 that "It is very much the custom in North Carolina to drink Drams of some kind or other before Breakfast; sometimes Gin, Cherry-bounce, Egg Nog &c... ."[78]

Apples and Cider

Apples played an extremely important role in early American life and particularly at Christmas. The ubiquitous apple was versatile, so it is no wonder that it took its place in Wachovia from the beginning for food and drink, but also later for Christmas celebrations as decorations on the pyramids and as gifts to children and adults. Curiously but appropriately, in *The School of Infancy* by John Amos Comenius, the Moravian teacher and bishop likened children to little fruit trees in their care and growth, a readily understood analogy in a rural society. He emphasized their delivery to teachers for "strength in mind and body" just as the trees are transplanted into orchards for better growth and productivity.[79] He said, "For young trees when transplanted elsewhere always grow tall, and garden fruit has always a richer flavor than forest fruit."[80] However, Comenius cautioned against early removal of children from their mothers, as "the shoot taken out to be planted while too tender grows weakly and slowly; but the firmer one grows strongly and quickly."[81]

Cider was an important apple product in early America. As early as 1799, Thomas Butner, the baker chosen to serve Salem that year, incurred the displeasure of the town administrators when he was found to be selling hard cider (alcoholic) to the local youths.[82] One writer has said that "'hard' cider is a twentieth-century term," as before then essentially "all cider was hard," due to lack of refrigeration to keep it sweet.[83] In order for the juice to ferment, the crushed fruit must contain a proper amount of sugar. Fermentation preserved the juice and produced an intoxicating beverage, which had to be closed to the air to prevent its turning to vinegar.[84] In this country, cider (or "cyder") was consumed in vast quantities and was inexpensive, three shillings a barrel in the late seventeenth and early-eighteenth centuries and as little as fifty cents a barrel later. Rich and poor alike drank it. Naturally fermented cider contains about 8 percent alcohol (16 proof). Many Americans did not consider it an alcoholic drink, hard or not. "[A]fter 1800...the annual per capita consumption of hard cider was 15 or more gallons."[85] One historian thinks that frontiersmen preferred cider to beer because of its higher alcoholic content.[86]

John Adams and Thomas Jefferson both enjoyed cider, as did many Americans who viewed water as untrustworthy to about 1825. George Washington along with Jefferson had cider carefully blended and made, using certain apples like the Hewe's Crab.[87] Although corn liquor was somewhat popular on the frontier, the better tasting, safer, and more easily made cider quickly became more popular. One author says that "virtually every homestead in America had an orchard from which literally thousands of gallons of cider were made every year. In rural areas cider took the place not only of wine and beer, but of coffee and tea, juice, and even water. Indeed, in many places cider was consumed more freely than water, even by children, since it was arguably the healthier more sanitary beverage."[88]

The same author continued, "Cider became so indispensable to rural life that even those who railed against the evil of alcohol made an exception for cider, and the early prohibitionists succeeded mainly in switching drinkers over from grain to apple spirits."[89] Finally cider was directly attacked, and some temperance zealots took axes to the orchards to chop down the trees. In spite of the opposition, cider remained a popular drink until the end of the nineteenth century. Another writer says that "sweet cider has been described as the 'Coca Cola' (as hard cider was the beer)

Sweeten a quart of cyder with double refined sugar, grate nutmeg into it, then milk your cow into your liquor...pour half a pint or more...of the sweetest cream you can get all over it.

of colonial America" and that the two ciders were "the country's 'national beverage' by the 1820s."[90]

There is a vivid account of the potency of cider royal for a youth as recounted in George Bahnson's diary. "Cider royal" was a form of strong cider, which was "hard cider mixed with distilled apple brandy or whiskey"[91] and perhaps sugar. Bahnson wrote:

During preaching our dear Aunt had a most shocking fright. Bernard had gone to Sol Transou's where Tryphonius at present at Salem is on a visit. They did not hear the bell ring & consequently did not go to preaching. Cider royal was handed about, & poor Bernard not knowing the deceitful character of that beverage began to feel sick, & was made fun of by some of the boys. All at once Wessly Cearney came into our room exclaiming: 'Der Bernhard ist versoffen!' [Bernard is drunk.] Fancy to yourself the fright of poor Aunt & H. Aunt ran out immediately to look for Bernard, whom she fancied in the creek, but he was before Transou's & came immediately upon her calling him. The poor boy continued to feel sick all day almost. It is unaccountable that the parents of Tryphonius did not pay stricter attention.

Perhaps though he had not drunk very much, but having taken no breakfast, any drink of such a description was apt to exercise more than common influence upon his stomach.[92]

Cookbook writer Amelia Simmons in 1796 gave a colorful receipt for the very popular syllabub made with cider, and one wonders at the logistics of fulfilling the instructions. She suggested: "Sweeten a quart of cyder with double refined sugar, grate nutmeg into it, then milk your cow into your liquor...pour half a pint or more...of the sweetest cream you can get all over it."[93]

Sweetness epitomizes the power of the apple, and that is how it ultimately, with the help of travelers, got out of the forests of the mountains of Kazakhstan to America. The term "sweet" may have had a connotation somewhat different then than we understand today. One author describes "sweet" as "a metaphor for a certain kind of perfection.... The best land was said to be sweet" [i.e "sweet land of liberty," "home sweet home"]; so were the most pleasing sounds, the most persuasive talk, the loveliest views, the most refined people, and the choicest part of any whole...it stood for fulfillment."[94] The author continued, "The fact that the apple was generally believed to be the fateful tree in the Garden of Eden might also have commended it to a religious people who believed America promised a second Eden."[95]

The apple is about 84 percent water, and is particularly desirable for its sugar. For the German Moravians, *Schnitz* was the word for the dried apples they preserved. A 1931 Salem cookbook provided a recipe for baconseasoned *Schnitz* with unsweetened dumplings.[96] Dried apples reduced the bulk of fresh apples considerably; fifty pounds fresh yielded about seven pounds dried. Compactness and perishability were two key factors.[97] Dried apples made a more easily mailed present, as Peter Wolle wrote on 9 January 1816 that he had sent *Schnitz* to his mother in Nazareth, Pennsylvania. He remarked that he hoped she "will enjoy many a good meal from them."[98] Apples could also be bartered as an important food commodity. Merchants like Elias Vogler in Salem advertised for dried fruit in the local paper. On 18 November 1865, Vogler had an ad in the *People's Press* that he was seeking to buy 500,000 pounds of dried fruit, including apples.[99] Cash or credit was given, and when a sufficient quantity had accumulated, the shipment would be sent off by rail to bigger cities. A traveler in North Carolina in 1872 reported that every house had "its orchard and dry house."[100] Fruit could be dried in the sun for about two days or slipped into an oven at the end of the baking cycle. Susannah Kramsch wrote in 1819, "Baked in oven. Put the first apples in to dry."[101] One could also put the apple slices into a loosely constructed dry house built around a fireplace or a stove.[102] There was a dry house built around the oven at the Salem tavern. The Moravian records reported the construction of a dry house for the town of Salem in 1789 "in order to take care of the rich harvest of fruit which God has given us."[103] The air and the heat dried the fruit slices, sometimes within twelve hours. If weather was bad, someone, perhaps a child, could string the slices, and hang them near a heat source, such as a fireplace or stove.[104]

Although a southern apple specialist estimates that there are more than 1,600 varieties of apples in the American South,[105] another source says there are about 7,000-7,500 varieties of apples in the world.[106] A U.S. government publication of 1905 listed the names of about 17,000 varieties of apples that appeared in American publications of the previous century.[107]

An early American horticultural specialist says, "During that era there was an apple for every community, for every function, whether for cider, storage, baking, drying, or eating out of hand; there was an apple for every taste, crunchy, soft, sweet, and tart, and an apple for every season, especially in the winter when few fruits or vegetables were available."[108]

Salem street scene, 1867. *OSHPC.*

FOOD AND BEVERAGES

The names of apples tantalize us with their past. Consider origin, appearance, use, and discoverers in the following list of apple names: Sheepnose, Bottle Greening, Oxheart, the Twenty-Ounce Pippin,[109] the Ladies Favorite of Tennessee, the Early Harvest and Cider Apple, the Clothes-Yard Apple, Jacob's Sweet Winter, the Plum Apple, the Hog Apple, Pumpkin Sweet, Snuff, Buttermilk, Summer Cheese, Watermelon, Payne's Late Keeper, and Morgan's Christmas. Today there are still North Carolina apples with American Indian names such as Junaluskee, Nequassa, Cullasaja, and Ellijay.[110]

No early recorded names of apples in Wachovia have been found until George Bahnson in 1835 mentioned Cheese Apples, "the only good winter apple tree" that he had.[111] An apple historian documents that there were many "Cheese Apples" or apples with "cheese" in the names. He suspects that they received the name because they looked "somewhat like a wheel or hoop of cheese."[112] In the Diary of the Bethania Congregation, 12 February 1845, it was noted, "Planted a Buckingham apple tree in the northwest corner of the garden behind the shed."[113]

On Christmas Eve 1862, Captain Charles Bahnson wrote in a letter home that the only Christmas they (he and some other soldiers) had was to try "some of Gellie's apple butter."[114] Apple butter was one delicacy often made with boiled down fresh apple cider and pared apples, stirred for hours in a kettle, and flavored with sugar, sometimes cinnamon, and perhaps cloves.[115] It was preserved in covered crocks in a cool, dry place. The buildings of Salem had capacious cellars and garrets where such foodstuffs could be stored to await consumption.

Through the years apples were mentioned countless times as snacks and treats for Salem children as well as decorations and gifts for Christmas. Schoolteacher Peter Wolle in 1816 remarked on receiving two apples along with a wax candle for Christmas.[116] He referred to the use of apples as missiles in the boys' hands when in an argument with his colleague Brother Daniel Wohlfahrt (Welfare) he disapprovingly recorded, "I told him that it was also not right to be in the room when the children were in the garden, since they then threw apples at each other, and that I believed he knew of no other way to keep order in school than with a ruler."[117] George Bahnson recorded on 18 December 1835 that "Amanda brought me cakes, cider & apples" at Jacob Conrad's house.[118] Indeed, one Moravian woman in Pennsylvania remembered that earlier in the nineteenth century as a child during Christmas "every evening before we went to bed we had Christmas cakes, sweet cider, and apples."[119]

Treats were especially enjoyed by nineteenth-century American children because they rarely were the first to be fed in a large family and almost certainly did not receive the choice of the bounty. In 1853, one wise and benevolent author calling herself "Aunt Fanny" deplored the second-

"Wendell Michael, 1807," featuring a man with his hands in apple butter crocks, from the Journal of Lewis Miller, vol. I, p. 23. *Collection of the York County Heritage Trust, York, PA.*

class treatment of some young-sters, describing meals of cold potatoes, meatless bones, and watery soups. She declared that they deserved equal considera-tion and furthermore stated, "I believe in great round apples and big slices of good plain ginger-bread" for the little ones.[120]

Well before Aunt Fanny's admonishments, Moravian com-munities in America were cele-brating children, who received at the lovefeast on Christmas Eve a candle, an apple or a cake, and a nicely printed Bible verse, perhaps in colored ink. Apples as gifts were mentioned by Mary Louise Johnston who wrote from the Salem Girls' School, where she was a student, to her father in Monroe, Georgia, on 14 January 1839, about the preceding Christmas. She described gifts in the school drawers of cakes, candy, almonds, raisins, and apples along with a lighted wax candle.[121]

In 1904 *The Wachovia Mor-avian* reported that at the Carmel church "a beautiful Christmas tree graced the occasion heavily laden with candies, apples and many other presents which were distributed."[122] Early European Christmas trees frequently had apples as adornments, reminis-cent of the apple-decorated trees in medieval church miracle plays depicting the Garden of Eden (See Chapter Two).

Sweets and Treats

Schoolteacher Peter Wolle highlighted sweets that he enjoyed in Salem in the second decade of the 1800s. Some of them were sweetmeats (preserved fruits); sugarcake; pies, both apple and peach; buns; cookies (thicker and usually called "cakes" in Wachovia); meringue balls; streusel; applecake; peppernuts (a kind of small, round cookie); and "appledumplings for supper, never eaten before in N. Carolina!".[123]

Also noted were "sweet milk for a desert [sic]", with which he was "very much delighted." This may have been possibly syllabub or posset.[124] Wolle paid homage in his diary to the beloved ginger cakes on 18 December 1818, when he spoke of preaching his "gingerbread-sermon…because everyone is now occupied with this favorite work."[125]

There is an account by a grandson of John and Christina Vogler of the childish pleasures involving sweet treats and fruits as experienced at his grandparents' home. F. H. Fries wrote, "The grandchildren loved to go there for they knew that the corner cupboard in the living room con-tained cake or candy, that would invariably be offered by Grand-mother, while Grandfather had apples from his trees or grapes off his vines that were kept by him in season, and later in Winter, dried persimmons, of which he was very fond."[126]

Drawing of the interior of Salem's Winkler Bakery, late-18th century. *OSMG.*

Sweets have always been appreciated as a special treat at Christmas, and sharing them together in good fellowship promoted bonding. As one anonymous writer proclaimed at an earlier time, "In Salem, family Christmas visiting still exists, and at every house there are brown Christmas cakes."[127] Colonel William A. Blair wrote about Moravian Christmas cakes in the 1930s: "no dainty tidbit, anywhere, was more characteristic of Salem, more generally made, or more highly prized."[128]

During Christmas everyone enjoyed at vesper and other times the Christmas cakes, renowned by all residents and visitors to Wachovia. Early in December 1862, Charles Bahnson while away at war wrote in a memorandum at the end of a letter to his father that he would like to have some apples and ginger cakes,

"for it would not appear like Christmas, to spend it without eating any of them."[129] That same year on Christmas Day he wrote that he "came very near having the toothache from thinking of my gingercakes & sugar... ."[130] Bahnson's father had noted in his diary in 1834 that the dough for the Christmas cakes was a "very important matter."[131]

Baking and sharing the legendary Christmas cakes were part of the winter pleasures, and the comments were frequent in describing this tradition. In 1835, Bahnson wrote on 21 December, "A disagreeable rainy day. But Christmas cakes were to be baked tomorrow & so I started off to get some molasses... ."[132] It was a source of pride for the housewives to produce cakes that could hold up under the scrutiny of their peers, and women toiled indefatigably to accomplish their goals, usually

producing more than a gallon of the delicacies. Susannah Kramsch noted in her diary on 15 December 1820: "baked Christmas cakes with the english sisters. All fatigued."[133] George Bahnson remarked on 18 December 1834, about his wife's efforts: "In the meantime our cakes had turned out very well, but my sweet H[ortensia] felt very tired having been on her legs all day, seeing to every thing, in order to produce Christmas cakes to her liking & worthy of the praise of others."[134] Birdie Goslen recorded in her diary 14-15 December 1892: "I will bake the ginger cakes tomorrow... . Finished baking our 1½ gallons by 5 o'clock...perfectly splendid."[135] An early-twentieth-century Salem woman observed, "With what kindly hypocrisy [sic] each guest comments upon the delicacy of flavor [of the "brown

Christmas cakes"] and returns at length to nibble her own store, complacently assured that her ancestral recipe is unsurpassed."[136] An assertion made in the introduction of a 1931 Salem cookbook was indicative of how women achieved success by repetition and tradition. It stated: "None of the recipes is kitchen-tested, oven timed or failure-proof; for our grandmothers depended more upon experience and intuition than upon mechanical devices for success in cooking."[137]

Although some recipes may have been reserved just for family, cookie cutters were shared. The cutters were expensive at that time, and so neighbors borrowed from each other to increase the variety of the shapes of their cakes. On 21 December 1834, Bahnson wrote in his diary, "On this day a great many people bake their christmas cakes, there being but few patterns [cutters] in town, they are borrowed in every house & consequently only few can bake at a time."[138]

Ingredients varied somewhat, but whatever the combination, Moravian ginger cakes were not always light or thin, as they are today. The thinly rolled spicy, ginger "cookies" sold commercially today have evolved out of this centuries-old tradition, coming from Germans in Pennsylvania and from Europe.[139] One could break a tooth on some of the early cakes, as the stiff dough often produced a hard cake that would last for months. Ginger cakes with beer was a favorite combination, served at the tavern and elsewhere. A receipt attributed to Salem's Winkler bakery and distributed by Old Salem Museums & Gardens today contains the following ingredients: molasses, brown sugar, cloves, ginger, cinnamon, margarine and shortening (earlier lard would have been used), soda, water, and about four pounds of flour. The yield will be about seven or eight pounds of cookies.[140]

Although women mentioned baking the ginger cakes in their diaries, they did not always write down the ingredients. Obviously, there was no need, as they knew by heart the receipts they used every Christmas season, or they had their mother's written ones as reference. A Christmas cakes receipt of Paulina Schober (1791-1869) of Salem, sister of Peter Wolle's wife Maria Theresa Schober and Van Zeveley's wife Johanna Sophia Schober, is a case in point. These women would have known what to do with such receipts, so the unintentional absence of the ingredient of ginger would not have been a problem. Paulina Schober's receipt reads: "Rub 2# Sugar with 2# butter to cream, by degrees add 2¼ flour and yelk [sic] of 8 eggs well beaten—2 spoonsful alcohol, the whites beaten to snow add last, spice ¼ oz. cin., ¼ oz. Cardamon & ¼ oz. cloves. roll out thin with flour & sugar."[141]

The 1931 Salem cookbook also has what its contributor Mrs. Della Tesh denominated a "Very Old Recipe" handed down from the past. It was meant to make a large quantity of Christmas cakes, as it calls for 15½ pounds flour along with 1¾ pounds lard, 1¾ pounds butter, one gallon of molasses, four pounds brown sugar, eight tablespoons cinnamon, four tablespoons cloves, two tablespoons ginger, and five tablespoons soda. The note suggested that a pint of brandy might be added, if desired.[142] A Moravian woman interviewed by a Quaker writer in Pennsylvania in 1882 remembered from her youth that before Christmas they "baked a great supply of cakes... and these lasted all winter."[143]

One quite different ginger cake variation, more like a cruller, was included in Louisa Vogler Senseman's receipts and called for molasses, lard, sugar, egg yolks, salt, cream, pearl ashes, cinnamon, flour, and orange peel, which when mixed and rolled out was cut into "stripes," fried in lard, and sprinkled with grated sugar.[144] The editor of Louisa's recipes observed that all the entries seemed to have been written at one time by the same hand. They were dated 1844-1854, the years when Louisa was married to Edwin, a minister. She and her husband in 1851 were called from Salem to serve in New Salem, a Moravian community in Illinois, so she may have been preparing for future occasions when she

Posset Receipt

Old Salem Museums & Gardens' early eighteenth-century century Manuscript Cookbook has a receipt for posset with eggs and without milk or cream. It calls for 20 beaten eggs, a pound of sugar, ale, and sack (white wine).[vi] In other receipts bread, almond paste or a porridge like oatmeal were sometimes added, and, of course, milk. Posset was especially pleasant on a cold winter day, perhaps around Christmas, when the nourishing drink was warmed over the fire or heated by the use of a hot poker thrust into the mixture. Since the curds resulting from the warm milk and alcohol rose to the top, these vessels often had a tubular spout that projected from the bottom upwards in order to sip the liquid and avoid the rest, which could be eaten with a spoon.[vii]

would not have female relatives to consult for such knowledge.[145] The 1931 Salem cookbook lists three other variations of this recipe.

The "inmates" of the Salem Girls' School (they frequently spoke of themselves in this manner) were not left out of the cake sharing at Christmas. As a matter of fact, the school made a point of creating an air of festivity with decorations and food because many of the students did not travel home during the holiday.

Students at the Girls' School frequently mentioned the cakes. Virginian Annie L. Ogburn wrote of her reminiscences from 1871 to 1875. She described the gifts of nuts, candies, and raisins in brown paper bags from the principal and commented with enthusiasm on the cakes. "[T]he largest paper bag of all, was filled with delicious dark brown Christmas cakes. They were given that name because they only appeared when Christmas came, and we never saw cakes like them at any other time; neither have I found their like any where else. What girl can spend a Christmas in the Academy and forget to remember them forever after!"[146]

On 23 December 1816, schoolteacher Peter Wolle, wrote that he and Mr. Vogler went to Lenert's shop in Salem "to buy some sugarthings for Christmas to present to the Pathen [god-children]."[147] The next day he received as a Christmas present two apples and a wax candle with three wicks from a Miss Baumgarten.[148] Ten days earlier he had recorded a business visit to Sister Schweinitz from whom he received "some Christmas cakes, which they had baked to day."[149] Several days later, on 5 January, he wrote that gingerbread and wine were bought "to host my children" testifying to the fact that children were given some alcoholic drinks as previously discussed.[150]

Wolle singled out cheese in his diary only once, in 1820, terming it "excellent" as enjoyed by his pregnant wife.[151] Most Salem residents probably did not have enough milk for making cheese and may have had to buy it at the store.

When Salem merchants began to advertise in the local paper in the second half of the nineteenth century, the ads reflected much about the sweets and other foods like cheese and fruits that were available and desired at that time. Hall & Hall at the Salem Confectionery in 1858 emphasized their "Large and Fresh assortment of Nuts, Figs, Raisins, Prunes, Dates, Currants, Preserved Ginger, Fig Paste, Crackers, Cheese, Cakes, Plain and Fancy Candies, Preserved Fruits, Lemon Syrup, Cigars,...Fresh Oysters, Ale & Lager Beer."[152]

Charles Winkler began his 22 December 1871 ad with the salutation "A MERRY CHRISTMAS!" He then proceeded to list "a large assortment of PURE CANDIES, both common and fancy, Nuts, Raisins, Oranges, Lemons, Figs, Currants, Citron, Prunes, &c. FRESH CAKES..."[153] In a circa 1880 broadside, C.A. Winkler advertised, "The well-known Christmas cakes not sold any where else."[154]

On 3 December 1874, in Salem, F. W. Meller advertised "FANCY GOODS & TOYS" as well as the fruits in Winkler's ad plus bananas, dates, fresh nuts, cakes and candies.[155] In 1879, his 27 November ad was headed "Headquarters of SANTA CLAUS" in which he offered "FOREIGN AND DOMESTIC FRUITS AND NUTS' and "All kinds of plain and French CANDIES," which were warranted to be "STRICTLY PURE."[156]

Both Wolle and Bahnson mentioned sugarcake in their diaries. Wolle referred to it on 4 July 1816, when he noted in English: "At 2 o'clock a private party had a refreshment of wine sangria and sugarcake."[157] Bahnson referred to sugarcake in 1835 when he remarked: "we happened to have sugarcake fresh from yesterday, which was a treat for us, en famille [in the family] at the vespertable."[158] Several years later he spoke of bringing home before Christmas a special present of sugarcake sent by a well-meaning parishioner to his young daughter, who regretfully had already gone to sleep and could not enjoy it.[159]

In 1836, Bahnson presented a vivid visual and auditory picture involving sugarcake: "According to promise we rode out to visit Ephraim Transou. Henry Wilson [child of their neighbor Dr. Wilson] went along with us, & behaved himself quite well. Our darling [Bahnsons' daughter Angelica] had much

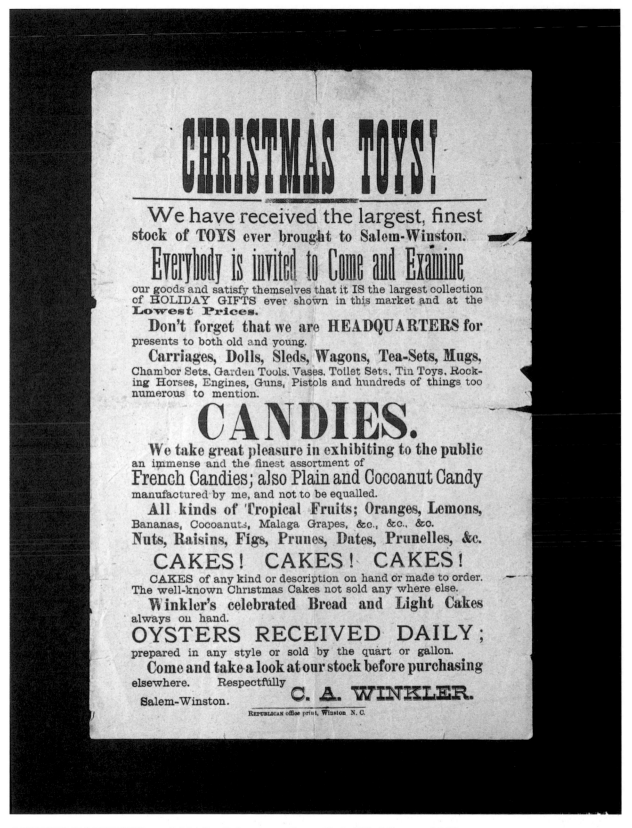

"CHRISTMAS TOYS!" broadside for Salem merchant C. A. Winkler, ca. 1880.
Courtesy of the Moravian Archives, Winston-Salem, NC.

Oranges

Oranges were considered special treats, one or two sometimes given at Christmas or perhaps to a sick person at other times. Susannah Kramsch, at home with her sick husband, spoke of receiving an orange from Mr. Bagge on 13 December 1821.[viii] From Josiah Smith's diary came a report on 23 December 1780 that he and his fellow Americans on board ship received "One Thousand Sweet Oranges" which were divided amongst 64 of them, a real Christmas treat.[ix]

Surprisingly for the climate, Johann Heinrich Leinbach of Salem mentioned on 13 June 1830, "This morning I grafted a couple of orange trees or bushes." No further reference to the outcome was noted.[x]

fuss with little William sometimes they played together & at other times they sung quite a loud duetto... . I have never seen any child being fed so much & so fast as this poor little thing... Little William swallowed large pieces of sugarcake which would have choked our darling once for ever."[160]

Sugarcake and its vesper connection have been of longtime interest. In 1859, the Moravian Historical Society met in Nazareth, Pennsylvania, on its second anniversary in the middle of December. The proceedings recorded that "the company discussed the sugar cake and other cakes peculiar to the vesper table."[161]

As with the Christmas cakes, there are few references to the ingredients used in sugarcake in the early Salem diaries. Although there are "sugar cake" receipts from an earlier period, they are quite different from the one that many Moravians make and use today. The modern recipe with lots of sugar may be a nineteenth-century innovation that has evolved and become a more recent "Moravian tradition." European antecedents for such cakes are not generally as sweet. Louisa Vogler Senseman did have a receipt for "Plain Cakes" that called for sugar, butter, water, cinnamon and pearl ash (wood-ash-derived potassium carbonate, which makes a white, alkaline salt).[162]

A receipt for "Moravian Sugar Cake" appeared in *The Moravian* in April 1863, in response to a query from "a lady subscriber, and in compliance with other repeated solicitations," telling us that perhaps sugarcake was just becoming widely popular among Moravians. The receipt was asserted to be "the genuine home-made sugar-cake which we have taken down from the lips of several experienced housekeepers."[163]

Lovefeast Food and Drink

With all the historic problems of production of food and drink for the beloved bonding service, the lovefeast remains one of the most cherished traditions of the Moravian Church and one that other non-Moravian churches have instituted in their own congregations. Lovefeasts were special services reserved for significant occasions, like Christmas. For a more complete discussion of the service, see Chapter Six.

The lovefeast was not a sacrament of the church but a liturgical service of bonding and fellowship much like the early Christian agape (also defined as a lovefeast). Food and drink, however, are not essential to a lovefeast, although they have always added to the appeal of the service. Current Moravian archivist Dr. Daniel Crews writes, "There is no hard and fast rule on what refreshments, if any, are served at a lovefeast."[164] Fellowship together is the most important aspect.

Baking for the lovefeast, although essential, was an undeniable chore for many people, and understandably they sometimes shirked their duty. It was suggested in 1844 in the Wachovia community of Friedland that if members and their children participated in the lovefeasts, then they should participate in the baking.[165] However, widows in Bethania were released from that obligation in 1846.[166] Money to pay for the wood as well as the labor for chopping could be expensive for a woman or a family with few funds.

As described in the Introduction to this book, in November of 1753, the first lovefeast in Wachovia took place within the shelter of a tiny structure abandoned the year before by a German named Hans Wagner. Amid the howling of nearby wolves, the carefully selected group of male settlers thanked God for their safe arrival. Although they did not divulge what they ate or drank, it may very well have been pumpkin broth or cornmeal mush, two staples of their diet.[167]

In Bethlehem, Pennsylvania one historian believes "tea and a roll were typical refreshments" for lovefeasts. "Coffee, chocolate, bread and water, and even a haunch of venison were served at times in 1744 and 1745," wrote Vernon Nelson.[168]

Lovefeast server Mattie Winkler at Salem's Home Moravian Church, Christmas 1939. *OSHPC.*

In Wachovia in 1779 at South Fork, the Christmas Eve lovefeast food consisted of honey cakes.[169] In 1789 in Salem it was decided that "Coffee shall be served at the Christmas lovefeast, instead of the tea hitherto used... ."[170] Also in 1789, Salem's Congregation Council suggested that "sangaree" (Moravian archivist Dr. Daniel Crews defines this as "a mixture of water and spiced wine")[171] might be served for lovefeasts in warm weather.[172] At the consecration for Salem's Home Moravian Church in 1800, beer and buns were served.[173] At the Springplace, Georgia, Moravian Indian Mission in 1805, on Christmas Eve, for the lovefeast they had "wheat bread and bush-tea (for lack of good tea)."[174] The missionary Byhans also experimented with an okra beverage when low on coffee; this was either entirely okra or mixed three parts to one part coffee. Byhan wrote that it

FOOD AND BEVERAGES

"tasted very nearly like coffee."[175] At the Georgia Indian Mission they also experimented with carrots, wheat, and chestnuts as coffee substitutes.[176] Note the request from the *Diener* (server) who prepared the lovefeasts in 1809 in Salem and wanted "a linen bag for straining the coffee; also a large coffee can, two or three tea-canisters, and several teaspoons."[177] Although coffee was often served to the children, in 1821 it was decided that tea would be used for the children at their lovefeast that year.[178]

Receipt for Moravian Sugar Cake[xi]

To gratify one of our lady subscribers, and in compliance with other repeated solicitations, we furnish herewith a recipe for making the genuine home-made sugar-cake which we have taken down from the lips of several experienced housekeepers.

Of well-risen wheaten bread dough take about two pounds. Work into it a tea-cupful of brown sugar, quarter of a pound of butter and a beaten egg. Knead well and put into a square pan dredged with flour. Cover it and set it near the fire for half an hour to rise. When risen, wash with melted butter; make holes in the dough to half its depth, two inches apart, fill them with sugar and a little butter. Then spread ground cinnamon and a thick layer of brown sugar over the whole surface. Sprinkle with a little essence of lemon. Put into the oven and bake in fifteen minutes.[xii]

An amusing incident concerning coffee in a children's lovefeast in Bethania on 24 December 1836 was recounted by George Bahnson. His young daughter Angelica was so energized by the consumption of her entire portion of caffeinated lovefeast coffee that she "was quite beside herself & ran about in the room from one chair to the next, at the same time expressing much joy at the decoration."[179] That year Bahnson also remarked on the state of the coffee for lovefeasts, which he proclaimed never good because of want of cream, even though there were a plentiful number of cows.[180]

By the mid-nineteenth century there were some specific mentions of lovefeast buns in Salem.[181] In 1845[182] and in 1851 it was noted that William Winkler had been baking the buns although not to complete satisfaction of the congregation.[183] Instructions for making lovefeast buns, titled "Formula for L.F. Buns," found in a folder at the Moravian Archives in Winston-Salem seems a likely "official" recipe. It starts with the base of one gallon water and calls for 1/2 ounce nutmeg, the juice and gratings of one orange and one lemon, six ounces malt, one pound and eight ounces eggs, five pounds pastry flour, eleven pounds eight ounces bread flour along with two pounds butter and one pound shortening. Before the buns rise for the last time, the directions say: "Dip letter in melted butter and stamp bun in top M or cut with razor blade." This is the only found mention of marking the lovefeast buns with the letter "M," a Moravian custom still in practice.[184] The same folder at the Archives provides the recipe for "Moravian Love Feast Cakes," which would yield 180 two-ounce cakes spiced with mace and cinnamon.[185]

The sweet accompaniment at lovefeasts probably continued to vary, as on Christmas Eve 1878, an article in a guide book published by Blum in Salem described the lovefeast offerings as cake and coffee handed around to all present by "ladies dressed in black with white muslin caps and aprons."[186] With the buns or cake, the "good coffee" so frequently mentioned in the diaries attest to the longevity of that tradition. Cream or milk was long preferred for lovefeast coffee. In 1876 at the New Philadelphia Moravian Church, located several miles from Salem, "in absence of coffee in the Lovefeast, milk, or water, according to choice, was used."[187] Today in the Moravian congregation at St. Croix, the Virgin Islands, Kool-Aid punch and large sweet buns are enjoyed."[188]

Vesper Food and Beverages

Traditionally in Wachovia, dinner was the main meal of the day when meat, vegetables, sometimes soup, and bread were served at noon or early afternoon. The nineteenth century saw the popularization of a mid-afternoon "coffee break," called vesper, or "fesper," as Lisetta Vogler spelled it in 1831 (the way the Germans would have pronounced it). More social than dinner, vesper was a family-oriented afternoon coffee time or teatime for the Moravians.[189] In winter when the days were short, sometimes vesper and supper (the evening meal) were combined, after which one retired early to bed.

Moravian *Records* editors Fries and Rights described vesper in the following way: "A favored custom of afternoon assembly of friends in a home where light refreshments were served. It was mainly a social custom but sometimes it found religious significance, such as in the singing of a birthday hymn or of prayers for travelers about to depart."[190]

Vesper undoubtedly grew out of the lovefeast, which originally had been used as a treat after the completion of some special church-related task, the arrival from or departure on a journe of a member of the congregation, the gathering of special friends and family at the conclusion of a funeral, a birthday, or special anniversary, or maybe the recognition of some special church visitor from another town. Whatever the reason, vesper gradually became an everyday occurrence, a time for people to stop their daily work and chores and enjoy tea or "good coffee" (frequently described as such by local diarists) a piece of cake, or other sweet treat such as a Christmas cake, or perhaps some bread and butter or bread and cheese. Children's birthdays began to be honored in this way when the family might invite the schoolteachers to share the occasion with some other friends as well.

To people like George Bahnson, coffee was the "nectar" of the repast.[191] In his diary entry of 9 July 1834 he wrote: "We staid there to vesper & supper. Vesper is taken in every family, & very complete. In winter they unite vesper & supper into one."[192] Supper could also be a meal of leftovers from dinner, or as the

offerings at the Girls' School called them: "warmed-overs" along with milk, pie, pancakes, cornmeal mush, and perhaps chocolate (as a drink).[193] A Moravian sister in Bethlehem told of generally having a supper at six o'clock of "cold meat, bread and butter, and pickles."[194]

To illustrate the gusto with which some people enjoyed their vesper, picture this scene: It is a warm North Carolina afternoon in July, about 170 years ago. George Bahnson has been visiting the Conrads in Bethania where he has encountered the local egocentric and presumptuous schoolmaster who conducts him by horseback to the farmhouse of another member of the Bethania congregation. The owner is a "simple but wellmeaning farmer" devoted to his religion and in stark contrast to the teacher. An older man named Vetter Michael is there along with several others. "Cousin" or "Old Man" (as "Vetter" might mean) Michael is hungry and ready for the goodlooking cakes and breads set out for afternoon coffee. He is "stowing away as hard as he could, large morsels of bread & cakes." One can imagine the crumbs falling with abandon![195]

Other foods served at vesper and documented in Wachovia were sugarcake, white bread, butter, cake, vespercakes, waffles, meringue balls, "good bread and excellent cheese," funnel cakes with and without honey, sweet potato cake, pretzels (probably sweet), applecake with cream, crullers (a small sweet cake in the form of a twisted strip fried in deep fat), gingerbread, and shavings with loaf sugar upon them. (No enlightening reference to "shavings" has been forthcoming, although an imaginative possibility might be slivers of cake or bread.)

By 1882 an elderly sister from Bethlehem felt that the two o'clock vesper had generally fallen out of use in that area, but she still liked to use it to entertain guests from out of town when preparing dinner or supper for them was not convenient. On those occasions she always served sugarcake and coffee. Her daughter, present at the interview, quickly added, "It would not be a vesper without the sugar-cake."[196]

Francis Henry Fries (1855-1931), son of Lisetta and Francis Fries, wrote fondly of vesper at his family home in Salem. "Vesper, given in the years succeeding the War, was the meal most dear to all who could attend. Punctually at three o'clock Mother came in...and served coffee and sugar cake to all the men of the family," including Mr. Pfohl, the bookkeeper at Fries Mills, "and others who might drop in." Fries wrote that "the beautiful custom of...a cup of coffee and a love feast bun or slice of freshly baked 'sugar cake' "was a simple but meaningful repast. His reminiscence of this family tradition was part of a history of the Fries family, which he prepared as a Christmas gift for his only daughter Rosa in 1930.[197]

John Vogler House in Salem.

Enslaved Holiday Celebrations and Charitable Holiday Meals

In Salem it seems that one treat for the enslaved African American members of the church was that they were generally not made to work on Christmas Day. On 18 December 1832, Minister Schmidt wrote, "Bro. Steiner visited me and consulted me about my call and the serving of the small Negro Congregation. As the Negroes are free at Christmas and as a general rule go away for visits, it was considered best not to have a preaching service on Christmas Day."[198]

Again on 17 December 1837, it was recorded, "[S]ince the Negroes are free for Christmas and New Year's Day, and only few can be expected to the services, therefore the Christmas celebration was today with the usual [Christmas] services but without a lovefeast. To the children small gifts of *pfeffernusse* [small round gingerbread biscuits] were distributed by some of the sisters to their joy."[199] On 23 December 1849, the Salem diarist wrote, "Since many of the Negroes have to work for their owners on Christmas Day when that falls on a week day,—and those who do not work visit their friends and acquaintances, we thought it best to take under consideration the important subject of our Savior's birth already today... ."[200]

Outside Salem a southern plantation celebration including the enslaved was described by J. Pierpont at the home of William Alston, near Georgetown, South Carolina, in 1805:

Dec. 25. Christmas. Throughout the state of South Carolina, Christmas is a holiday, together with two of the succeeding days, for all literary seminaries, but more especially for the Negroes.

On these days the chains of slavery with which the blacks are loaded and in which they toil unceasingly for their masters, are loosed.... Children visit their parents, husbands, their wives, brothers and sisters each other, who live at a distance, and partake the pleasure of social connexions of which they are deprived during the remaining part of the year.

On the morning of Christmas Col Alston gave orders that as many beeves might be butchered as to supply all with meat, which as a general thing is not allowed them. No less than 21 bullocks fell sacrifices to their festivity.[201]

Gifts to the enslaved were mentioned by Moravian Mary Fries Patterson on 26 December 1864, when she wrote to her sister Carrie in Salem: "This morning we...gave a stew to all the Negroes."[202] In a period dictionary, "storepond" is one definition of a "stew," which was a holding pond for fish to be kept fresh and accessible for the table. Thomas Jefferson had two fish ponds built at Monticello in 1812 for just such a purpose.[203] In this context Patterson probably used "stew" to refer to goods gathered over a period of time to be presented all together on one occasion as Christmas gifts.

By contrast, a quite different celebration planned as a posthumous gift to some children by a Salem enslaved church member was recorded. After the death of John Emanuel, who was with his wife Sarah among the first members of the 1823 log church for African Americans in Salem, it was noted in his memoir: "A peculiarity of his should not be left unnoticed. Since his baptism in the year 1803, on January 6 [Epiphany: the coming of the Magi to see the baby Jesus] each year on this day, formerly in Bethania and later in Salem, he took pleasure in inviting a number of children of our members to an afternoon vesper, which they enjoyed together. He was a great friend of the children, who loved him, and often on Sundays a number of them would go to talk with him. He left in writing the notice that next year on January 6 he was going to have such a vesper with the children invited. He was beloved also by the grown people."[204]

Firewood and the Yule Log

For the Moravians to produce baked treats such as Christmas cakes and lovefeast buns much forethought and planning was required, which included the use of copious amounts of firewood in the fireplaces, stoves, and outside bake ovens—no small matter in earlier times. Collecting and chopping wood was just one of the chores at a time of year that also traditionally included such labor-intensive activities as hog butchering.

In order to cook all the "home materials," an ample supply of wood was essential.[xiii] Five days before Christmas in 1785, George Washington noted that he had "some Carts and Cutters" brought from his plantations "to assist in laying in a Stock of Fire wood for Christmas."[xiv] In 1815 at the Moravian Indian Mission in Georgia, Brother and Sister Gambolds's report included a similar remark: "...busy the whole day bringing in wood in order to have a sufficient supply in house during the Christmas season.[xv] Bethania minister George Bahnson, after receiving a load of wood two days before Christmas 1836, helped the deliverer in "cleaning the yard for the holy days."[xvi] In the 1840s, Colonel Openheart, the benevolent patriarch of a South Carolina plantation and a character in a southern story created by Charlestonian William Gilmore Simms, spoke his mind to his wife on the subject of celebrating Christmas. Regardless of circumstances such as bad crops and rising debts, according to the Colonel, the Yule "log must be kindled at Christmas though he may have never another left in his wood-yard."[xvii] Without fire, it was a comfortless and cheerless world in the cold months.

The Yule Log is an English custom, in which a fine, large tree with the widest girth was chosen to be felled and burned. As long as the Yule Log burned the workers of the estate received a respite from labor. To prolong the burning some intrepid workers often soaked the log with water. As the Yule Log burned down, a small portion would be saved to start the fire under the next year's log as a token of good luck.

Woodpile outside of Salem's Miksch House.

Postcard featuring the "bringing in" of the Yule Log, twentieth century. *Author's collection.*

A southern tradition often practiced by the enslaved was "Christmas Gift!" This was a game of surprise, initiated on Christmas morning as a means of getting a little gift from the owner and his family. One had to shout out the phrase "to catch" the other person first in order to obtain the gift. Most families were prepared for these occasions and had the little tokens ready. It should be noted, however, that while this was a common tradition in the South, there is no mention of the custom in Wachovia.

Feeding the poor was an important aspect of the nineteenth-century Christmas, and there were numerous stories to encourage both adults and children to share with those less fortunate. Newspapers and magazines exhorted the public not to forget the needy.[205] An early Pennsylvania Christmas verse appeared in 1800:

Lovefeast Coffee

Lovefeast Coffee recipe as taken from a 1931 Salem cookbook prepared by the Dorcas Co-Workers of the Salem Home.[xviii]

3 pounds coffee, any good grade

1 gallon whole milk or ½ gallon single cream

4 pounds sugar

7 gallons water

Get water boiling hot. Put grounds loosely in a bag and leave in boiling water for 15 minutes. Take out the bag and add sugar and milk just before taking from the stove.

Contributed by Mr. W. J. Hege

Come ye rich, survey the stable
Where your infant saviour lies;
From your full o'erflowing table
Send the hungry good supplies.[206]

Through the years there were many opportunities to perform charitable works, both in the cities and the outlying districts. As mentioned in Chapter Four, *The Moravian* of 1864 urged, "...as a thank-offering to Christ at Christmas, let men bring their gifts—to the doors of poverty, to the bedside of the sick, to the hospitals where our brave soldiers are suffering, to the tents of the defenders of our country, to the homes where their families dwell."[207]

Brother Zevely from Salem reported in 1836 that some people he encountered while doing missionary work in the Blue Ridge Mountains of Virginia had no bread, but existed on potatoes, beans, and cabbage and often had no meat or milk. He had tears in his own eyes when approached by a weeping mother with "half starved children" who begged for help in keeping them all from perishing. She pled: "O Grandfather, do save mine and my children's lives. We have had not one mouthful of bread for two weeks, and we have ate up all our Irish potatoes, and it does appear we must perish except you help us."[208]

Such accounts were duly passed on to the Home Mission Society in Salem, which did what it could. Elsewhere, others did likewise, as Mahala Roach in Mississippi in 1856 wrote that she sent dinner, "some both cooked and uncooked to our neighbors."[209] In Pennsylvania a newspaper article in 1857 wrote of one man's reminiscence of Christmas as a boy on his parents' very modest farm when, nevertheless, "there were great baskets of provisions sent to the poor family at the foot of the hill."[210]

Children were involved in ministering to the needy by

words and deeds. The Juvenile Missionary Society, made up of scholars from the Salem Sunday School, in 1872 were urged from their "hearts and hands" to help the poor with the necessaries of life.[211] A letter in 1869 from a little girl named Carrie in Salem to *The Moravian* newspaper's "Mr. Moravian Letter-Bag" is a touching reminder of how children can magnificently rise to the occasion, in this case to provide materials for a mission ship to carry spiritual food to the heathen. She wrote, "Here is a little gold dollar which was given to me during the war. I prize it very much, but I can't see that it is doing any good lying all the time idle in my mama's box; so I made up my mind that I would give it to you when you came to see us. It will help to buy a plank for the ship that is to tell the poor heathen of a Savior's love... ."[212]

The Wachovia Moravian described a visit to the Poor House by a group of Salem women calling themselves the Helping Hand Society in December 1895. The society had been making such visits for thirty-eight years. On this year there was "beside every plate...a paper bag containing Christmas cakes, an orange, an apple and some candy; and at each plate some little gift suited to the wants of the individual for whom it was intended."[213]

Ultimately, in the matter of food and drink for the revival of spirits at a bleak time of year for both rich and poor, the Bethania minister Bahnson summed it up well when he remarked after New Year's in 1835 on the conviviality of the occasion: "The dinner... was exquisite, & did which I cannot deny revive my somewhat drooping spirit. Not only the treat of good victuals but the animated & interesting conversation, caused a person to feel very comfortable."[214]

The St. Philips brick church in Salem.

Chapter 6
Music and Services

Morning Star, O cheering sight!
Ere thou cam'st, how dark earth's night!
...in me shine;
Jesus mine;
fill my heart with love divine.

— from "Morning Star," a popular Moravian Christmas hymn by Francis F. Hagen

Moravian Musical Traditions for Christmas and Everyday

Imagine a snowy Christmas Eve Sunday morning in Friedberg, North Carolina, in 1876. After breakfast, Moravian minister David Smith and his son Theodore struggle to hoist a melodeon into the carriage. The instrument is to be used for the consecration service of a new church in Eden. Father and son feel in an expansive, joyful, Christmas mood as they pass by houses along the way, and so the boy begins to play hymns as he and his father sing. What a sight and sound to behold for the appreciative listeners![1]

The Moravians love music, and from the earliest days they have been known for a musical culture both advanced and sophisticated. The Moravian Church has always shared and celebrated God's love through participatory music in its services, particularly at Christmas and Easter, but also on secular festal occasions such as the Fourth of July as well as in the daily lives of the people. Children

have been unfailingly incorporated into and encouraged in this musical tradition. As an example of the deeply ingrained use of music in every aspect of the lives of Moravians, the following amusing story is told of a condescendingly critical question asked by an outsider about their distinctions between sacred and secular music. The question was flawlessly re-joined by a Moravian youth. The boy had just played a selection of Haydn in a chamber

Drawing of Moravians practicing music, 1795. *Collection of Moravian Historical Society, Nazareth, PA.*

The Trinity Moravian Church band at Christmas, 1914. *OSHPC.*

music society concert on a Saturday afternoon. The outsider, a disapproving New England minister, asked him what instrument he would have used on Sunday to worship the Lord. The youth quickly replied with the following retort: "And shall you, sir, pray with the same mouth tomorrow with which you are now eating sausages?"

The Unity of the Brethren was "the first among Protestant Churches to publish a Hymnbook in 1505,"[2] and it was in the people's language, not in Latin. As subsequent editions were issued, the hymns created a powerful influence in the church and community, as they not only enlivened the worship services, but crossed class barriers in illuminating for everyone the Gospel of Christ with free grace through Him. In fact, a contemporary writer points out that the theology of the church is best expressed through its hymnody and its

liturgy.[3] In order to fully illustrate the extent to which music permeated and influenced every part of Moravian lives in early days, a number of diverse examples, which are not all holiday references, have been sprinkled throughout the chapter to emphasize this very important point.

In contrast to the Moravians, Lutherans, and Catholics, who always included Christmas in their religious observances, other denominations performed much less music than the Moravians, or none at all, in the colonies in the early days. The Anglican Church, for example, did not allow hymns and carols in the service, as they were thought to be too secular,[4] although there would be, instead of the colorful pageantry, perhaps a touch of greenery and the reading of the liturgy concerning Christmas. The Quakers did not celebrate nor did the strict Calvinistic Presbyterians and the Baptists until later.

George Bahnson reported in 1834 that the Methodists declared openly, "The Moravians will burn in hellfire for having lovefeasts on Sundays."[5] Even as late as 1855, New York newspapers reported that Methodist, Baptist, and Presbyterian churches would be closed on Christmas Day because "they do not accept the day as a Holy One."[6] These churches, believing that "no biblical support existed for the holiday," considered Christmas a "pagan ritual masquerading as Christian."[7]

However, adhering to their traditions and greatly inspired by the moment, the first Moravian settlers to arrive in Wachovia in the late fall of 1753 (in a little less than six weeks travel time from Bethlehem) were so thankful to reach the shelter of Hans Wagner's abandoned cabin that they relished the singing of a verse extemporized by Brother Gottlob:

We hold arrival Lovefeast here,
In Carolina land,
A company of Brethren true,
A little Pilgrim Band,
Called by the Lord to be of those
Who through the whole world go
To bear Him witness everywhere,
And naught but Jesus know.[8]

It was a frequent practice among eighteenth-century Moravians to create poems and verses on such meaningful occasions and fit them to familiar tunes.

At the beginning of Wachovia on the evening of 25 December 1753, in the midst of the wilderness, the first settlers of Bethabara "sang hymns relating to the holy Christ-child."[9] On the preceding evening they had held their "first Christmas Eve Watch meeting in North Carolina," as well as a lovefeast.[10] Soon they were regularly worshipping with the *Singstunde* ("song service"). Although these early Moravian settlers were busily hewing fields out of

...musical instruments were used to elevate and solemnize the experience in Salem at the ceremonial laying of the "Foundation Stone" of the Single Brothers' House... .

forests, they were ever mindful of their music. Indeed, musical instruments received high priority. On 23 February 1754 the Bethabara settlers stopped work early to have an evening lovefeast, memorably writing, "the Lovefeast was announced with our new trumpet, which we have

made from a hollow tree, and no trumpet in Bethlehem has a better tone."[11]

That same trumpet may have been used in 1755 when a weeping neighbor came to the Bethabara settlement in the middle of the night to say that upon returning home from searching for strayed horses he had found his wife and children missing. At the close of their morning prayer service, the Moravian men continued to blow the trumpets used during the meeting in hopes that any attackers would be frightened away. The sound of the instruments led to safety the terrified but unharmed family, who had been hiding in the woods from a pillaging band of strangers.[12]

Musical instruments came steadily to Wachovia. In 1755, trumpets were sent from Bethlehem,[13] where the first spinet (harpsichord) had arrived from London in January 1744.[14] In

Salem's Single Brothers' House.

An interior room in the Salem Tavern decorated for Christmas.

November of the same year, for the Sabbath lovefeast at Bethabara, flutes were used for the first time.[15] In 1756, the hymn singing was accompanied by two violins;[16] in 1759, a death was announced by French horns;[17] by 1762, "a little organ" had "been set up";[18] and, in 1768, Wachovia had received "a set of trombones," whose "use on solemn days and festivals...strengthened and edified our congregation."[19]

Also in 1768, musical instruments were used to elevate and solemnize the experience in Salem at the ceremonial laying of the "Foundation Stone" of the Single Brothers' House, where the procession was led by musicians.[20] When the framing of the building was raised, "the musicians blew their trumpets from the top of the house."[21] For specific occasions like the laying of a cornerstone, the liturgy provided selected hymns. Using these hymns along with musical instruments to signify an important event in community life illustrates the priority of music to the Moravians as an underlying expression of "their spirit of faith and fellowship."[22]

In 1771, when Josiah Martin, the Governor of North Carolina, arrived in Salem, he was greeted outside town by a party of men, including "our trombonists...preceding the chariot in which he sat until he reached the lodging prepared for him."[23] That welcoming gesture was repeated for the arrival of President George Washington on 31 May 1791. "As he approached the town several tunes were played, partly by trumpets and French horns, partly by the trombones."[24] On the first night of his stay Washington requested "some music during his evening meal." It was, of course, furnished, as it was for the second evening. Washington and his party attended a *Singstunde* "with instrumental selections" at which "they expressed their pleasure... . In the evening the wind instruments were heard again, playing sweetly near the tavern."[25] This was not the first time that Washington had visited a Moravian town and heard their music. He had enjoyed just such an occasion in Bethlehem as a visitor in 1782.

The Moravians' use of instrumental music, according to minister and musician Christian Latrobe (1757-1836), had many attributes, including being "recommended by the Brethren as a most useful substitute for all those idle pursuits, in which young people too often consume their leisure hours." He continued that since it provided most pleasing effects, its use was encouraged in many aspects of life.[26] The towns' night watchmen, for example, as they made their rounds while calling out the hour, might sing a hymn "to edify sleepless people,"[27] or create a verse to include the time of day.

With music as a necessity of life, it was natural to establish in Salem a *Collegium Musicum*, a musical society patterned after those of Europe, as well as the Pennsylvania Moravian towns of Bethlehem, Lititz, and Nazareth where such societies were established as early as the 1740s. One may liken this group to a chamber music society with a large diversified selection of secular music. Thus, Salem, for a ten-year period beginning in 1780, had the assistance of Johann Fredrich Peter (1746-1813), whom one writer has called "the most brilliant of all Moravian musicians." Peter brought with him from Europe copies of a number of symphonies and quartets of the leading composers. The "sweet music" Washington heard on his visit to Salem may have been taken from these copies and was probably played by violins, a viola, violoncello, a flute, two horns, and two clarin trumpets.[28]

Salem schoolteacher and musician Peter Wolle described the arrival of what he thought was the first bassoon in Salem in October 1816. "Joy prevailed to a great degree when the wagon which was to bring our bassoon arrived... . All the world crowded together to see that new kind of machine, never seen before at this place." Disappointingly, the only man who could blow it was not to be located until the evening, when it was tried with the clarinets to everyone's satisfaction.[29] A few days later Wolle was busily polishing the "cliffs of the clarinets" so that they would "not be outdone by those of the bassoon."[30] All of this was in anticipation of the coming Christmas, as the musicians were already meeting at the church to plan the "christmas pieces" they would use.[31]

Music was also an integral part of home life. Peter Wolle, after his marriage and move to Bethania as minister, spoke of playing the piano and singing "for quite a while" after his birthday vesper in 1820.[32] Salem residents of some means like the Bagges, the Schweinitzs, and the Vierlings had pianos in their homes, which offered their families opportunities for musical entertainment.

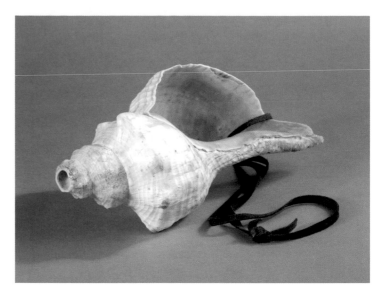

The conch shell and lantern used in the role of Salem's night watchman during twentieth century museum events. *Author's collection.*

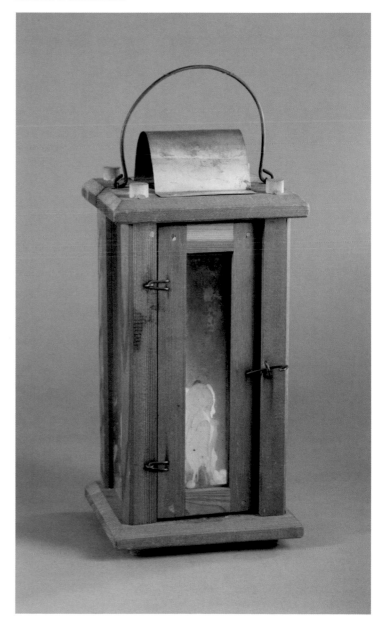

In 1818, Wolle went to the estate sale of the deceased Dr. Vierling, where he remarked on the sale of some music, a "good" violin, and a piano that sold for $180, a price greater than its original cost![33]

Music was used by the creative schoolteacher Wolle in innovative experiments to interest his students in natural science. He scattered sand on a fragment of glass and "drew a violin bow across it—did the same with water in a glass," and used a pendulum to denote a correct beat.[34] At the Schweinitz house he played the piano while watching their little son "with pleasure as he listened to me with understanding."[35] As would be expected, Wolle gave music lessons to children.[36]

The services and programs at the Moravian churches and their schools throughout their history have used music as a major focus. In 1787 in Bethania "the children came in wagons and on horseback to attend the Christmas Eve vigils... . Including five Negro children from town, there were 102."[37] In 1788 in Salem "a large number of children could not attend the Christmas Eve services because of the intense cold and insufficient clothing."[38] The children's Christmas lovefeast in Bethabara on 24 December 1788, included music on the "clavier, violin, and flute." (A "clavier" was probably either a forte piano or clavichord[39]).[40] By the late 1700s, a clavichord or forte piano had been purchased for the Girls' School in Salem, and lessons

On the afternoon of Christmas Day 1816, Wolle wrote that they "blowed some parties in the square, as the weather was so agreeably warm." If temperatures allowed, playing music outside for these special events often occurred.

were offered to those who showed promise.[41] Singing classes and lessons on a clavier and violin were also offered to the little boys.[42] The Girls' Boarding School offered music as a special course for which there was a small extra fee, and girls taking piano lessons could purchase sheet music for themselves.[43] "Singing school" was held for all the students.[44] By 1857 the school had its "first full-time male professor of music."[45]

Peter Wolle often described the church music practices in Wachovia. He wrote on 22 December 1816, "At 3 o'clock was the trial of the music for the holidays."[46]

Much satisfaction was obviously derived from the practice. "At the trial of music Mr. H. Leinbach and Haman blowed the flutes to some pieces, which has not been heard this long time; it was very agreeable."[47] That particular year Wolle remarked with amusement on the crying of children and the breaking of cups as an accompaniment to the music at the children's lovefeast on Christmas Eve.[48]

On the afternoon of Christmas Day 1816, Wolle wrote that they "blowed some parties in the square, as the weather was so agreeably warm."[49] If temperatures allowed, playing music outside for these special events often occurred. On New Year's Day 1817, the good weather allowed them to play their wind instruments from the church gallery for the enjoyment of everyone.[50] Wolle recorded on 1 January 1818, that a group played on the square with "clarinette, cornet, bassoon, and violincello; it was not perfect, but still a pleasure to the many listeners."[51]

To explain the zeal with which Wolle and other Moravians pursued their heritage of musical excellence, one may consider the contents of an article written by Colonel William A. Blair, which appeared in the Winston-Salem *Journal and Sentinel* just before Christmas in 1936. "In the beginning those old Bohemian brethren used, in part, the Gregorian tunes, that ritual music collected and arranged by Gregory the Great, between the years 555 and 600 A.D., but, they also

This instrument, called a rostrum, made in Salem, 1820-25, by John Vogler, was used to rule paper for writing music. *OSMG.*

gathered and adopted other tunes and songs wherever they could be found, and composers arose within their own brotherhood, itself, some of whose productions are still in use."[52] Indeed, at Bethabara on Christmas Eve of 1755, it was recorded that Brother Henrich "made an address, and also read from the large Hymnbook hymns written in all centuries concerning the night of Christ's nativity, drawing special attention to one written by Count Zinzendorf thirteen years ago."[53] Moravian archivist Dr. Adelaide Fries noted that many twentieth-century hymns "date from Bishop [Christian] Gregor's 1784 tunebook."[54] Gregor was a "distinguished hymnologist of the Church."[55] This hymnbook was mentioned in Salem as "the new Unity Hymn Book" for which they were grateful to have received more copies.[56] It was printed in Barby, Germany, in 1783 and contained "the words for seventeen hundred and fifty hymns" along with "a topical index and an index of first lines."[57] Individuals in town who had bought the book were asked to bring them to preaching services.[58]

The hymn to which Brother Henrich referred in 1755 was probably the tune commonly known as the Bethlehem Christmas Hymn by Zinzerdorf. Sometimes leaders used familiar tunes for which they simply created or extemporized words as they went, guided by divine inspiration. Count Zinzendorf, "a gifted poet,"[59] followed this practice on the occasion of Christmas Eve 1741 in Bethlehem as the congregation followed his repetition "with fervor and emotion" of the words for the hymn of thirty-seven stanzas, "Happier is for us no night than that which brought us the Wonder Child.... These stanzas were printed with the title '*In der Christnacht zu Bethlehem*, 1742' and were called 'Bethlehem Christmas Hymn', also, 'The Pennsylvania Christmas Hymn.' "[60] The Liturgy and Hymn Book noted the words of the songs

Frontispiece for a nineteenth-century copy of the music for "Morning Star." *Courtesy of the Moravian Music Foundation, Winston-Salem, NC.*

along with the tune numbers. There might be close to two hundred hymns sung to one tune.

A hymn which has come to be intimately associated with children and with the Moravian Christmas is "Morning Star." Adelaide Fries explained the origin of the composition in a small booklet called "Moravian Customs Our Inheritance."[61] She wrote, "On the evening of the Fourth Sunday in Advent we use the Morning Star

anthem, the words of which were written by Johann Scheffler, a physician of Silesia, Germany, who lived 1624-1677; translated by Bennet Harvey, Jr., a Moravian minister of England, living 1829-1894."[62] The hymn had been translated even earlier by Martin Hauser (1799-1875).[63] The tune was composed by Francis F. Hagen (1815-1907) in 1836 when he was a teacher at the Boys' School in Salem. The hymn was performed for the first time that year on

Christmas Eve in Salem and was dedicated to the children of Home Church, which had been Hagen's childhood church.[64]

By the mid-nineteenth century, "Morning Star" was habitually performed during Christmas with a child as soloist and the congregation responding antiphonally.[65] In 1907, it was recorded, "Sunday evening, December 22nd, the Morning Star Anthem was sung in the beautifully decorated church, so ushering in the happy Christmas season.... . The evening service was particularly pretty this year because the lighted tapers were given to all, instead of only the children."[66]

Music contributes greatly to the elevation of the soul in any church service, but certainly as an added tool in mission efforts. In 1806, an American Indian mother at the Moravian Indian Mission in Georgia enjoyed the singing during a Christmas *Singstunde* and the service's message. She was told that "we [Moravians] do not sing just for the fun as the Indians do, but with our singing we praise God, our Savior and also pray to him."[67] The poor woman wept with emotion as the children interpreted the meaning of the Gospel to her.

The *Singstunden* were song services of themed music chosen for a special occasion. In Wachovia there were close to two thousand hymns in the Moravian book.[68] Congregational singing was enjoyed as a heritage from John Huss at the Bethlehem Chapel in Prague,[69] and it was enhanced by the variety of "solo and choir anthem[s],"[70] like "Morning Star."

In 1807, Karsten Petersen and Christian Burkhardt, craftsmen from Salem who were sent to bring the Gospel to the Creek Indians in Georgia, stopped at the Springplace mission for a visit. Moravian missionary Anna Gambold had composed a "well-written hymn," which the children had learned by heart to sing for the visitors. The

Music contributes greatly to the elevation of the soul in any church service, but certainly as an added tool in mission efforts.

men wrote an account in which they said, "It is not to be expressed in words, how sweet their voices are... ."[71] Old Salem Museums & Gardens owns a memory book presented to Karsten Petersen in 1807 at Springplace. It contains many examples of artwork and Biblical verses entered by the American Indian students who attended school there at that time.[72]

A touching and amusing account that reflects the essence of the Moravian love for music was expressed by the Springplace missionary Gottlieb Byhan in 1807. He wrote in a letter to Christian Benzien in Salem that he had been working for three or four years on an organ "like the one in the Brothers' House" but, of course, cruder, and "mostly made out of fence rails."[73] He said that he had no suitable leather for bellows and no proper case, which in any event would need to have been of clapboard, but he was, nevertheless, able to play it on Christmas Eve for the first time, and "it brought much joy to our children." He went on somewhat tongue-in-cheek: "I am expecting a scolding from you because you will be thinking, 'You could put your time to something better!'"[74]

The organ "in the Brothers' House" to which Byhan referred was built in 1762 and bought

from the Bethabara congregation by the Single Brothers, to be "installed as the first organ in the *Saal* [worship and meeting hall or chapel] in the Single Brothers' House in Salem."[75] This small organ is thought to have been made in Pennsylvania by Johann Gottlob Klemm and David Tannenberg.[76] The Moravian records spoke of it as the first organ they had heard played in North Carolina. It remained in the Salem Single Brothers' House until 1823 when at the closing of the choir house it was given to the Friedberg congregation. Its subsequent history is not known.[77]

The one-manual organ completed by David Tannenberg in 1798 for the *Gemein Haus*, or Congregation House, in Salem, is now in the *Saal* of the Single Brothers' House. Early on, it suffered at least one indignity, as described in the records, "Rats ate the leather on the bellows of our organ, but it has been replaced."[78] The organ continues to be played, particularly on special occasions such as the Candle Tea of Home Moravian Church.

Today in the specially designed James A. Gray Auditorium in the Visitor Center at Old Salem Museums & Gardens stands one of the most significant pipe organs in the history of organ-building in America. It represents the second instrument commissioned by the Salem Moravians from this country's first American-trained organ builder, David Tannenberg (1728-1804), who had learned the skill under the tutelage of fellow Moravian organ builder Johann Klemm. The latter had moved from Dresden, Germany, to Pennsylvania. The organ's "high degree of technical and artistic sophistication" made it especially well suited to the Moravian use of other instruments with it.[79] This organ was commissioned to be used in Home Moravian Church in Salem, completed in 1800. Some

The 1800 David Tannenberg organ built for Salem's Home Moravian Church and now installed in the Old Salem Museums & Gardens Visitor Center.

German painted image with a lovefeast depicted in the left corner, 1746.
Courtesy of the Moravian Archives, Herrnhut, Germany.

of the organ's case was made in Salem, and the installation was accomplished by Tannenberg's son-in-law, Philip Bachmann. Tannenberg, of an advanced age for the time (he was 72 years old), was unable to make the trip to North Carolina. The restoration of the organ in 2004 allows programs and concerts by various musicians to take place at Christmas and throughout the year.

In February of 1806, a little over a year before Byhan's homemade organ was played for the first time in Springplace, three Cherokee men stopped in Salem on their way home after a meeting with President Thomas Jefferson. Brother Wohlfahrt, a former Springplace missionary, showed them the town, including a visit to the new church where "the organ was played for the singing."[80] If the Cherokee visitors were present at Springplace on Christmas of 1807, they would have been able to make a comparison between the magnificent Tannenberg instrument of Salem and the homely one of Byhan; both, however, were made with love to express the soaring tributes of the Moravians to the Creator of all mankind. "Hands to Work and Hearts to God" was a maxim befitting the purpose of both instruments.

Services

Although some denominations celebrated Christmas with various services, those of the Moravians were particularly well crafted in their universal appeal. It was customary in Salem to preach a sermon on the morning of Christmas Day as part of a traditional liturgical service and to have some kind of service in the evening. Choirs might have brief services in the afternoons. The evening service "of praise" could be a lovefeast, a *Singstunde*, or a combination of the two.[81] From the early 1800s, the Girls' School students presented dialogues based on Biblical text and included music sometime during the week of Christmas. As Sunday Schools developed, the scholars often presented programs and concerts, which were well attended, even drawing visitors from the outside communities.

Sermons sometimes were taken from the text for the day. The Daily Texts are a uniquely binding aspect of the Moravian Church, dating from 1731 when the texts were first published, and continuing today. The Daily Texts were the inspiration of Count Zinzendorf, who personally drew the watchwords from a collection he had made from the Bible. These selected verses were designed to give people daily food for spiritual thought. Naturally, they could be used all during the holy season of Christmas as the basis for sermons and meetings. The texts are usually selected several years ahead in Herrnhut, Germany, by a group of ministers. A watchword (*losung* or *loosung*) is chosen from suitable Old Testament verses and paired with a related New Testament verse. The selections are disseminated to the churches, which today publish them in an established format of books printed annually and sold to members. Sometimes in the early days with the vagaries of transportation, the texts did not arrive in time for the first of the year. Peter Wolle in 1818 remarked on that fact in his diary and asserted that he had copied some for their use until the shipment arrived.[82] Today the Daily Texts are printed in about fifty different languages.[83]

There is a comfort to any person who is worshipping privately anywhere in the world on a particular day to know that other people all over the world are using the exact same text on that day. A sense of commonality is thus established. Indeed, other denominations use the texts as well. In the eighteenth century, the Daily Texts were "the main source of the topics for the addresses delivered each day."[84] Often a hymn stanza or a portion thereof was chosen to go with the verse.[85] Consequently, one had the means for a thematic private contemplation, or, in the case of a minister, an appropriate topic for a sermon. As Peter Wolle noted on 10 December 1816, he had delivered a "German sermon to the children upon the text of the day."[86]

In the eighteenth century, the Communion service was sometimes called by Moravians the "Supper of the Lamb,"[87] the "Lord's Table," or the "Soldiers' Meal."[88] In the early days the term

1780 engraving of a Moravian lovefeast. *OSMG.*

"soldier" was applied to those devout members "fighting" for their cause.[89] *Abendmahl*, which means "evening meal" in German, refers to the last meal of Jesus and his disciples. The taking of bread and wine to represent the body and blood of Christ was considered to be the most important religious event in which a member could participate.[90] Communion, which generally took place monthly, could be withheld from members whose behavior warranted such treatment. At Christmas, communion was part of one of the services. Customs through time changed, and the records noted that before Christmas in 1802 although "it had been customary for members to prostrate themselves in prayer during the Holy Communion.... This has become difficult, for lack of room, and in future all will kneel."[91] The Sabbath, or Saturday, was a day of rest, as was Sunday. Communion and lovefeasts were often held on the Sabbath and, of course, during Christmas, which was a meaningful time for baptisms, as well.[92] The baptism of Salem's "only negro, Sambo," who received the name Abraham on 26 December 1780,[93] was noted as "an especially blessed day."[94]

The Lovefeast

The lovefeast or *Liebesmahl* is not a sacrament of the Moravian church. However, it is a much-loved liturgical custom that began on 13 August 1727 in Herrnhut somewhat in the manner of the "early Christian love-feasts, called agapae" and continues today.[95] The tradition of the lovefeast started in Herrnhut on 13 August 1727 when a particularly moving service caused people to linger afterwards, reluctant to withdraw from the prevailing mood of goodwill, unity, and brotherly love. Count Zinzendorf sent for some food and drink, and in the simple act of sharing a meal and a significant spiritual moment together,

The tradition of the lovefeast started in Herrnhut on 13 August 1727 when a particularly moving service caused people to linger afterwards, reluctant to withdraw from the prevailing mood of goodwill, unity, and brotherly love.

the Moravian lovefeast was born on a day that is also recognized as the Renewal of the Moravian Church.[96]

The concept is sometimes used locally by other denominations. It has always been an occasion of music, fellowship, and perhaps simple food, although refreshments are not required. (See Chapter Five for examples of food and beverages offered at lovefeast services in Wachovia and other areas.) At Christmas the music for the lovefeast is selected with the theme of the birth of Christ. A portion of Beethoven's Mass was performed during love-feast in 1859 in Bethlehem.[97]

During the lovefeast service the distribution of "burning wax tapers"[98] to represent Christ as the light of the world contributed immeasurably to the effect, and sometimes the room was darkened to increase the power of the symbolism. Such a practice occurred at the lovefeast at New Philadelphia Church in Wachovia on 24 December 1870: "The candles and preparatory operation

of closing the shutters afforded the usual excitement to the children."[99] Today the lights are still dimmed or cut off during this part of the service in order to give full impact to the meaning of the burning tapers, an emotionally charged experience.

Lovefeasts are generally held by the whole congregation today, but earlier they were also frequently "held for many small occasions by smaller groups,"[100] such as choirs or work groups, like the seamstresses and knitters, the cobblers and tanners, and the washerwomen in Bethlehem.[101] Birthdays, weddings, and anniversaries were all "semi-social gathering[s]"[102] to which one might invite friends and families to join in singing hymns in unison, while eating and drinking together. Such diverse groups as the *Collegium Musicum*, which would be performing during Christmas, and the brethren who were learning the Indian language perhaps in preparation for being missionaries, would be given lovefeasts in gratitude as special treats.[103] In 1745 in Bethlehem, a working lovefeast was held at midnight for the fifty sisters who volunteered for a night watch. "In one night they stripped more feathers in preparation for the little children whose births are expected than several sisters would have been able to do in perhaps a quarter of a year."[104] Adelaide Fries remarked that the first lovefeast in Salem took place on Christmas Eve of 1771.[105] Peter Wolle wrote on 18 December 1814 that a "very agreeable Lovefeast" was held for the musicians, Dieners, Choir Dieners, Attenders of the Sick, and Fremdendiener (hosts to visitors.)" Afterwards they practiced "the pieces for Christmas."[106] It came to be a popular custom to have a lovefeast for the people who helped in decorating the church at Christmas.[107] Before Christmas in 1816, Wolle noted that such lovefeasts were "the salary or compensation for services during the year."[108] Their

The Allen sisters serving tea in the Salem Tavern, 1953. *OSHPC.*

importance was so great that hurt feelings could be the result of not receiving an invitation. Wolle remarked on Sunday, 22 December 1816, "Then was lovefeast for the masters in the branches of trade carried on for the congregation, but myself was not invited, though I am sure I am serving as master in a more extensive manner than any of the rest!"[109]

Sometimes reports of current events and letters were read at lovefeasts. Not having today's modern communication inven-

tions, church members relished the news from a single copy of a newspaper, infrequent letters from faraway friends, sermons from renowned church leaders, and mission reports from remote corners of the Earth. The hour required for the minister to read such material was time well spent. Strangers, as guests, might be included on such occasions.[110]

The diversity of nationalities[111] of the visitors was taken into account, and special English services were sometimes provided for their benefit. In Bethlehem

on Tuesday, 5 January 1745, a lovefeast in English was held for a group of forty, which included Swedes, Scots, Irish, French, Welsh, Norwegians, Swiss, and Germans. What they had in common was that they all worked "among the English." (A later music historian remarked that at such meetings "it became a custom to let everybody sing in his native tongue,"[112] which sometimes meant as many as thirteen languages soaring upward together.) The diarist of this event recorded that they had resolved to have a short meeting in

127

English daily at about one o'clock because they recognized that there was a necessity for the understanding of the English language for the German Moravians as well as for the rest of the attendees.[113] In Salem in 1786 a similar resolve was reached to have Sunday afternoon English language services when possible for the benefit of English-speaking workers in town; in fact, the workers had made the request.[114]

The power of such a service as a lovefeast in the church was illustrated in Bethania in February 1835, by the Moravian minister George Bahnson. He wrote of a family that had separated itself from the congregation because of a dispute with some other members. On a certain festival day the family's son Tryphonius sneaked to a lovefeast without his parents' knowledge. When they discovered the reason for his disobedience, they were so affected that they returned again as faithful members of the church. Bahnson concluded that it was "a remarkable instance how a child by its simplicity can lead back to the right path its parents although they ought to be wiser in every respect."[115]

The students at the Salem Girls' School always enjoyed the church lovefeasts and other Christmas celebrations. Most December or January issues of the school publication, *The Academy*, had an article entitled "Christmas" or "The Holidays" in which the school's affairs were described in detail. News frequently included Salem happenings, church events, and local merchants' fare. The following "lively and fresh" description of the 1877-1878 year at the Academy was admired enough to be put in the *North-Western North Carolina Guide Book*, published by Blum in 1878:

We shall never forget the Merry Christmas and Happy New Year of 1877-8 at the Academy. We had ample illustration of the Moravian

The diversity of nationalities of the visitors was taken into account, and special English services were sometimes provided for their benefit...a lovefeast in English was held for a group of forty, which included Swedes, Scots, Irish, French, Welsh, Norwegians, Swiss, and Germans.

faculty for making such festive seasons thoroughly enjoyable whilst maintaining a strict regard for spiritual profit. The rejoicings of the Church imparted their glow to our holiday pleasures, which were purified and sweetened by being brought into contact with heavenly things, and all this without any appearance of affectation or artificiality, and without any undue repression of youthful spirits.[116]

The article continued:

On Christmas Eve we attended love-feast. We found the church beautifully decorated with festoons and arches of evergreens. The joyful words whose import every Christian feels, especially at Christmas, greeted our eyes in letters of living green from the gallery, "Glory to God in the highest and on earth peace, good will towards men." The service comprised the reading of the account, in the gospels, of our Saviour's birth, prayer, and singing by the congregation and choir, the latter

accompanied by the deep-toned organ and a large orchestra. Ladies dressed in black with white muslin caps and aprons, handed cake and coffee to all present. Burning tapers were brought in on trays, and distributed, one to each child, emblems of the light which Christ brought into the world. They surely impressed the minds not only of the children, but of their elders as well. How beautiful was the scene in the church, the bright lights and the happy faces, and how fortunate the children to be so pleasantly instructed in regard to the spiritual Light, whose advent was commemorated by the service.[117]

The following story illustrates the active participation in the lovefeast service by children. Moravian Margaret Blair (McCuiston), who began to keep a diary in 1908, shortly thereafter recorded her small brother's (John Fries Blair, born 1903) first lovefeast. Not aware that the congregation politely waited until everyone had been served before eating the buns, young Margaret took a substantial bite immediately upon receiving hers, thus embarrassing her mother. In order to prevent her son from making the same mistake, Mrs. Blair hurriedly cautioned him to wait until he saw the bishop start to partake. The boy carefully noted the moment and cried "at the top of his voice, The bishop has began [sic]!"[118]

Young people were just a portion of those who enjoyed and actively participated in lovefeasts. Elias Vogler, instrumental in the African American Sunday School program at Salem's St. Philips, in 1868 had a Christmas lovefeast prepared there. The records state that many "whites were present as guests" and among "the scholars (some...grown men and women, and themselves parents) recited a Christmas dialogue prepared by the teachers, and they did it very creditably to their teachers and themselves."[119]

Dialogues

The participation of adults in dialogues—plays or conversations concerning the birth of Christ—may have been confined to Moravian mission efforts like St. Philips. School students were generally the main presenters. The Salem Girls' School was an integral part of the community, and the pupils were always organized to give dialogues at Christmas, sometimes presented in the *Saal* ("meeting hall") of the *Gemein Haus* ("congregation house"). Dialogues often attracted a large audience, sometimes necessitating several performances. Author Frances Griffin remarked that the inspector (head master or principal), who was the creator of the dialogues, "being a minister, always seemed to let his inclination to preach get the better of dramatic instinct... . Consequently, what came out of the mouths of eleven- and twelve-year-old girls as 'conversation' is little short of astounding."[120] The reader will recall from Chapter Three that in 1835 the young minister George Bahnson attended a Christmas dialogue with his wife at the Salem Girls' School. He described it as made up of "rather...strange contents, being a kind of dogmatical exposition of the whole Christian doctrine, from the manger to the cross—It could not be called a Christmas dialogue."[121]

There is at least one complete early dialogue extant, presented in 1808, with the names of the girls and the parts they took. It is interspersed with songs.[122]

Eliza Vierling Kremer (1811-1899) in her adult reminiscences described the dialogues from her time as a young teacher at the Salem Girls' Boarding School in 1826: "Christmas was a season of great enjoyment to inmates of the Academy. Where we now have the Sunday School entertainments, we had our Christmas dialogues—prepared by the Principal—the discourse relating to the birth and life of the Saviour, interspersed with anthems suitable to the occasion."[123]

Louisa Lenoir, a student at Salem in 1819, wrote to her mother in Fort Defiance, North Carolina, about Christmas in the Moravian community that year. This is the earliest and fullest description of a Christmas celebration including a dialogue in Salem, and Louisa pronounced it "new and interesting" in spite of her "imperfect account." She wrote of attending a preaching service in the chapel on Christmas Eve. The next day at three o'clock the girls presented their dialogue, which included the birth of Jesus as well as His presentation in the Temple. Ten or twelve of the girls stayed behind a curtain to sing an anthem as an introduction to the dialogue which then began with the pronouncement "Hark! What mean those happy voices, sweetly sounding to my ear." They all then joined "in conversing about the birth of Jesus."[124]

Between Christmas and New Year's Day, Louisa wrote that the students spent their time "pleasantly." One of the teachers sometimes read to them from a novel, but she hastily assured her mother that "it contained more of history & less of love than Novels generally do, it was the Crusades." Classes resumed on the Monday after New Year's. Her comments about several of her fellow students, at least some of them cousins, attest to their zeal in their studies. She remarked that Sophia

was "so engaged in reading history that she cannot take time to write home. Cousin Julia is reading Ramsey's United States & Laura has commenced Modern Europe."[125]

Miranda Miller Scarborough, a student in Salem in 1835, elaborately described in October, 1890 the Christmas dialogues held in the chapel when she was a girl. Her description gives us the best idea of what the performances were like. The placement of the piano behind a curtain "mellowed" the music and caused the "angelic chorus" to sound as if from afar, even "emblematic of the angelic chorus on the plains of Bethlehem... . The girls taking part in the dialogue were dressed in white, with lace caps enveloping the head like a fleecy halo in the rather dim light of lamp or candle. The subject of the dialogue was 'the old, old story,' ever new, taken without change from the Gospels, and arranged in a conversational style. A group of maidens around a well discussed the wondrous news of the birth of the Saviour in a manger at Bethlehem, of the story of the

One music historian calls the ode "the most elaborately planned musical form in the Moravian Church. Also called a psalm, the ode was comprised of hymn texts and scriptural excerpts that were chanted or sung as anthems."

shepherds, and the hearing of the angels' song; then the older ones quoted some of the prophecies in the Old Testament relating to the birth of the Saviour... ."[126]

The dialogue was obviously a popular event for school and church groups of all kinds, some-what in the manner of plays and concerts today. On 26 December 1868, a Sunday School group presented a dialogue. "At 2 p.m. the scholars of the 'factory' S.S. [Sunday School] had a Christmas dialogue after which they received presents from their kind teachers."[127]

As we have earlier observed, like other institutions in Salem, the African American church continued to participate in a similar celebration. "On December 25, Xmas day" in 1871, "there was a Christmas dialogue and singing at night. Sr. Maria Crist, the superintendent of S. School, had taken great pains in training the scholars."[128]

Odes were often part of such dialogue programs. The Old Salem Museum & Gardens collection has a carefully preserved printed ode of 1830 belonging to Lisetta Maria Vogler and perhaps used in a Christmas dialogue. In 1816, John Gambold enclosed in a letter to Van Vleck in Salem the "Spring Place Christmas Eve Ode" which he said had been done by "Little Mother" (Anna Rosina Gambold)

the month before.[129] Moravian archivist Adelaide Fries believed that odes came into general use locally in 1798 when a printing office opened in Salisbury and the church ordered 150 copies of an ode for the "Great Sabbath Lovefeast."[130] So pleased were they with the appearance of the odes that they continued their use for other events. Fries speculated that the congregation did not receive copies but that they were for the use of the minister, the choir, and of course, the student chorus presenting the dialogues. She said that generally most people would know the words for the hymn and would simply "fall into the singing as soon as the first words of a stanza were heard."[131] One music historian calls the ode "the most elaborately planned musical form in the Moravian Church. Also called a psalm, the ode was comprised of

hymn texts and scriptural excerpts that were chanted or sung as anthems."[132] He stated that it resembled a Lutheran cantata, but was less formal and had more congregational singing. In contrast, a dialogue allowed for other types of music to be mingled together: anti-phonal chants, solos, duets, and recitations.[133]

As we have seen, singing Christmas hymns was always emphasized in the schools. Note this entry for the protocol of the school in Nazareth in December, 1792: "It was wished that the children of the 2 & 3 room might / the Advent Season having just begun / frequently sing Christmas verses and hymns." In 1793, a notation was again made: "With respect to Christmas, several things were regulated, and frequent singing of Christmas verses recommended."[134]

The African American children at the log church in Salem sang Christmas anthems, which "Sr. Denke had taken great pains to teach them to sing to the musick" [sic].[135] Diligent instruction had started on 3 January 1841, when Abraham Steiner observed that they wanted to continue the practice "with the intention of giving the Negroes better knowledge of our church tunes."[136] By 1843, on a cold, snowy day when no one was expected to be at the log church, the minister heard as he approached from a distance "songs from the Sunday School Union hymnbook." He discovered "a fine little group...gathered around the warm stove" and was touched by what he sensed as "the Lord's presence... very near."[137]

When Sunday Schools became popular in Wachovia, students began to give programs during the week of Christmas. The time and day varied, but the performances were always well received and many congregation members attended them, as well as the Christmas dialogues. On 28 December 1881 in Salem, the pastor reported, "This evening the Colored Sunday School gave its Christmas Entertainment. The recitation and hymns had been very diligently taught by the Northern teachers of the Colored Day School and succeeded admirably."[138]

John Vogler's (1783-1881) grandson F. H. Fries reminisced about Vogler's Sunday School trips: "He must have had a good voice, for old friends from the foot of the Blue Ridge mountains were fond of telling how he and Van Zevely would visit their Sunday Schools from time to time, and they would always know of his approach, for they would hear his voice at a distance, through the forest, singing 'Children of the Heavenly King, as ye journey sweetly sing.'"[139]

Reconstructed St. Philips log church in Salem.

Salem Home Church's Candle Tea

Although the Candle Tea still presented today in Salem is not a service, it has elements of the lovefeast with its music, nativity, candles, and food in fellowship, and it is a *Putz*-based tradition. Therefore, for those reasons and because the community at large accepts it as a much beloved Christmas tradition, it has been placed in this chapter. The Candle Tea is such an extremely popular fund-raising project of Home Moravian Church that rarely are there not long lines of people patiently waiting in cold, rain, or snow. As the program observes, the proceeds from the tea "are used to benefit those in need throughout the community and the world."[140] Intrinsically, and most importantly, the tea is a way for modern Moravians to strengthen their own ties to the revered traditions of the historical church and to ensure their meaning and relevancy for future generations.

A possible precursor of Home Church's Candle Tea was a small tea room set up in the kitchen of the Salem Tavern where the Allen sisters were then living in 1928. The sisters had a *Putz*, served tea, and offered candles for sale.[141]

The history of the Home Church Candle Tea began in 1929 when Miss Maggie Pfohl suggested that a Christmas *Putz* be a project of the Ladies' Auxiliary to be open to the public as a fundraiser. Miss Pfohl and Miss Helen Vogler built the first *Putz*, which was opened on December 16 for three weeks and attracted 2,746 people and raised $399. In succeeding years the locations for the Candle Tea have changed. In 1937, a women's study and worship group of the Home Church accepted sponsorship of a "Candle Tea" (without the *Putz*) in the Single Brothers' House. Miss Ella Butner, who at that time made all the candles used for lovefeasts, demonstrated candle making while members of the study group dressed in costume and acted as hostesses. Refreshments were served and a large food table was featured with a sale of baked goods donated by the ladies.

In 1941, a Nativity was added to the sub-basement of the Single Brothers' House and for the first time the tea and the Nativity were combined. In 1943, notices were sent to schools to invite children. In 1945, the growth of the project prompted the taking on of the responsibility by the entire Home Moravian Church's Women's Auxiliary and the formation of a year-long committee. Candle trimming was added in 1946 and the sale of foods discontinued.

In 1949, the *Putz* featuring a miniature town of Salem was introduced as part of the Candle Tea and continues as an ongoing element with the addition of a

"First Fruits" by John Valentine Haidt, 1747. *Courtesy of the Moravian Archives, Herrnhut, Germany.*

MUSIC AND SERVICES

Images of the Salem *Putz* at Home Moravian Church's Candle Tea. *Courtesy of Women's Fellowship, Home Moravian Church.*

Epiphany, a continuation of the celebration of the birth and baptism of Jesus, which began with Advent, commemorates the traditional revelation of the Baby to the Wise Men who were guided to the manger by the star on January 6.

new (one-inch-to-eight-feet scale), meticulously constructed building or landscape embellishment every year in order to depict the town as it was at the beginning of the nineteenth century. Currently, during each Christmas season the small town rests peacefully under a light coating of "powdered granite" snow laid on with an old-fashioned popcorn popper.[142] Tiny details create added realistic interest, such as the laundry frozen on a line, a cart incapacitated by a broken wheel, well-trodden paths to the "necessary houses," a turning mill wheel, and deer grazing in God's Acre.

In 1951 a new exit from the Single Brothers' House for Candle Tea visitors, by then numbering in the thousands, was necessary. In 1952, the secular and the religious scenes—the *Putz* and the Nativity—were separated into two rooms.[143]

The Candle Tea continues to be an Advent tradition of Home Moravian Church and still consists of some narratives, Christmas music played on the Tannenberg organ, candle demonstrations

and sales, the partaking of coffee and sugarcake, the viewing of the Salem *Putz* and the Nativity, and a reading of the Christmas story. In essence, in appealing to all the senses, the Candle Tea has become a firmly established Winston-Salem tradition that has endured for three-quarters of a century, and many local residents would not feel that Christmas was complete without it. It is also a way for Home Moravian Church to preserve and disseminate the awareness of long-cherished customs. The Candle Tea is held in the 1786 part of the historic Single Brothers' House (1769) during the early Advent season. Other Moravian churches in Wachovia have developed their own versions of this popular custom.

Of course, Advent is not just a Moravian custom, as most Christian churches celebrate it. Advent begins on the first of the four Sundays leading up to the Saviour's day of birth. "Advent" comes from the Latin word meaning "coming," and it refers to the preparation for the coming of the Christ child. Christian Gregor, called the father of Moravian music, composed in 1783 an anthem called "Hosanna," which is often sung during Advent. Salem's Edward Leinbach also composed an antiphonally rendered "Hosanna."[144] The hymn "Morning Star" is generally sung on the third or fourth Sunday of Advent and also on Christmas Eve.

Epiphany, a continuation of the celebration of the birth and baptism of Jesus, which began with Advent, commemorates the traditional revelation of the Baby to the Wise Men who were guided to the manger by the Christmas star on 6 January. Epiphany is often referred to as Twelfth Day, which the English and other cultures as far back as 900 marked with festivities signifying the end of Christmas. In a 5 February 1816 letter, John Gambold described Epiphany as "time...spent...with our 'First Fruits' in conversations and stories of other missions."[145] The subject of missions was usually a theme for the liturgy of the day in the Moravian Church.[146]

An intriguing mention from Sunday, 1 December 1907, by the Salem minister Rondthaler, was that of looking in "upon the pleasant Advent pastime of the Siewers children, a custom which has come down from the Herman family long ago."[147] No further light has been shed on that particular family custom, but it does illustrate how family traditions become beloved for generations and therefore provide continuity to lives. As Colonel William A. Blair so aptly stated in 1936, "Early Moravians in Salem put emphasis on worship, on pleasure for the children and the gathering of families."[148] That tradition continues to exist today.

Endnotes

Chapter 1: Moravian Christmas Traditions and the Evolution of the Holiday

1. *The Moravian*, vol. 8, no. 52 (24 December 1863) 206.

2. *The Moravian*, vol. 15, no. 51 (22 December 1870) 202.

3. *The Wachovia Moravian*, vol. 2, no. 22 (December 1894) 1.

4. John Amos Comenius, *The Orbus Pictus* (Syracuse, NY: C. W. Bardeen, 1887. Reissued Detroit, MI: Singing Tree Press, 1968) vii, viii.

5. Ibid, title page.

6. August Gottlieb Spangenberg, Benjamin La Trobe, ed. *An Exposition of Christian Doctrine, as Taught in the Protestant Church of the United Brethren, or Unitas Fratrum*, third English edition from original 1778 edition (Winston-Salem, NC: Southern Province of the Moravian Church, 1959) 97.

7. *Engel* = angel. See Vernon H. Nelson, ed., Kenneth G. Hamilton and Lothar Madeheim, Trans. *The Bethlehem Diary*, vol. II, January 1, 1744 - May 31, 1745 (Bethlehem, PA: The Moravian Archives, 2001) Glossary, 377. Adelaide Fries wrote that an infant was baptized a few hours after birth. (Fries, *Records*, vol. 1, 203). Children were generally not named until baptism. Interestingly, George Bahnson, whose baby was not baptized immediately, referred to her up to baptism as "future Angelica" (George Frederick Bahnson, *Personal Diary of George Frederick Bahnson, 1834-1838*. Transcribed by Alice North Henderson and Dr. Peter Meyers. (Old Salem Museums & Gardens Research Center) 23 October 1835, 409.

8. Adelaide L. Fries, *Records of the Moravians in North Carolina*, vol. 1, (Raleigh: North Carolina Historical Commission, 1922) 203-04.

9. In Salem there is a "guardian angel" story told about Eliza Vierling (1811-1899) as a child playing near a woodpile at the back of her parents' barn. She suddenly burst into the kitchen to report to her mother that she had just seen an angel on the woodpile. At the moment that Sister Vierling, accompanied by her daughter, rushed to the spot to investigate, the huge stack of wood came crashing to the ground at exactly the spot where the little girl had been playing. Eliza's miraculous escape from death was thus attributed to her guardian angel. From Mary Barrow Owen, ed. *Old Salem, North Carolina*, "The Vierling House," Edwin L. Stockton. (Winston-Salem, NC: The Garden Club of North Carolina, 1941, reprint 1946) 81.

10. Adelaide Fries, "Moravian Christmas Customs," Christmas Box, Moravian Archives, Winston-Salem, NC. Also, Fries, *Records*, vol. 5, 2154, n. 14.

11. Peter Wolle in his diary tells a story of a child who lived apart from his missionary family for seventeen years. See Paul Larson's *An American Musical Dynasty: A Biography of the Wolle Family of Bethlehem, Pennsylvania*. (Bethlehem: Lehigh University Press, 2002) 22. As we all have been, the Moravians were a product of their times. Thus, reading the life of one Johann Christian Till (1762-1844), it is not surprising to hear him say, "In my childhood, I underwent a great deal of harsh treatment, especially since child rearing at that time consisted more of blows with the stick than of loving remonstrances." He asserted that one such punishment "with the rod...was carried out with such force that frequently my bloody shirt would stick to my skin..." Craig D. Atwood and Peter Vogt, eds. *The Distinctiveness of Moravian Culture* (Nazareth, PA: Moravian Historical Society, 2003) 82.

12. See Carl Bridenbaugh's *Myths & Realities, Societies of the Colonial South*, Part III, "The Back Settlements"(New York: Atheneum, 1980).

13. Salem became a part of the newly created Forsyth County when Stokes County was divided in 1849.

14. *The Moravian*, vol. 13, no. 52 (24 December 1868) 206.

15. *The Moravian*, vol. 15, no. 51 (22 December 1870) 202.

16. *The Moravian*, vol. 8, no. 2 (8 January 1863) 7.

17. "Domestic Fiction, 1820-1865." Online: http://www.wsu.edu/~campbelld/amlit/domestic.htm. Accessed 28 Jan. 2007.

18. Marion Harland, *Marion Harland's Complete Cookbook*. (St. Louis: The Marion Co., 1906) 89.

19. Beecher and Stowe, *American Woman's Home* (Hartford, CT: The Stowe-Day Foundation, 1994) dedication.

20. *The Moravian*, vol. 1, 1856, children's column.

21. *The Moravian*, vol. 14, no. 51(23 December 1869) 202.

22. Noah Webster, *The American Spelling Book; Containing The Rudiments of the English Language for the Use of Schools in the United States* (Philadelphia: Jacob Johnson & Co., 1805), 43.

23. Gratifyingly for our theme, Webster even included in the 1805 edition a definition of New Year's Day, a then popular alternative to Christmas for holiday celebrations, as he said: "Then people express to each other their good wishes, and little boys and girls expect gifts of little books, toys and plums."

24. Rowena McClinton, *The Moravian Mission among the Cherokees at Springplace, Georgia*. Dissertation Ph.D. thesis (Lexington, Kentucky: University of Kentucky, 1996) 95.

25. Arnold Arnold, *Pictures and Stories From Forgotten Children's Books*. (New York: Dover Publications, 1969) 2.

26. Anne M. Boylan, *Sunday School: The Formation of an American Institution, 1790-1880* (New Haven, CT: Yale University Press, 1988) 44.

27. Fries, *Customs and Practices of the Moravian Church* (Bethlehem, PA: 2003) 90.

28. "Negro Project Around Salem," Book IV (unpublished typescript, Old Salem Museums & Gardens) 14.

29. Ernest M. Eller, ed. *The School of Infancy* by John Amos Comenius (Chapel Hill: UNC Press, 1956) 57.

30. The term *Fremde* was often employed for those visiting and not part of the church. It could be used for familiar neighbors as well as total strangers. Sometimes in Salem a person called a *Fremden Diener* (*Diener*: servant, not literal here) would be used to introduce the town to important strangers, as was done for George Washington. Thus, the correct interpretations of the little town would be sure to be received.

31. Evelyn Wilson, *Dr. George Follett Wilson Journal* (Greenville, SC: A Press, 1984) 38.

32. John Guilds, ed. *The Writings of William Gilmore Simms*, Vol. V, "Maize in Milk" (Columbia: USC Press, 1974) 315-318.

33. Walker's 1828 dictionary: "squibs" is defined as: "small pipes of paper filled with wildfire," in other words, firecrackers.

34. Stephen Nissenbaum, *The Battle for Christmas* (New York: Alfred A. Knopf, 1997) 73.

35. The subject of Christmas was addressed in other Dickens's works, including *Christmas Stories and Christmas Books*. The essence of Christmas as selfless love was beautifully expressed in *The Cricket on the Hearth*.

36. There are some scholars who believe that a man named Henry Livingston wrote this poem, but it is generally attributed to Moore. See endnote 36 in Chapter Four.

37. Alfred Shoemaker, *Christmas in Pennsylvania: A Folk-Cultural Study*, second edition (Mechanicsburg, PA: Stackpole Books, 1999) 39.

38. *Kriss Kringle's Christmas Tree* (Philadelphia: E. Ferrett & Co, 1846) 74.

39. *The Moravian*, vol. 2, no. 52 (24 December 1857) 414.

40. *The Moravian*, vol. 3, no. 52 (24 December 1863) 206.

41. Marion Harland, *The Christmas Holly* (New York: Sheldon and Co., 1867) 85-86.

42. Earnest McNeill Eller, *Salem Star and Dawn* (Winston-Salem, NC: Woman's Fellowship Moravian Church South, 1912) 62.

43. Eller, *The School of Infancy*, introduction, 52.

44. Harland, *Marion Harland's Complete Cookbook,* 89.

45. Mrs. Julien Ravenel, *Charleston the Place and the People* (New York: MacMillan, 1912) 385.

46. Winifred Kirkland, *Where the Star Still Shines* (Winston-Salem, NC: Woman's Auxiliary, Home Moravian Church, n.d.) 29.

47. *The Wachovia Moravian* (December 1895).

48. Kirkland, 29.

Chapter 1 Sidebar Endnotes

i   Fries, "Moravian Christmas Customs.

ii   Ibid.

iii *The Moravian*, vol. 8, no. 17 (23 April 1863) 72.

iv   Fries, *Records*, vol. 6, 2861.

v   John Walker, *A Critical Pronouncing Dictionary* (Hartford: Silas Andrus, 1828).

vi   In 1859 in Salem it was noted, "Several young brethren have applied for permission to decorate the church at Christmas. Pleasing as it is to have the church decorated on the occasion, the Board nevertheless hesitated to give its consent. When in former years the church was decorated, it gave rise to protracted evening gatherings of young people of both sexes in the chapel, and caused various complaints at the time. The originators are well meaning persons, but cannot exercise a controlling influence. At all events the warden is to be consulted, and even if there should be no objection from that side, the superintendence of the preparations by married persons of weight must be secured."

vii Committee in Bethania, February 14, 1816, as recorded by Jon Sensbach, *A Separate Canaan* (Ann Arbor: UMI Dissertation Services, 1993), 503.

Chapter 2: The Christmas Tree and the Pyramid

1. Springplace Diary, Springplace, Georgia, 21 December 1805 (Moravian Archives, Winston-Salem, NC).

2. Clement Miles in *Christmas Customs and Traditions* (New York: Dover, 1976) 276, noted that in Sweden parlor floors were strewn with juniper or spruce or straw before Christmas. The custom obviously originated in Europe.

3. Mrs. Vann was Chief James Vann's wife. The chief, in spite of his bouts of uncontrollable, murderous rage and random mean-spiritedness fueled by alcohol, was instrumental in encouraging the Moravians to come to Springplace, primarily because he wanted education for the children of the Cherokee Nation. He sent his own son Joseph to the school and provided some slave labor for the mission; the missionaries in turn helped him in constructing his fine new home, which today is a museum with the Georgia State Parks and Historic Sites, where they decorate for Christmas in the Moravian style.

4. Springplace Diary, 21 December 1805.

5. Springplace Diary, 21 December 1806.

6. See Chapter Three for an extensive explanation of the *Putz*.

7. *Lewis Miller: Sketches and Chronicles* (York, PA: The Historical Society of York County, 1966) 45.

8. E-mail correspondence with Justine Landis, Curator, York County Heritage Trust, 17 February 2005.

9. Winterthur Yuletide Interpretive Manual (Henry Francis Dupont Winterthur Museum, Winterthur, Delaware) Trees, 1.

10. Springplace Diary, 24 December 1814, Moravian Archives, Winston-Salem, North Carolina.

11. Tanya Gulevich, *Encyclopedia of Christmas* (Detroit: Omnigraphics, 2000) 143.

12. Craig Atwood, *Community of the Cross: Moravian Piety in Colonial Bethlehem* (University Park: The Pennsylvania State University Press, 2004) 162.

13. The Rev. Dr. Edmund Schwarze. *History of the Moravian Missions Among Southern Indian Tribes of the United States.* (Bethlehem, PA: Times Publishing Co. for Transactions of the Moravian Historical Society, Special Series, vol. 1, 1923) 83-84.

14. William C. Reichel, *A History of the Moravian Seminary for Young Ladies* (Philadelphia: J. P. Lippincott & Co., 1858) 146.

15. Schwarze, 84.

16. Springplace Mission Papers, Box M: 411, 7 December 1806, Moravian Archives, Winston-Salem, NC.

17. Paula Welshimer and John Bivins Jr., *Moravian Decorative Arts in North Carolina: An Introduction to the Old Salem Collection.* (Winston-Salem, NC: Old Salem, Inc., 1981) 88.

18. Schwarze, 113.

19. Springplace Mission Records, 2 January 1813, 1: 1.

20. Springplace Diary, 29 December 1807: "Caesar came to the house to show the verses he and his relatives had received the previous year. He was told that the reason he did not receive one this year was because of his 'apathy towards God's word.' "In a letter to Christian Benzien from John Gambold on 7 December 1806, Gambold mentioned "The verses with the Springplace borders," which may make those from Anna's brush unique to that area and particularly desirable to people like Caesar and his family. (Springplace Correspondence, 7 December 1806).

21. Schwarze, 114.

22. Although a search for this artwork was undertaken, it was not located. Herman Viola, the former director of the Smithsonian Institution's National Anthropological Archives and Curator Emeritus at the Smithsonian's National Museum of Natural History, has written many books as a specialist on the history of the American West, including one on Thomas McKenney. Viola believes that McKenney sent such work to certain well-placed people in positions of authority in the hope of support and contributions. He suggested that a likely candidate to receive Darcheechy's work may have been John C. Calhoun, the Secretary of War for the State Department. (See Schwarze, *History of the Moravian Missions Among Southern Indian Tribes of the United States* for additional information on Calhoun's policy concerning "the civilization of the Indian.") Viola stated in a telephone conversation that the artwork may have been tucked away in the voluminous papers of Calhoun found in various libraries around the country. It could also have been destroyed by a disastrous fire at the Smithsonian castle in 1865 in which many of the Indian portraits and artwork were lost (phone conversation with Viola, 14 August 2005).

23. Springplace Diaries, 15:1, 14 November 1818.

24. Springplace Mission Correspondence, 15 August 1810, 1:24, M 412.

25. Springplace Diaries, 25 December 1807.

26. James Henry spoke of Christmas garlands interwoven with "the bouquet of chaste flowers" in Moravian decorations; James Henry, *Sketches of Moravian Live and Character.* (Philadelphia: J. B. Lippincott, 1859) 159.

27. Springplace Correspondence, 15:1, 9 September 1821.

28. Fries, *Records*, vol. 5, Minutes of Salem Boards, 27 December 1786, 2146.

29. Ibid.

30. Phillip V. Snyder, *The Christmas Tree Book: The History of the Christmas Tree & Antique Christmas Tree Ornaments* (New York: The Viking Press, 1976) 25.

31. Alfred L. Shoemaker, *Christmas in Pennsylvania: A Folk-Cultural Study* (Kutztown, PA: Pennsylvania Folklife Society, 1959; reprint, Mechanicsburg, PA: Stackpole Books, 1999).

32. Shoemaker, 53.

33. Ibid.

34. Shoemaker, 119.

35. Diary of Caroline Fries (Shaffner), 1861-1864, Fries and Shaffner Papers #4046, Southern Historical Collection, UNC, Chapel Hill. Caroline, known as "Carrie," born in 1839, was the oldest daughter of Lisette Vogler Fries and Francis Fries. Her maternal grandparents were John Vogler and Christina Spach. The diary is part of the papers, but a more legible typescript was prepared for 67 pages of the diary, from which these excerpts were taken.

36. Ibid. See Chapter Six for a detailed discussion of dialogues presented by the Salem Girls' School students.

37. Fries and Shaffner Papers, #4046.

38. Shoemaker, 55.

39. Fries and Shaffner Papers, #4046.

40. Kostbarkeiten, Herrnhut: Archives, "November page," 2000.

41. Adelaide Fries, "Christmas Customs," 1936, Folder Q645.4, Moravian Archives, Winston-Salem, North Carolina.

42. John Lewis Krimmel, Sketches, Henry Francis Dupont Winterthur Museum, Winterthur, DE.

43. William Woys Weaver, *The Christmas Cook* (New York: Harper Collins, 1990) 52.

44. Ibid, 51-52.

45. Gulevich, 141.

46. Elaine Dow, *Christmas, a Potpourri* (Topsfield, MA: Historical Presentations, 1986) 36.

47. Gulevich, 246-249.

48. Weaver, 54.

49. Gulevich, 141-142.

50. Snyder, 19.

51. William Sandys, *Christmas Carols, Ancient and Modern* (London: Richard Beckley, 1833) xix.

52. Snyder, 12-13.

53. Weaver, 53.

54. Snyder, 11.

55. Ibid, 12.

56. Weaver, 54.

57. Snyder, 13.

58. Ibid, 14.

59. Daniel J. Foley, *The Christmas Tree* (Philadelphia and New York: Chilton Co., 1960) 42.

60. Snyder, 14.

61. Miles, 265.

62. Sandys, xli.

63. William Sandys, *Book of Days* (London: John Russell, 1840) 135.

64. There are similar recorded occurrences of British royal family members having Christmas trees, even in the late 1700s.

65. Snyder, 33.

66. Ibid.

67. Winterthur Yuletide Interpretive Manual, "Trees in American Homes", 2, Winterthur Museum, Winterthur, DE.

68. Charles Dickens, *A Christmas Tree* (Sydney, Australia: P.I.C. Pty Ltd, 1988).

69. Old Salem Museums & Gardens Christmas interpretive material, 2000, Gene Capps.

70. Shoemaker, 46.

71. Ibid.

72. Rt. Rev. Edward Rondthaler, D.D., LL.D, *The Memorabilia of Fifty Years,* 1877 to 1927 (Raleigh, NC: Edwards & Broughton Co., 1928) 59.

73. Shoemaker, 47-48.

74. *Kriss Kringle's Christmas Tree. A Holiday Present for Boys and Girls* (New York and Philadelphia: E. Ferrett & Co., 1846) preface.

75. Snyder, 157.

76. Ibid, 159-160.

77. Jenny Lind was so popular that even cake receipts were named after her, as was true for other famous persons. See Emily-Sarah Lineback's *Preserving the Past: Salem Moravians' Receipts & Rituals* (Boonville, NC: Carolina Avenue Press, 2003) 69-70, for several local "Jenny Lind" cakes from the Vogler collection of receipts.

78. Snyder, 109.

79. Hans Christian Andersen, *The Christmas Tree* (NY: McLoughlin Brothers, n.d.)

80. Harnett Kane, *The Southern Christmas Book* (New York: David McKay, 1958) 190.

81. Foley, 82.

82. Snyder, 157.

83. Ibid, 167-168.

84. Gulevich, 146.

85. Ibid.

86. Internet site: "Closed for Christmas," http://www.christianitytoday.com:so/leaders/newsletters/2005/cln51212.html, accessed January 4, 2007.

87. Robert Brenner, *Christmas Revisited* (West Chester, PA: Schiffer, 1986), 13.

88. Ibid.

89. Dow, 29.

90. Dr. Daniel Crews, ed., *Records of the Moravians*, vol. 13 (Raleigh: North Carolina Department of Archives and History, 2006) Memorabilia of Salem Congregation, 1871, 6940-41.

91. Crews, *Records*, vol. 13, 24 December 1874, 7120.

92. Albert Oerter, *Diary of the Colored Church in Salem*, Moravian Archives, Winston-Salem, NC.

93. Ibid.

94. Colored Church, No. VIII Diary, 26 Dec. 1874, Moravian Archives, Winston-Salem, NC.

95. Kane, 196.

96. *The Wachovia Moravian*, January 1897.

97. Ibid, 1899, 1904.

98. Ibid, 3 January 1898.

99. *Guide Book of N.W. North Carolina Containing Historical Sketches of the Moravians in NC: A Description of the Country and Its Industrial Pursuits* (Salem, NC: L.Y. and E.T. Blum, Printers, 1878) 21.

100. *The Academy, A Monthly Journal of Salem Academy*, vol. 8, no. 61, 107.

101. "Cantata" is defined as "a composition for one or more voices usually comprising solos, duets, recitatives, and choruses and sung to an instrumental accompaniment. (*Meriam Webster's Collegiate Dictionary, 10th edition*). Walker's 1828 dictionary defines it simply as a song.

102. *The Academy, A Monthly Journal of Salem Academy*, vol. 8, no. 62, 114.

103. Thor Martin Johnson, "Christmas in Herrnhut in 1936," Christmas Box, Folder Q645.4, Moravian Archives, Winston-Salem, NC.

104. Reinhard Martin, "Christmas in the German Moravian Church," Christmas Box, Folder Q645.7, Moravian Archives, Winston-Salem, NC.

105. Dr. William N. Schwarze, Archivist, Bethlehem, "Transcription of Items from the Bethlehem Diary Relating to Early Celebrations of Christmas in Bethlehem, Pennsylvania," 14; Dr. Charles H. Rominger, *The Pennsylvania German Folklore Society*, vol. 6, "Early Christmases in Bethlehem, PA, Bethlehem, 1941."

106. Ibid.

107. Ibid, 489.

108. Extracts from Theodor Bechler, *Ortsgeschichte von Herrnhut*, Herrnhut, 1922.

109. Weaver, 54.

110. "Smokers" are whimsical incense burners in which the mouths of the figures (some Christmas-related, such as the gift-bringer images) emit the smoke.

111. Snyder, 102.

112. Miles, 266.

113. Peter Wolle Diary, 19 February 1816, 163.

114. Ibid, 1 January 1818, 321.

115. Ibid, 23 December 1829.

116. Susannah Kramsch Diary, Moravian Archives, Winston-Salem, NC.

117. Crews, *Records*, vol. 13, Salem Diary, 1872, 6983.

118. Ibid, Bethania, 24 December 1874, 7120.

119. Brenner, 23.

120. Shoemaker, 61.

121. Snyder, 38-39.

122. Shoemaker, 61.

123. Snyder, 29, 107.

124. Snyder, 40.

125. Ibid.

Chapter 2 Sidebar Endnotes

i. Schwarze, 113.

ii. Ibid.

iii. Ibid, 114.

iv. Springplace Correspondence, #14:2.

v. Carolus Linnaeus was a Swedish botanist who developed the system of categorizing plants and animals.

vi. Schwarze, 114.

vii. Springplace Correspondence, 15:1, Sept. 9, 1821.

viii. Springplace Correspondence, July, 14, 1821, 13: 2, Letter to Van Vleck from Johann Renatus Schmidt.

ix. Ibid.

Chapter 3: The Putz and Other Decorations

1. John Walker, *A Critical Pronouncing Dictionary* (Hartford: Silas Andrus, 1828).

2. Richmond E. Myers, *Christmas Traditions* (Bethlehem, PA: Acorn Graphics, 1985) 35.

3. Ibid, 35-36.

4. Ibid, 41. The minister was Dr. A. D. Thaeler of Bethlehem.

5. Daniel S. Grosch, a booklet entitled "Constructing a Christmas Putz" reprinted from an article in *The Moravian* (Bethlehem, PA and Winston-Salem, NC: The Board of Christian Education, Moravian Church in America, n.d.) 2. Found in Christmas Box, Folder Q645.4, Moravian Archives, Winston-Salem, NC.

6. Rt. Rev. Edward Rondthaler, D.D., LL.D, *The Memorabilia of Fifty Years, 1877 to 1927* (Raleigh: Edwards & Broughton Co., 1928) 223.

7. Myers, 69.

8. *The Academy*, vol. XII, December 1889, Salem College Library.

9. Adelaide Fries, *Records*, vol I, 233.

10. Fries, "Christmas Customs," Christmas Box, Folder 4: 7, Moravian Archives, Winston-Salem, NC.

11. Springplace Diaries, 24 December 1806, Moravian Archives, Winston-Salem, NC.

12. Springplace Diaries, 24 December 1805. Christmas historian Clement Miles wrote that in Sweden parlor floors were strewn at Christmas with "sprigs of fragrant juniper or spruce-pine, or with rye-straw." Clement Miles, *Christmas Customs and Traditions* (New York: Dover, 1976. Reprint of *Christmas in Ritual and Tradition, Christian and Pagan*, T. Fisher Unwin, 1912) 276.

13. James Henry, *Sketches of Moravian Life and Character* (Philadelphia: J.B. Lippincott, 1859) 155-162.

14. Daniel Crews, *Records*, vol. 13, 26 December 1874, 7121.

15. The blood and water (unction) of the wounds of Jesus were an important part of the life of eighteenth century Moravians. These aspects were "mentioned repeatedly in sermons, prayers, and hymns . . . The congregation was often called the Congregation of Blood to indicate its identification with Jesus' sufferings. Blood was especially important in Communion" in which the wine symbolized the "blood of the Savior." (Vernon H. Nelson, Editor, *The Bethlehem Diary, vol. II*, 1 January 1744 - 31 May 1745 (Bethlehem, PA: The Moravian Archives, 2001) Glossary, 378-379. This was true of other denominations as well. "The Anglican hymn 'Rock of Ages' " speaks of the symbolic cleansing of the guilt of a sinner by the blood and water from the pierced wounds of Jesus' side. The lines are: 'Let the water and the blood, from Thy riven side which flowed, be of sin the double cure, cleanse me from its guilt and power.' " (Ibid., "unctuous," 398).

16. Springplace Correspondence, Gambold to Van Vleck, 4 January 1816.

17. George F. Bahnson Diary, 1 January 1835, 356-357.

18. Mary Theobald and Libbey Oliver, *Four Centuries of Virginia Christmas* (Richmond: The Dietz Press, 2000) 38.

19. Kalmia, the American laurel, was named by Swedish naturalist Carolus Linnaeus (1707-1778) to honor fellow countryman and botanist Peter Kalm. Linnaeus "established the modern scientific method of naming plants and animals." (*The World Book Encyclopedia*, vol. 12 (Chicago: Field Enterprises, 1973).

20. *The Academy*, vol. 5, no. 44, November/December 1882, 15 but numbered 11.

21. *The Academy*, vol. 9, no. 72, January 1887, 198.

22. Ibid.

23. Jedediah Morse, *Geography Made Easy: Being an Abridgement of the American Universal Geography* (Boston: Thomas & Andrews, 1816) 201.

24. Diary of Birdie Goslen, 13 December 1891, Moravian Archives, Winston-Salem, NC.

25. Old Salem Museums & Gardens, acc. 750.1.

26. Adelaide Fries, Christmas Box, "Home Church," A:6 - H:1, 16 June 1949, Moravian Archives, Winston-Salem, NC.

27. *The Twin-City Daily Sentinel*, "Christmas in Salem Now and In Years Past," Saturday Evening, 16 December 1911.

28. *Winston-Salem Journal and Sentinel* article, n.d. but stated to be about 1963-64 by Richard Starbuck of the Moravian Archives. Christmas Box, Folder Q645.7, Moravian Archives, Winston-Salem, North Carolina.

29. Louisa Lenoir, Letterbook, Salem, 15 June 1819, Rare Books, Southern Historical Collection, Wilson Library, Chapel Hill, NC.

30. Miranda Miller Scarborough, October 1890, Rare Book Room, Salem College Library.

31. Gene Capps, Christmas Interpretive Material, 2002, Old Salem Museum & Gardens.

32. Springplace Diaries, 24 December 1805, Moravian Archives, Winston-Salem, NC.

33. *The Moravian*, vol. 8, no. 1, 1 January 1863, 2.

34. C. Daniel Crews and Lisa D. Bailey. *Records of the Moravians in NC 1856-1866*, vol. 12, "Diary of the African Church," 25 December 1866 (Raleigh: Department of Archives and History, 2000) 6635.

35. George F. Bahnson Diary, 24 December 1835.

36. The following mention, preceding the above, describes a birthday celebration for Hortensia, equated in happiness with Christmas, with the anticipation of their own babe (Angelica) to come. "Sr. Lydia had secretly made a very nice Putz on which appeared goody & two pair of most lovely little shoes for an expected stranger & future sojourner in our family, God willing!. . . Liturgy 35 was sung in the evening, whereupon we illuminated the little houses which we brought along from Bethlm, sat round in the room, & looked at them, feeling almost as happy as children at Christmas." George F. Bahnson Diary, 15 March 1835, 277.

37. George F. Bahnson Diary, 24 December 1837, 1310.

38. Birdie Goslen Diary, Moravian Archives, Winston-Salem, NC.

39. Reinhard Martin, "Christmas in the German Moravian Church," Christmas Box, Q645: Folder 7, Moravian Archives, Winston-Salem, NC.

40. The word *tableaux*, plural, was used for graphic descriptions or representations; arrangements of a scene. Patterson refers here to the *Krippe*, or Nativity scene, which was a part of the larger *Putz*. Fries-Bahnson Correspondence 1859-68, 17 December 1864, Moravian Archives, Winston-Salem, NC.

41. *The Twin-City Daily Sentinel*, "Christmas in Salem Now and In Years Past," Saturday Evening, 16 December 1911.

42. Springplace Diaries, 17 December 1807.

43. Springplace Diaries, 24 December 1807.

44. Ibid.

45. Springplace Diaries, 21 December 1812.

46. Peter Wolle Diary, 20 December 1814, 55.

47. George F. Bahnson Diary, 20 December 1834, Bethania, 232.

48. Ibid, 23 December 1837, 1309.

49. Crews and Bailey, *Records of the Moravians in North Carolina*, vol. 12, Private Diary of R.P. Leinbach, 6506.

50. George F. Bahnson Diary, 22 December 1834, 234.

51. Ibid, 28 August 1834, 187..

52. Peter Wolle Diary, 28 December 1809, 15.

53. C. Daniel Crews and Lisa D. Bailey, *Records*, vol. 12, 6216, 6271, 6640, 6644.

54. Peter Wolle Diary, 1814, 53, 54, 55.

55. Ibid, 1816, 162-63.

56. Ibid, 6 December 1818.

57. Springplace Correspondence, 1:1, 2 January 1817.

58. Peter Wolle Diary, 1 January 1819, 348.

59. Rondthaler, 252.

60. Henry, 155-162, excerpts in Folder 2, Q645, "Christmas," Moravian Archives, Winston-Salem, NC).

61. Vangie Roby Sweitzer, *Christmas in Bethlehem: A Moravian Heritage* (Bethlehem, Pennsylvania: Central Moravian Church, 2000) 20.

62. Peter Wolle Diary, 1 January 1819.

63. Sweitzer, 9.

64. Ibid, 10.

65. George F. Bahnson Diary, 24 December 1837, 1310.

66. Ibid, 25 December 1837, 1312.

67. Ibid, 27 December 1838, 1507.

68. Myers, 43.

69. Ibid.

70. Crews and Bailey, *Records*, vol. 12, 7 December 1859, 6322.

71. Altred Shoemaker, *Christmas in Pennsylvania* (Mechanicsburg, PA: Stackpole Books, 1999) 153.

72. Rondthaler, 38.

73. Ibid, 197.

74. *The Moravian*, vol. 16, no. 1, 5 January, 1871, 2. John Bunyan lived during the period of 1678-1684 and wrote about the dream of a man named Christian whose pilgrimage through life with Bible in hand took him from the City of Destruction to the Celestial City. His life's journey appealed so widely that it was, indeed, second only to the Bible in popularity for a long period of time in history (*Encyclopaedia Britannica*, vol. VII (Chicago, 1974) 1007.

75. *The Wachovia Moravian*, vol. II, no. 23, January 1895.

76. The author is taking the liberty of making *Putz* a plural English word. It is, of course, a German word that has made the transition to English usage in speaking of this particular aspect of the Moravian Christmas.

77. *The Twin-City Daily Sentinel* "Christmas in Salem Now and In Years Past," Saturday Evening, 16 December 1911.

78. *The Academy*, 25 December, 1878, 31.

79. Ibid, vol. 7, no. 51.

80. Winifred Kirkland, *Where the Star Still Shines* (Winston-Salem: Woman's Auxiliary, Home Moravian Church, no date) 29.

81. Adelaide Fries, "A Moravian Christmas," manuscript in Christmas Box, Q645, Folder 4:10, Moravian Archives, Winston-Salem, NC. This became a newspaper article in the *Winston-Salem Journal & Sentinel*, 27 Dec., 1931.

82. Fries, *Moravian Customs*, Salem College Library, Rare Books, 1936.

83. Ibid.

84. *The Moravian*, vol. IX, no. 1, 1 January 1864, 2.

85. Henry, 206.

86. Ibid.

87. Grosch, n.p.

88. Tanya Gulevich, *Encyclopedia of Christmas* (Detroit: Omnigraphics, 2000) 408.

89. A mid-twentieth century author wrote what has become a classic about the power of the Moravian Christmas *Putz*, or crib. It is titled *Snow Over Bethlehem* (Katharine Milhous, New York: Charles Scribner's Sons, 1945), and relates the story of how Sister Anna Johanna and others were able to make a memorable Christmas for a group of children being moved from Nazareth to Bethlehem as a precaution against a possible hostile Indian attack in 1755.

90. Gulevich, 409.

91. Fries, *Moravian Customs*, 21,

92. *Neue Krippelbilder*, article, no other identification.

93. Ibid.

94. Martin, n.p.

95. Fries, Christmas Box, Q645, Folder 6, 16 June, 1949, Moravian Archives, NC.

96. Fries, *Customs and Practices of the Moravian Church*, 52.

97. Ibid, 52-53.

98. Ibid.

99. Ibid.

100. From a brochure prepared by The Moravian Church in America, South, no date.

101. Elizabeth Trotman, article from *Winston Salem Journal and Sentinel*, "Moravian Stars to Shine on City for Christmas," 22 November 1959, Christmas Box, Q645, Folder 6, Moravian Archives, Winston-Salem, NC.

102. Kirkland, 43.

103. James Boeringer, *Morning Star* (Cranbury, NJ: Associated University Presses, 1986) 18.

104. *Richmond Newsleader*, 25 December 1928, interview with Mrs. Martha Vandergrift.

105. Advent from the Latin *adventus*: the coming of Christ at the Incarnation.

106. Flora Ann Bynum, *The Christmas Heritage of Old Salem*, "The Moravian Advent Wreath" (Williamsburg, VA: The Williamsburg Publishing Co., 1983).

107. Moravian Christmas brochure, no other information.

108. Phillip V. Snyder, *The Christmas Tree: The History of the Christmas Tree & Antique Christmas Tree Ornaments* (New York: The Viking Press, 1976) 28-29.

109. Shoemaker, 74.

110. Ibid, 57-65.

111. Snyder, 91.

112. Shoemaker, 100.

113. Ibid, 99.

114. *The Moravian*, vol. 15, no. 51, 22 December 1870, 204.

115. Shoemaker, 59.

116. *The Moravian*, vol. 16, no. 1, 5 January 1871, 2.

117. George Johnson, *Christmas Ornaments, Lights, and Decorations*, vol. 1 (Paducah, KY: Collector Books, 1997) 16.

118. John K. Winkler, *Five and Ten* (Babson Park, MA: Spear and Staff, 1940) 56-57.

119. Ibid, 86-91.

120. Snyder, 62.

121. Rondthaler, 154.

122. *The Wachovia Moravian*, vol. II, no. 22, 1, December 1894, Salem, NC.

123. *The Wachovia Moravian*, vol. VIII, no 93, December 1900, 1.

Chapter 3 Sidebar Endnotes

i.   Snyder, *The Christmas Tree*, 95.

ii.   Johnson, 11

iii. Ibid., 13, and Snyder, 86

iv.   Ibid.

v.   Snyder, 81.

Chapter 4: The Evolution of the Gift Bringer and Gifts

1.   New York *Sun*, 21 September 1897.

2.   *Bible*, First Corinthians, Chapter 13.

3.   *The Moravian*, vol. 14, no. 52, 30 December 1869, 207.

4.   Ibid, 26 December 1856.

5.   Ibid, 25 December 1857.

6.   Ibid, vol. 14, no. 52, 30 December 1869, 207.

7.   Woden: an earlier form of Odin, became one of the principal gods in Norse mythology, a war god and protector of heroes, who rode an eight-legged horse. Woden's day was Wednesday.

8.   Thor: deity common to all the early Germanic peoples, a great warrior benevolent to all mankind. His name represented thunder, and he may have been the son of Odin. He was sometimes equated with the Roman god Jupiter, who was the god "whose worship embodied a distinct moral conception." Thursday comes from Thor's Day (*Encyclopaedia Britannica*, 15th edition [Chicago: William Benton, 1974], entry for "Thor").

9.   Saturnalia was the festival of Saturn, in ancient Rome beginning on December 17 and honoring the god of agriculture, often in a very unrestrained celebration.

10. Phillip V. Snyder, *December 25* (New York: Dodd, Mead, & Co., 1985) 208-209.

11. An article in the *Encyclopaedia Britannica, Micropaedia*, vol. 7 (Chicago: William Benton, 1974) 324, states that in 1969 the feast day of Nicholas, along with that of some other saints, was dropped. They all are now commemorated together on January 1.

12. Louise Carus, editor, *The Real St. Nicholas* (Wheaton, IL: Quest Books, 2002) back cover.

13. Snyder, 210.

14. Gerry Bowler, *The World Encyclopedia of Christmas* (Toronto: McClelland & Stewart, 20002) 17.

15. Tanya Gulevich, *Encyclopedia of Christmas* (Detroit: Omnigraphics, 2000) 239.

16. Penne Restad, *Christmas in America: A History* (New York: Oxford University Press, 1995) 210.

17. Gulevich, 355.

18. Gulevich, 521.

19. Bowler, 92.

20. Restad, 56.

21. Marion Harland, *The Christmas Holly* (New York: Sheldon and Co., 1867).

22. Restad, 55.

23. Taken from an unattributed nineteenth-century colored print of a young girl with a schoolbook in one hand and a laurel wreath in the other.

24. Phebe Earle Gibbons, *Pennsylvania Dutch & Other Essays* (Philadelphia: J.B. Lippincott & Co., 1882, reprinted Mechanicsburg, PA: Stackpole Books, 2001), 45 and 407.

25. Gulevich, 621.

26. *Kriss Kringle's Book*, 1842, published in Philadelphia by Thomas, Cowperthwait & Co.; *Kriss Kringle's Christmas Tree: A holliday (sic) present for boys and girls* published in Philadelphia in 1845 by E. Ferrett & Co. (Alfred Shoemaker, *Christmas in Pennsylvania : A Folk-Cultural Study* (Kutztown, Pennsylvania: Pennsylvania Folklife Society, 1959; Mechanicsburg, Pennsylvania: Stackpole Books, 1999) 36.

27. Restad, 55-56.

28. William Sandys, *Christmas Carols, Ancient and Modern* (London: Richard Beckley, 1833) xcii-xciii.

29. *The Academy*, vol. 10, no. 82, 277.

30. John Walker, *A Critical Pronouncing Dictionary* (Hartford: Silas Andrus, 1828).

31. Shoemaker, 4.

32. Gulevich, xiii.

33. Washington Irving, *Diedrich Knickerbocker's History of New-York* (New York: Heritage Press, 1940) 75.

34. Stephen Nissenbaum, *The Battle for Christmas* (New York: Alfred A. Knopf, 1997) 55.

35. Arthur Hosking, "Is Santa Claus an American?" *Liberty* (New York: Liberty Magazine, 30 December 1933)

36. It is generally accepted that Moore was indeed the author of the poem, although there are some who attribute it to Henry Livingston, Jr. (1748-1828). Arguments include that Livingstone wrote light, whimsical verse in the same meter as the famous poem and that he had a much less grave and sober personality than Moore, which would make him the more likely creator. Don Foster, Author Unknown: *On the Trail of Anonymous*, Chapter 6: "Yes, Virginia, There *Was* a Santa Claus" (New York: Henry Holt, 2000). No concrete, definitive evidence has ever been found to substantiate the Livingston family claim.

37. The English use "Happy Christmas"; the Americans prefer "merry." Joe Wheeler and Jim Rosenthal, *St. Nicholas, A Closer Look at Christmas* (Nashville, TN: Thomas Nelson, Inc., 2005) xi.

38. Restad, note 15 on page 183.

39. Sarah Bahnson Chapman, ed., *Bright and Gloomy Days: The Civil War Correspondence of Captain Charles Frederic Bahnson, A Moravian Confederate* (Knoxville: University of Tennessee Press, 2003) 44.

40. Restad, 47.

41. Ibid, 49.

42. Ibid, 148.

43. Ibid.

44. Ibid.

45. *The Moravian*, vol. 14, no. 52, 30 December 1869, 207.

46. Nissenbaum, *The Battle for Christmas* (New York: Alfred A. Knopf, 1997). This is a theme of the book which has the subtitle: *A Social And Cultural History Of Christmas That Shows How It Was Transformed From An Unruly Carnival Season Into The Quintessential American Family Holiday.*

47. Snyder, *December 25*, 231.

48. *The Academy*, vol. 3, no. 28, 29.

49. *The Wachovia Moravian*, January 1903, 7.

50. Sally Kevill-Davies, *Yesterday's Children: The Antiques and History of Childcare* (Woodbridge, Suffolk, England: Antique Collectors' Club, 1998, reprint from 1991) 6-8.

51. John Guilds, ed., *The Writings of William Gilmore Simms, Volume V* (Columbia, SC: University of South Carolina Press, 1974) 317.

52. Ibid.

53. George F. Bahnson Diary, 10 June 1835, 322.

54. Springplace Correspondence, 21:2, Schmidt to Van Vleck, 18 October 1821.

55. Ibid, 24:1, 12 November 1821.

56. Ibid, to Brothers and Sisters, 11 January 1822, 24.

57. Gulevich, 237-38.

58. William Sandys, *Christmastide Its History, Festivities and Carols* (London: John Russell Smith, 1852). Marchpane or marzipan, a confection of crushed almonds or almond paste, sugar, and egg whites shaped into various forms

59. Bowler, 92.

60. Gulevich, 240.

61. Ibid; Bowler, 92.

62. Apples, fruits, and nuts according to an old children's rhyme are part of an ancient tradition of the foods of Christmas in Germany. Apples represented the "Tree of Knowledge in Paradise," nuts, the "difficulties and mysteries of life," and fruits, the bounty of Christmas. Peter Andrews, ed., *Christmas in Germany* (Chicago: World Book Encyclopedia, 1974) 24.

63. Gulevich, 240.

64. Bowler, 92.

65. Rick Steves and Valerie Griffith, *European Christmas* (Emeryville, CA: Avalon Travel, 2005) 160.

66. *Journal and Letters of Philip Vickers Fithian: A Plantation Tutor of the Old Dominion, 1773-1774*, Hunter Dickinson Farish, ed. (Charlottesville, The University Press of Virginia, 1983) 39-40.

67. *NC Historical Review*, Vol. XXI, No. 4, October, 1944, 375.

68. Snyder, *December 25*, 95.

69. The Diary of Robert Gilmor, *Maryland Historical Magazine*, vol. XVII, no. 3, September 1922, 232-234.

70. Ibid.

71. George F. Bahnson Diary, 2 January 1835, 358-359.

72. Snyder, December 25, 61.

73. Transcription of items from the Bethlehem Diary, by Schwarze, Pennsylvania German Folklore Society, 25.

74. Ibid, 24 December 1757, 27. It is interesting to note that the Moravian Book Shop in Bethlehem "is recognized as the oldest book shop in America," since 1745, according to Moravian author Vangie Roby Sweitzer. (*Christmas in Bethlehem: A Moravian Heritage* [Bethlehem, Pennsylvania: Central Moravian Church, 2000] 41.) In fact, the shop advertises itself on its business card as the "World's Oldest Bookstore." Salem's Moravian Book and Gift Shop, preceded by the Moravian Book Room, opened in the late 1960s and now is located in the former "mammoth" general store of Elias Vogler, built in 1867 (Charles Vogler, editor, *Descendants of Philipp Christoph Vogler, Books I and II* [Camden, ME: Penobscot Press for Philip Christoph Vogler Memorial, Inc., 1994] 355.)

75. Old Salem Museums & Gardens Research Center files.

76. Ibid.

77. Adelaide Fries, *Records*, vol. 1, Bethabara Diary, 1760, 233.

78. Ibid.

79. Fries, *Records*, vol. 5, 15 December 1784, 2043.

80. Springplace Diary, 22 December 1806.

81. Ibid, 29 December 1807.

82. Springplace Correspondence, 7 December 1806.

83. This 1805 greeting is in MESDA storage. It is often on display at Christmas. The same verse appears in *The Liturgy and Hymns of The American Province of the Unitas Fratrum or The Moravian Church* (Bethlehem: Moravian Publication Office, 1895) 48.

84. Springplace Diary, 30 December 1807.

85. Springplace Correspondence, Folder 6: 31, 8.

86. On 28 June 1806, indigo for dyeing was mentioned as one of the crops, along with rice, cotton, turnips, pumpkins, and Cherokee tobacco. The notation was made that lots of hoeing and weeding were required. (Springplace Correspondence, Gambold to Benzien, M 411:5:10, 3).

87. Craftsmen Christian Burkhardt and Karsten Petersen "built a complete loom and set it up in a little house for weaving on the Springplace premises, for the use of the missionaries" in 1807. The Rev. Dr. Edmund Schwarze, *History of the Moravian Missions Among Southern Indian Tribes of the United States* (Bethlehem, Pennsylvania: Times Publishing Co. for Transactions of the Moravian Historical Society, Special Series, vol. 1, 1923) 87.

88. Springplace Correspondence, 30 January 1808, Folder 6:35.

89. Springplace Diary, 25 December 1812.

90. Springplace Correspondence, Gambold to Brother Peter in Salem, 31 December 1812.

91. Rowena McClinton, *The Moravian Mission among the Cherokees at Springplace, Georgia*. Dissertation thesis, Ph.D. (Lexington: University of Kentucky, 1996) 522.

92. Springplace Correspondence, 1:4-6, to Brother Simon from Gambold, 25 December 1819.

93. *The Publications of the American Tract Society*, vol. 4 (New York: American Tract Society, n.d. but inscribed 1830) title page quotation from the Bishop of Durham.

94. *Julia Changed, or, The True Secret of a Happy Christmas* (Philadelphia: American Sunday School Union, 1832).

95. Springplace Correspondence, 2:2, to Van Vleck, 7 February 1820.

96. *Journal of Johann Heinrich Leinbach*, unpublished, Old Salem Museums & Gardens Library, April 13, 1830, 4.

97. C. Daniel Crews, *Mountain Gospel* (Winston-Salem, NC: Moravian Archives, 1993) 37-38.

98. Ibid, 9.

99. Ibid.

100. Eliza Vierling Kremer, "Bits of Old Salem Gossip," Salem College Library, Rare Books.

101. Peter Wolle Diary, 23 December 1816, 267.

102. Ibid, 24 December 1816, 267.

103. Susannah Kramsch Diary, Moravian Archives, Winston-Salem, NC.

104. Lecture by Mary Audrey Apple, Old Salem Museum & Gardens, 4 December 2004.

105. Thomas Gray, *The Old Salem Toy Museum* (Winston-Salem, NC: Old Salem, 2005) 37.

106. Fries, *Records*, vol. 6, 31 January 1804, Auf. Col., 2776.

107. Elisabeth Sommer, Research report on toys in Salem 1785-1900, 10 May 2001, 2.

108. Ibid.

109. MESDA files. Antoinette Emilie Schulz was born 21 May 1825.

110. Ibid.

111. *Daily National Intelligencer*, Washington, D.C., 22 December 1818, 3-4.

112. Margaret Law Callcott, ed., *Mistress of Riversdale, The Plantation Letters of Rosalie Stier Calvert, 1795-1821* (Baltimore: The John Hopkins University Press, 1991) 287.

113. A testimony to the bond between the Vogler father and son is found in a letter dated 11 May 1858, in which Elias wrote, "If any body had a good dear old pappy I have it."(E. A. Vogler Letter Book 1857-60, Letter to William E. Albright, Philadelphia, 122, private collection).

114. Crews, *Mountain Gospel*, 22. Zevely actually cited the third commandment, which Moravians at the time considered to be "Remember the Sabbath and keep it holy." This is the third commandment in the Lutheran and the Catholic churches. At that time the Moravians were using the Lutheran numbering of the commandments. In other Protestant and Jewish churches this commandment is usually number four, if they are numbered.

115. Richmond E. Myers, *Christmas Traditions* (Bethlehem, Pennsylvania: Acorn Graphics, 1985) 30.

116. George F. Bahnson Diary, 1 December 1836, 812.

117. Ibid, 9 December 1836, 819.

118. Louisa Hagen (Sussdorff) Diary, 24 December 1837.

119. Whether this wreath was created from an embellished watercolor, paper flowers, dried flowers, or greenery is unknown.

120. Fries Papers, MESDA files.

121. Reminiscences of Sarah H. Rand, Salem College Library.

122. *The Academy*, 29 December 1879, 31.

123. Reminiscences of S.F. Academy, 1871-1875, Anna L. Ogburn, Lombardy Grove, Mecklenburg, Va., Salem College Library.

124. Dr. Roy Ledbetter, "Moraviana: Christmas Eve," *The Moravian*, December 1996, 8-9.

125. From a brochure entitled "Christingles," no other information listed.

126. Adelaide Fries, "Moravian Customs," 25, Moravian Archives, Winston-Salem, North Carolina.

127. Stephen Nissenbaum, 122.

128. Ibid.

129. *The Moravian*, vol. 6, no. 52, 26 December 1861, 415-416.

130. Eleven-year-old Lisetta Vogler kept a travel journal of a trip taken that year with her parents and two siblings in which she described on 13 September "the now beautifully illuminated Broadway" which her father said "was far superior to any street in Philadelphia." (Frances Griffin, ed. *The Three Forks of Muddy Creek*, vol. 7, "Lisetta's Journey," 36.)

131. Restad, 33-34.

132. Ibid, 34.

133. Calathumpian bands were roaming mobs "banging and blowing on homemade instruments, intent on creating mischief to match their noise," Penne Restad, *Christmas in America: A History* (New York: Oxford University Press, 1995) 39. A type of frolick they definitely were, sometimes with fearful aspects, which ultimately led to a call for national intolerance for such bold and aggressive raucousness, including strong drink.

134. *The Moravian*, "Christmas in Philadelphia," 1 January 1863, vol. VIII, no.1, 1.

135. Snyder, *December 25*, 105.

136. *People's Press*, 25 November 1859.

137. Aesop's Fables had long been popular in Salem. Schoolteacher Peter Wolle recorded in January 1816, that he "and the children read some of Aesop's fables from the *Children's Friend (Kinderfreund)*, which amused them very much"(Peter Wolle Diary, 20 January 1816, 140).

138. *People's Press*, 13 December 1867.

139. Paula Welshimer and John Bivins, Jr., *Moravian Decorative Arts in North Carolina: An Introduction to the Old Salem Collection* (Winston-Salem, North Carolina: Old Salem, 1981) 88.

140. Regina Vogler, Autograph Book, MS 6:4//MC 9:I. Moravian Archives, Winston-Salem, NC.

141. Emery is a granular substance of corundum employed for grinding and polishing, which was stuffed into fanciful shapes like strawberries and used to clean rust from needles and pins, thus testifying to the constant women's chore of sewing being made a little more pleasant by such accoutrements.

142. Fries and Shaffner Papers, #4046, Series B: 1864, vol. 3, Southern Historical Collection, University of North Carolina, Chapel Hill, NC. Carrie, born in 1839, was the oldest daughter of Lisetta Vogler Fries and Francis Fries of Salem.

143. *The Moravian*, vol. 5, no. 1, 5 January 1860, 8.

144. *Louisa May Alcott, The Novels of, Little Women* (Ann Arbor: State Street Press, 2001) 9.

145. Ibid, 21.

146. Ibid, 28.

147. *The Moravian*, vol. IX, no. 52, December 1865, 206.

148. C. Daniel Crews, *Records*, vol. 13, 6981.

149. Ibid, 6981-82

150. Diary of the African Church in Salem, James Hall, pastor, Christmas excerpts, 1, prepared for the author by Richard Starbuck, Moravian Archives, Winston-Salem, NC.

151. Crews, *Records*, vol. 13, 6981.

152. Ibid, 28 December 1910.

153. Karal Ann Marling, *Merry Christmas: Celebrating America's Greatest Holiday* (Cambridge, Massachusetts: Harvard University Press, 2000) 2.

154. Salem Diary, 25 December 1887, Moravian Archives, Winston-Salem, NC.

155. *The Academy*, December 1879, 30.

156. Ibid, vol. II, no. 92, January 1889, 362.

157. Ibid, vol. 5, November-December 1887, 13.

158. Fries-Bahnson Correspondence, 1887, Moravian Archives, Winston-Salem, NC.

159. Ibid, 6 January 1888, Moravian Archives, Winston-Salem, NC.

160. *People's Press*, 9 December 1886.

161. Sincere thanks to Brad Rauschenberg for offering the use of these papers to my editor Gary Albert for inclusion in this book.

162. Nannie Haskins Williams Diary, vol. 1, #3179, Southern Historical Collection, UNC, Wilson Library, Chapel Hill.

163. The forty-five day German Christmas season included St. Thomas Day when a rich fruitcake was baked and people danced until the wee hours of the morning (Andrews, Peter, ed. *Christmas in Germany* (Chicago: World Book Encyclopedia, 1974) 24). Many folk customs have originated for St. Thomas Day, including the "barring out" of the schoolmaster by his pupils in order to have a holiday and/or tasty treats, a popular southern tradition, mentioned in Philip Vickers Fithian's *Journal and Letters of: A Plantation Tutor of the Old Dominion, 1773-1774,* Hunter Dickinson Farish, editor, Charlottesville, Virginia: The University Press of Virginia, 1983. In Germany it was a time for "forecasting the future" by young women employing certain devices for determining their future husbands (Clement Miles, *Christmas Customs and Traditions* (New York: Dover, 1976. Reprint of *Christmas in Ritual and Tradition, Christian and Pagan*, T. Fisher Unwin, 1912, 225). In England it was an occasion for poor people to beg for money and foodstuffs in return for which they might present "a sprig of holly or mistletoe" (Ibid, 226).

164. Margaret McCuiston, *Christmas Recollections of Margaret McCuiston* (Winston-Salem, NC: John Blair, 1980) 18-19.

165. Richmond E. Myers, *Christmas Traditions* (Bethlehem, PA: Acorn Graphics of Oaks Printing Co., 1985) 69.

166. The booklet by Fries has an accompanying gift card with her signature. It is in the Christmas Box at the Moravian Archives, Winston-Salem, NC.

167. William C. Reichel wrote in *A History of the Moravian Seminary for Young Ladies* (Philadelphia: J.B. Lippincott & Co., 1858, 18) that "very high literary attainments were not the principal object" in the school. "It was to develop the intellect by patient and laborious teaching, to discipline the mind to habits of reflection and self-control, to render knowledge subservient to usefulness in society, and *the religion of the heart the crown of all*" [author's emphasis]. This heart religion was the direct communion with the Creator in what was often described as a "child like faith." That direct and personal communication was self-enabling in helping one to achieve the most potential with one's God-given talents.

168. Cherokee Mission Papers, 25 January 1804, Folder #4, Box M-411, Springplace Correspondence, 1804-1805, letter to Gotthold Reichel in Salem.

169. *The Moravian*, 26 December 1856.

Chapter 4 Sidebar Endnotes

i. Tanya Gulevich, *Encyclopedia of Christmas* (Detroit, Michigan: Omnigraphics, 2000) 353-359.

ii. *Harper's New Monthly Magazine*, vol. 27, July and August, 1863 (New York: Harper & Brothers, 1863) 306-307.

iii. Ibid, 309.

iv. Gerry Bowler, *The World Encyclopedia of Christmas* (Toronto: McClelland & Stewart, 2000) 92.

v. Also spelled "Calends," the first day of each month in the ancient Roman calendar. The Kalends of January was a time of celebration for the New Year.

vi. Jock Elliott, *Inventing Christmas: How Our Holiday Came to Be* (New York: Harry Abrams, 2001) 69.

vii. Moravian Archives, MS 16:2, Mc 81 XIII, Winston-Salem, NC.

viii. *Early American Life Christmas*, Vol. XXXVII, 2006 (Shaker Heights, Ohio: Firelands Media Group LLC., 2006). "A Festive Fancy," Peter F. Stevens, 18.

ix. Robert Brenner, *Christmas Revisited*, (West Chester, PA: Schiffer), 58.

x. *The Academy*, vol. 3, no. 29, 36.

xi. Ibid, vol. 7, no. 52, January 1885, 51.

xii. *People's Press*, 9 December 1886.

xiii. Online: *History of St. Nicholas Magazine:* http://en.wikipedia.org/wiki/st.nicholas magazine. Accessed: January 13, 2007.

xiv. *St. Nicholas*, vol. IX, 1882, 183 and 264.

Chapter 5: Food and Beverages

1. Alfred L. Shoemaker, *Christmas in Pennsylvania: A Folk-Cultural Study* (Kutztown, PA: Pennsylvania Folklife Society, 1959; Mechanicsburg, PA: Stackpole Books, 1999) xiv.

2. Ibid, referring to a Christmas dinner invitation, 1786.

3. Joe Gray Taylor, *Eating, Drinking, and Visiting in the South: An Informal History* (Baton Rouge, LA: Louisiana State University, 1982) 8.

4. Mrs. Margaret Hunter Hall, *The Aristocratic Journey: Being the Outspoken Letters of Mrs. Basil Hall Written during a Fourteen Months' Sojourn in America 1827-1828*, Una Pope-Hennessy, ed. (New York: G. P. Putnam's Sons, 1931) 208-209. Thanks to Chuck LeCount, Historic Brattonsville, South Carolina, for bringing this quote to my attention.

5. Ibid, 81.

6. Shoemaker, 108. See William Woys Weaver, *Sauerkraut Yankees: Pennsylvania German Foods & Foodways* (Philadelphia: University of Pennsylvania Press, 1983; Mechanicsburg, PA: reprinted by Stackpole Books, 2002)170-172, for traditional recipes for making sauerkraut.

7. George F. Bahnson Diary, 10 December 1835, 456.

8. Dorcas Co-Workers of the Salem Home, compilers. *Pages from Old Salem Cook Books* (Winston-Salem, NC: Dorcas Service League, 1947 [a reprint from 1931]).

9. Salem College Library, Rare books, VF - 1839.

10. Peter Wolle Diaries, 1809-1821, 28 October 1814, 39.

11. Springplace Correspondence, M 411:5:4, 2, 23 March 1806.

12. George F. Bahnson Diary, 1 January 1836, 684-685..

13. Ibid, 12 June 1834, 17.

14. Adelaide L. Fries, *Records of the Moravians in North Carolina*, vol. 1 (Raleigh: State Department of Archives and History, reprinted 1968) 139.

15. Audrey Hume, *Food* (Williamsburg, VA: Colonial Williamsburg Foundation, 1978) 20.

16. Sandra Oliver, ed., *Food History News* (Isleboro, ME: Autumn, 1991) 1- 4.

17. George F. Bahnson Diary, 1 July 1834, 103.

18. Hume, 16, referring to comments of Nicholas Cresswell.

19. Sarah Bahnson Chapman, ed., *Bright and Gloomy Days: The Civil War Correspondence of Captain Charles Frederic Bahnson, A Moravian Confederate* (Knoxville: University of Tennessee Press, 2003) 103.

20. Dorcas Co-Workers of the Salem Home, 37.

21. George F. Bahnson Diary, 21 November 1834, 211. For a similar "fresh meat walk," a historical fiction children's book entitled *The Great Turkey Walk* by Kathleen Karr (New York: Farrar, Straus & Giroux, 1998) describes a 900-mile turkey walk with 1,000 turkeys from Missouri to Colorado in 1860, initiated by a fifteen-year-old boy named Simon.

22. Peter Wolle Diary, 2 Januay 1816, 124.

23. Ibid, 17 January 1816, 138.

24. Second to the lead teacher

25. Fries, *Records*, vol.7, 3341.

26. *Journal of Johann Heinrich Leinbach*, unpublished, Old Salem Museums & Gardens Library, 54 or 66, depending on type-script.

27. Adelaide L. Fries and Douglas LeTell Rights, *Records of the Moravians in North Carolina*, vol. 8 (Raleigh: State Department of Archives and History, 1954) 4109.

28. George F. Bahnson Diary, 14 December 1836, 975.

29. Dorcas Co-Workers, 66.

30. George F. Bahnson Diary, 11 December 1834, 228.

31. Fries and Rights, *Records*, 4151, extracts from the Diary of Bethania, 11 December 1834.

32. Shoemaker, 15.

33. Weaver, 42.

34. Weaver, 43.

35. Ibid, 46-47.

36. Ibid.

37. Salem Board Minutes, 2 February 1808, from *Aufseher Collegium*. Items to be sold in the shop, as listed by Br. Kramsch were given under the date of February 1. Among the many goods were hog bristles (Fries, *Records*, vol. 6 2926).

38. Hume, 12.

39. Salem Tavern Inventory, 1791, Moravian Archives, Winston-Salem, NC.

40. Hume, 95.

41. *William and Mary Quarterly*, Excerpts from the Diary of Mrs. Nathan Blodget, 1796, 3rd series, vol. III, no. 2 (April, 1946) 288.

42. Peter Wolle Diary, 12 September 1816, 230.

43. Ibid., 20 September, 1816, 232.

44. Fries, *Records*, vol. 1, 163.

45. Passenger pigeons were common during this period before killed to extinction. Note the following reference to such occurrences near Salem in 1760: "In December, immense quantities of wild pigeons made their appearance and roosted near by for nearly a month. When together, at night, they covered only a small tract of woods, but were clustered so thick upon the trees as to break down the largest limbs by their weight The noise made by them in coming to their camp at night, as well as the fluttering, &c. during the night, and thus breaking up in the morning, was heard at a considerable distance. The spot was marked for many years." Rev. Levin T. Reichel, *The Moravians in North Carolina: An Authentic History* (Salem, North Carolina: O. A. Keehln and Philadelphia: J. B. Lippincott and Co, 1857) 200-201.

46. Amelia Simmons, *American Cookery* (Hartford, Connecticut, 1796; New York: facsimile by Dover, 1984; reprinted, Bedford, MA: Applewood Books, 1996).

47. Kay Moss and Kathryn Hoffman, *The Backcountry Housewife* (Gastonia, NC: Schiele Museum, 1994) 37.

48. Simmons, 23.

49. Peter Wolle Diary, 15 October 1816, 244.

50. George Bahnson mentioned the abundance of watermelons referring to "one large fellow" weighing 25 to 30 pounds; George F. Bahnson Diary, 28 Aug. 1834, 187.

51. Peter Wolle Diary, 13 November 1816, 254.

52. *Journal of Johann Heinrich Leinbach*, unpublished, Old Salem Museums & Gardens Library, June 8, 1830, 9. Dewberries resemble blackberries and are related, but they grow on a trailing bramble.

53. Hume, 30

54. Libbey Hodges Oliver and Mary Miley Theobold, *Four Centuries of Virginia Christmas* (Richmond, Virginia: Dietz Press, 2000) 2.

55. Anna Paulina Schober, Recipe Book, January 1805, collection of Old Salem Museums & Gardens.

56. George F. Bahnson Diary, 26 December 26, 1836, 838.

57. Ibid.

58. Richard J. Hooker, *Food and Drink in America: A History* (Indianapolis: Bobbs-Merrill, 1981) 157.

59. George F. Bahnson Diary, 25 December, 1834, 236.

60. Hunter Dickinson Farish, ed., *Journal and Letters of Philip Vickers Fithian, A Plantation Tutor of the Old Dominion, 1773-1774* (Charlottesville, Virginia: The University Press of Virginia, 1983) 52.

61. George F. Bahnson Diary, 1 January, 1835, 355.

62. Ibid, 14 January 1835, 366.,

63. Ibid, 3 December 1834, 224.

64. Ibid, 31 December 1836, 845.

65. Ibid, 25 November 1835, 445.

66. Ibid, 26 November 1835, 447.

67. Ibid.

68. An epergne, of French derivation, is "an ornamental stand or dish for holding fruit, flowers, etc., used as a centerpiece" (*Random House Webster's College Dictionary*). These centerpieces were often imported from England, of Sheffield plate with cut glass dishes, which held the sweetmeats, nuts, fruits, tarts, and other dainties so popular for dessert.

69. *NC Historical Review*, vol. XXI, no. 4 (October 1944) 375.

70. Joanna B. Young, *Christmas in Williamsburg*, The Colonial Williamsburg Foundation (New York: Holt, Rinehart and Winston, Inc., 1970) 43.

71. Fries, *Records*, vol. I, 160.

72. Fries, *Records*, vol. 2, 697.

73. Ibid., 899.

74. Ibid

75. Fries, *Records*, vol. 4 , 1545.

76. Ibid., 1576.

77. Mary Fries Patterson, 26 December 1864. Fries & Shaffner Papers, #4046, Series B: 1864, Southern Historical Collection, Wilson Library, University of North Carolina, Chapel Hill, North Carolina.

78. *Journal of a Tour to NC by William Attmore*, 1787, ed. Lida Tunstall Rodman (Chapel Hill, North Carolina: The University of North Carolina, 1922) 41. Published under the direction of The North Carolina Historical Society, The James Sprunt Historical Publications, vol. 17, no. 2.

79. John Amos Comenius, *The School of Infancy*, Ernest M. Eller, ed. (Chapel Hill: University of North Carolina Press, 1956) 116.

80. Ibid.

81. Ibid, 116.

82. Penelope Niven, *Old Salem: The Official Guidebook* (Winston-Salem: Old Salem, 2004) 74.

83. Michael Pollan, *Botany of Desire: A Plant's-Eye View of the World* (New York: Random House, 2001) 21.

84. The diary of Susannah Kramsch on 22 September 1819 noted, "Crissy fixed vinegar from cyder."

85. W.J. Rorabaugh, *The Alcoholic Republic: An American Tradition* (New York: Oxford University Press, 1979) 9.

86. Ibid, 113.

87. Old Salem Museums & Gardens has Hewes Crab and another early fine dessert apple called Esopus Spitzemberg planted in the museums' Nightwatchman's Orchard.

88. Pollan, 22.

89. Ibid.

90. Peter J. Hatch, *The Fruits and Fruit Trees of Monticello* (Charlottesville: University of Virginia Press, 1998) 61.

91. Rorabaugh, 111.

92. George F. Bahnson Diary, 22 November 1835, 441.

93. Simmons, 31.

94. Pollan, 17.

95. Ibid, 20.

96. Dorcas Co-Workers of the Salem Home, 35.

97. Creighton Lee Calhoun, Jr., *Old Southern Apples* (Blacksburg, VA: McDonald and Woodward, 1995) 27.

98. Peter Wolle Diary, 9 January 1816, 131.

99. Charles Vogler, ed., *Descendants of Philipp Christoph Vogler, Books I and II* (Camden, ME: Penobscot Press for Philip Christoph Vogler Memorial, Inc., 1994) 60.

100. Calhoun, 27.

101. Susannah Kramsch Diary, 1819-1823, 26 July 1819.

102. Calhoun, 28.

103. Fries, *Records*, vol. 5, 31 July 1789, 2268.

104. Ibid.

105. Calhoun, 2.

106. Maguelonne Toussaint-Samat, translated by Anthea Bell, *History of Food* (New York: Barnes & Noble, 1998) 626.

107. Hatch, 59-60.

108. Ibid, 60.

109. The name "pippin" derives from apples from trees originally raised from a pip or seed, according to Hatch, *The Fruits and Fruit Trees of Monticello,* 61. *Merriam-Webster's Collegiate Dictionary* defines "pippin" as "a crisp tart apple having usually yellow or greenish-yellow skin strongly flushed with red and used especially for cooking."

110. Pollan (47), Calhoun (41-294), and a North Carolina "apple sleuth" named Tom Brown have provided the colorful names of these apples. See the books of Pollan and Calhoun for even more. Tom Brown from Clemmons, North Carolina, a dedicated apple detective, broadcasts new finds in public locations like general stores, folk fests, and local papers. He tells of locating a hard, purple, elongated apple, which he began to carry around to country stores, and sure enough, someone said, "Oh, yes, that's a Plum Apple!"

111. George F. Bahnson Diary, 2 October 1835.

112. Calhoun, 183.

113. Minnie J. Smith, *Records of the Moravians in North Carolina*, vol. 9 (Raleigh: State Department of Archives and History, 1964) 4870. Calhoun describes this variety as "the quintessential southern apple. . . versatile for eating, cooking, drying, and cider" (Calhoun, 55).

114. Chapman, 24 December 1862, 45.

115. An early Salem receipt calls for four pounds of sugar and no spices (Manuscript Cookbook, R706:5C, Moravian Archives, Winston-Salem, North Carolina).

116. Peter Wolle Diary, 24 December 1816, 267.

117. Ibid, 6 July 1815, 96. Bishop Comenius himself was not opposed to discipline, but counseled parents that the rod of correction and the words of reproof will produce wisdom, for "He who attains to manhood without discipline becomes old without virtue" (*School of Infancy*, 103).

118. George F. Bahnson Diary, 18 December 1835, 669.

119. Phebe Earle Gibbons, *Pennsylvania Dutch & Other Essays* (Philadelphia: J.B. Lippercott Co., 1882) 196.

120. Fanny Fern, *Little Ferns for Fanny's Little Friends* (Auburn, NY: Derby & Miller, 1854) 296.

121. Salem College Library, VF - 1839.

122. *Wachovia Moravian*, January 1904.

123. Peter Wolle Diary, 25 September 1816, 234.

124. Ibid, 16 October 1816, 244.

125. Ibid, 20 December 1818, 346.

126. Francis Henry Fries, *The History of the Fries Family A.D. 810-1930*, Old Salem Museums & Gardens Research Center, 196.

127. MESDA, Fries vertical file.

128. "Moravian Christmas," 20 December 1936, *Winston-Salem Journal and Sentinel*.

129. Chapman, 39.

130. Chapman, 44-45.

131. George F. Bahnson Diary, 17 December 1834, 337.

132. Ibid, 21 December 1835, 672.

133. Kramsch Diary, 15 December 1820.

134. George F. Bahnson Diary, 18 December 1834, 669.

135. Birdie Goslen Diary, Moravian Archives, Winston-Salem, NC.

136. MESDA files, Vogler twentieth-century memoir.

137. Dorcas Co-Workers of the Salem Home, Introduction.

138. George F. Bahnson Diary, 21 December 1834, 340.

139. A local expert and former teacher of a class at Old Salem on making these cookies cautions that the dough be kept in a cool place, but not in the refrigerator, and that to achieve such thinness only a small quantity be rolled out at a time on a floured cloth-covered board (Jackie Beck, telephone conversation, 19 September 2005).

140. Old Salem Museums & Gardens, "Winkler Bakery Recipe Postcards." Online: http//old salem.org (accessed 11 December 2006). More local Christmas cake receipts may be found in editor Emily-Sarah Lineback's book, *Preserving the Past: Salem Moravians' Receipts & Rituals* (Boonville, NC: Carolina Avenue Press, 2003) 73-75.

141. Old Salem Museums & Gardens interpretive materials, Christmas, 2000, documented by Carol Hall.

142. Dorcas Co-Workers of the Salem Home, 85.

143. Gibbons, 196.

144. The Old Salem Domestic Skills Program published Senseman's collection, edited by Carol Hall: *L. L. Senseman, Salem, NC, 1844-1854, Receipts* (Winston-Salem, NC: Old Salem, Inc., 1988)

145. Hamilton, *Records of the Moravians in North Carolina*, vol. 10, 5641. Senseman, pastor at Friedberg and Hope, wrote on November 9, 1851, "Today we were surprised by a call to New Salem, Illinois. I opened the Sunday School with a sense of sadness." After a laborious journey beginning on December 4 of that year, they reached their destination in January. His wife Louisa and their new infant daughter died on August 15, 1854 in New Salem. The name of the town was changed to West Salem in 1854 because another "New Salem" already existed in Illinois (Dr. C. Daniel Crews and Richard W. Starbuck, *With Courage for the Future: The Story of the Moravian Church, Southern Province* [Winston-Salem, NC: Moravian Church in America, Southern Province, 2002], 286, note 2).

146. Reminiscences of Salem Female Academy, Anna L. Ogburn, Lombardy Grove, Mecklenburg, Va., Salem College Library.

147. Peter Wolle Diary, 23 December 1816, 267.

148. Ibid.

149. Ibid, 14 December 1816, 263.

150. Ibid, 5 January 1817, 278.

151. Ibid, 8 January 1820, 370.

152. *People's Press*, Hall & Hall advertisement, 15 October 1858.

153. *People's Press*, Charles Winkler advertisement, 22 December 1871.

154. Recipes, R 706.10, Moravian Archives, Winston-Salem, North Carolina.

155. *People's Press*, F. W. Meller advertisement, 3 December 1874.

156. Ibid, 27 November 1879.

157. Peter Wolle Diary, 4 July 1816, 213.

158. George F. Bahnson Diary, 13 September, 1835, 560.

159. Ibid, 7 December 1837, 1301.

160. Ibid, 2 May 1836, 576.

161. *The Moravian*, vol. IV, no. 50, 15 December 1859, 397.

162. Senseman, n.p.

163. *The Moravian*, vol. VIII, no. 18, 30 April 1863.

164. Crews and Starbuck, footnote 1, 165.

165. Smith, *Records*, vol. 9, 4817.

166. Ibid, 4928.

167. Fries, *Records*, vol. 1, 79.

168. Vernon H. Nelson, editor, *The Bethlehem Diary*, vol. II (Bethlehem: The Moravian Archives, 2001) 390.

169. Fries, *Records*, vol. 1, 409.

170. Fries, *Records*, vol. 5, 2281.

171. Crews and Starbuck, footnote 1, 165.

172. Ibid.

173. Crews and Starbuck, 165.

174. Cherokee Mission Papers, Folder 4, Springplace Letters, 1804-1805, 27 January 1805, Gottlieb Byhan to Gotthold Reichel, Moravian Archives, Winston-Salem, NC.

175. Cherokee Mission Papers, Folder 6: 3, 17 October, 1808.

176. Ibid.

177. Fries, *Records*, vol. 7, 3093.

178. Ibid, 3482.

179. George F. Bahnson Diary, 24 December 1836, 837.

180. Ibid, 31 January 1836, 498.

181. Kenneth G. Hamilton, *Records of the Moravians in North Carolina*, vol. 10 (Raleigh: State Department of Archives and History, 1966) 5520.

182. Smith, *Records*, vol, 9, 4846.

183. Ibid, 5574.

184. Recipes, R 706.5, Moravian Archives, Winston-Salem, North Carolina.

185. Ibid.

186. *Guide Book of N.W. North Carolina . . . Containing Historical Sketches of the Moravians in NC, A Description of the Country and Its Industrial Pursuits* (Salem, NC: L.Y. and E.T. Blum, Printers, 1878) 21.

187. Crews, *Records*, vol. 13, 24 December 1876.

188. Christmas Folder, #6, Moravian Archives, Winston-Salem, NC.

189. Travel Journal of Lisetta Vogler, "Lisetta's Journey," *The Three Forks of Muddy Creek*, vol. 7: 35.

190. Adelaide L. Fries and Douglas LeTell Rights, *Records of the Moravians in North Carolina*, vol. 8 (Raleigh: State Department of Archives and History, 1954) 4196.

191. George F. Bahnson Diary, 28 December, 1836, 840.

192. Ibid, 9 July 1834, 98.

193. *Salem Academy and College Through the Years* (Winston-Salem, NC: Salem College Alumnae Association, 1951) 5.

194. Gibbons, 196.

195. George F. Bahnson Diary, 11 July 1834.

196. Ibid, 196-97.

197. Unsigned typed manuscript entitled "The Francis L. Fries Home," Fries Files, Old Salem Museums & Gardens Research Center.

198. John Adam Friebele, *Diary of the Small Negro Congregation In and Around Salem*, trans. Elizabeth Marx, Book III, 12, Moravian Archives, Winston-Salem, NC.

199. Ibid, 36.

200. Ibid, Book VI, 32.

201. *S.C. Historical Magazine* (July, 1986) 152-153.

202. Diary of Mary Fries Patterson, 26 December 1864.

203. Damon Lee Fowler, ed. *Dining at Monticello* (Monticello, Virginia: Thomas Jefferson Foundation, Inc., 2005) 49.

204. Fries and Rights, *Records*, "The Negro Church," vol. 8, 25 August 1835, 4196.

205. Shoemaker, 17.

206. Ibid.

207. *The Moravian*, vol. IX, no. 52, 22 December 1864, 206.

208. C. Daniel Crews, *Mountain Gospel* (Winston-Salem, NC: Moravian Archives, 1993) 33.

209. Harnett Kane, *The Southern Christmas Book* (New York: David McKay, 1958) 192.

210. Shoemaker, 15.

211. Crews, *Records*, vol. 13, 6981.

212. *The Moravian*, vol. 14, no. 1, 7 January 1869.

213. *The Wachovia Moravian*, December 1895.

214. George F. Bahnson Diary, 2 January 1835, 359.

Chapter 5 Sidebar Endnotes

i. Letter from Alexander Campbell McIntosh of Alexander County to his wife, December 1848, #1212, McIntosh Family Letters, 1848-1849, Southern Historical Collection, Manuscripts Department, Wilson Library, University of North Carolina, Chapel Hill, North Carolina.

ii. Syllabub is milk or cream usually mixed with warm alcohol of some kind, sweetened and spiced as a drink but also sometimes thickened with gelatin to be served as a dessert. Some say syllabub is the forerunner of the popular southern eggnog. A 1931 Salem cookbook lists "Sillabub" ingredients of flavored and sweetened whipped milk mixed with frothed whites of eggs (Dorcas Co-Workers of the Salem Home, 94).

iii. Ibid.

iv. *Journal of a Tour to NC by William Attmore*, 1787, ed. Lida Tunstall Rodman (Chapel Hill, North Carolina: The University of North Carolina, 1922) 43. Published under the direction of The North Carolina Historical Society: The James Sprunt Historical Publications, vol. 17, no. 2.

v. Peter Wolle Diary, 26 May 1816, 202.

vi. Manuscript Cookbook, Old Salem Museums & Gardens Research Center.

vii. The visitor to MESDA may see several multi-handled communal drinking cups or "tygs" for posset in the early period rooms.

viii. Susannah Kramsch Diary, 13 December 1821, Moravian Archives, Winston-Salem, North Carolina.

ix. Josiah Smith's Diary, 1780-1781, The *South Carolina Historical and Genealogical Magazine*, vol. XXXIII, no. 2 April 1932 (Baltimore: The Williams & Wilkins Co.) 192.

x. Journal of Johann Heinrich Leinbach, 1830-1843, unpublished, Old Salem Museums & Gardens Research Center, 12 or 14, depending on typescript.

xi. *The Moravian*, vol. VIII, no. 18, 30 April 1863. From section on local news of Bethlehem.

xii. Winkler Bakery today in Old Salem Museums & Gardens sells a pack of recipe postcards of the popular Moravian foods such as sugarcake, gingerbread, lovefeast buns, molasses cookies, pumpkin muffins, chicken pie, white bread and honey wheat bread. Currently the bakers include yeast and mashed potatoes in the ingredients for their sugarcake. Cookbook editor Lineback included a local [Vogler] Sugar Cake with mashed potatoes in *Preserving the Past*. Emily-Sarah Lineback, ed. *Preserving the Past: Salem Moravians' Receipts & Rituals* (Boonville, North Carolina: Carolina Avenue Press, 2003) 51. Three of the four recipes for sugar cake in the 1931 Salem cookbook call for mashed potatoes (Dorcas Co-Workers of the Salem Home, 83-84). An early yeast was made from boiled potatoes with some brown sugar or from hops, water, rye flour, sugar, and eggs (Lineback, 42).

xiii. Nannie Haskins Williams Diary 1869-1890, Tennessee, Kentucky, vol. 1, #3179, Southern Historical Collection, Wilson Library, UNC, Chapel Hill, North Carolina.

xiv. *Washington, George, The Diaries of. 1771-1785*, vol. II, 1785, John C. Fitzpatrick, ed. (Boston and New York: Houghton Mifflin Co., 1925) 458.

xv. Rowena McClinton, *The Moravian Mission among the Cherokees at Springplace, Georgia*. Dissertation thesis Ph.D. (Lexington, Kentucky: University of Kentucky, 1996) 9 December, 358.

xvi George F. Bahnson Diary, 23 December 1836.

xvii John Guilds, *The Writings of William Gilmore Simms*, Vol. V, "Maize in Milk" (Columbia: University of South Carolina Press, 1974) 315.

xviii. Page 95.

Chapter 6: Music and Services

1. C. Daniel Crews and Lisa D. Bailey, *Records of the Moravians in North Carolina*, 1867-1876, vol. 13 (Raleigh: North Carolina Department of History and Archives, 2006) Friedberg Diary, 7225.

2. *The Liturgy and Hymns of the American Province of the Unitas Fratrum or The Moravian Church* (Bethlehem: Moravian Publication Office, 1895) Preface, 3.

3. Craig Atwood and Peter Vogt, eds., *The Distinctiveness of Moravian Culture*, Nola Reed Knouse, "Gott sah zu seiner Zeit," A Moravian Chorale from the 1544 *Gesangbuch der Bruder in Behemen und Merherrn* (Nazareth, PA: Moravian Historical Society, 2003) 9.

4. Robert Doares, "Colonial Church Christmases," *Colonial Williamsburg Journal of the Foundation* (Christmas edition, 2005) 28-30.

5. George F. Bahnson Diary, 17 August 1834, 178.

6. *Christianity Today* Online: http://www.christianitytoday.com/leaders/newsletter/2005/cln51212.html. Accessed January 3, 2007.

7. Ibid.

8. Fries, *Records of the Moravians in North Carolina*, vol. 1 (Raleigh, NC: State Department of Archives and History, 1968), 79.

9. Ibid, 86.

10. Ibid.

11. Ibid, 96.

12. Ibid, 134, Bethabara, 19 July 1755.

13. Ibid.

14. William C. Reichel, *A History of the Moravian Seminary for Young Ladies* (Philadelphia: J.B. Lippincott & Co., 1858) 38.

15. Fries, *Records*, vol. 1, 15 November 1755, 148.

16. Ibid, 26 August 1755, 172.

17. Ibid, vol. 3, 1438.

18. Ibid, vol. 1, 241.

19. Ibid, vol. 1, 369.

20. Ibid, 30 Aug. 1768, 374.

21. Ibid, 17 May, 1769, 391.

22. Hans T. David, *Musical Life in the Pennsylvania Settlements of the Unitas Fratrum* (Winston-Salem, NC: Moravian Music Foundation Publications, no. 6, 1959) 13.

23. Fries, *Records*, vol. 2, 620.

24. Ibid, vol. 5, 2324.

25. Ibid, 2325.

26. David, 12.

27. Ibid, 13.

28. Donald M. McCorkle, "The Collegium Musicum Salem: Its Music, Musicians and Importance" (Winston-Salem, NC: The Moravian Music Foundation, October 1956, 487; Reprinted from *The North Carolina Historical Review*, vol. XXXIII, no. 4, October 1956: 487).

29. Peter Wolle Diary, 6 October 1816, 240.

30. Ibid, 13 October 1816, 243.

31. Ibid.

32. Ibid, 5 January 1820, 369.

33. Ibid, 3 January 1818, 323.

34. Ibid, 2 January 1815, 58.

35. Ibid.

36. Ibid, 2 January 1816, 125; 4 January 1816, 127.

37. Fries, *Records*, vol. 5, 2206.

38. Ibid, 2227.

39. *Encyclopaedia Britannica*, 978.

40. Fries, *Records*, vol. 5, 2251.

41. Griffin, Frances, *Less Time for Meddling: A History of Salem Academy and College, 1772-1866* (Winston-Salem, NC: John F. Blair, Publisher, 1979) 29.

42. Fries, *Records*, vol. 6, 2744.

43. Griffin, 105.

44. Ibid, 199.

45. Ibid, 256.

46. Peter Wolle Diary, 22 December 1816, 266.

47. Ibid, 267.

48. Ibid, 24 December 1816, 268.

49. Ibid, 25 December 1816, 268.

50. Ibid, 1 January 1817, 276.

51. Ibid, 1 January 1818, 321.

52. "Moravian Christmas," *Journal and Sentinel*, Winston-Salem, NC, Sunday, 20 December 20, 1936. Found in Folder 6, Q645:6: Moravian Christmas in Salem, Moravian Archives, Winston-Salem, NC.

53. Fries, *Records*, vol. 1, 150.

54. Adelaide Fries, *Customs and Practices of the Moravian Church* (Bethlehem, PA: Interprovincial Board of Communication, Moravian Church in North America, 2003) 44.

55. *The Liturgy and Hymns of the Unitas Fratrum*, preface, iv.

56. Fries, *Records*, vol. 5, 2004.

57. Ibid, 2018, n. 38.

58. Ibid, 2184, 24 May 1787.

59. David, 8.

60. From transcription of items from the *Bethlehem Diary*, William Schwarze, 24 December 1742, 9. For text in both German and English of the thirty-seven stanzas, see Hamilton, *The Bethlehem Diary*, vol. 1, 217-228.

61. Adelaide Fries, "Moravian Customs Our Inheritance" (Winston-Salem, NC: Salem Academy Library, 1936) 18.

62. Ibid. Fries got the date wrong, it seems. It has been corrected here to 1836.

63. Ibid.

64. James Boeringer, *Morning Star* (Cranbury, NJ: Associated University Presses, 1986) 18.

65. Ibid.

66. Rt. Rev. Edward Rondthaler, D.D., LL.D, *The Memorabilia of Fifty Years, 1877 to 1927* (Raleigh, NC: Edwards & Broughton Co., 1928) 252.

67. Cherokee Mission Papers, Folder #5, 49, Box M-411, 1806-1807, Moravian Archives, Winston-Salem, NC.

68. Fries, *Records*, vol. 1, 2020.

69. Fries, "Moravian Customs," 8-9.

70. Fries, *Records*, vol. 1, 202.

71. Schwarze, *Moravian Missions Among Southern Indian Tribes*, 87.

72. Karsten Petersen Memory Book, 1807-1813, Springplace, Georgia. Blue paper cover with paper label which says: "Andenken, von Springplace, fur Br. Petersen," Old Salem negative no. S-7196. The book contains twelve watercolors with verses, prayers, etc., written by other people working and living at Springplace. Collection of Old Salem Museums & Gardens.

73. Cherokee Mission Correspondence, Folder # 5, 48-49, Box M-411, 1806-1807, Moravian Archives, 4 January 1807 to Christian Lewis Benzien.

74. Ibid.

75. *Splendid Service: The Restoration of David Tannenberg's Home Moravian Church Organ*, see Paula Locklair's essay, "...one of the finest instruments I have made... : The Home Moravian Church Organ," (Winston-Salem, NC: Old Salem, 2004), 24.

76. Ibid, 21.

77. Ibid, 24.

78. Fries, *Records*, vol. 6, 2629, 18 June 1799. To illustrate the ability of rats to create havoc, in 1755 the shoemaker in Bethabara had to take "down his house to kill the rats, which have done much damage. Many were found." Since it was a log house they were able to lay them up again by the next day (Fries, *Records*, vol. I, "Diary of the Brethren and Sisters in the Wachau," 148).

79. *Splendid Service: The Restoration of David Tannenberg's Home Moravian Church Organ*, see Foreword by George Taylor and John Boody (Winston-Salem, NC: Old Salem, 2004), vii.

80. Fries, *Records*, vol. 6, 2846.

81. Fries, "Moravian Customs," 26.

82. Peter Wolle Diary, 2 January 1818, 322.

83. Vernon H. Nelson, editor. Kenneth G. Hamilton and Lothar Madeheim, translators, *The Bethlehem Diary, vol. 2, January 1, 1744 - May 31, 1745* (Bethlehem, PA: The Moravian Archives) 382.

84. Ibid, glossary, vol. 2, 382.

85. Ibid.

86. Peter Wolle Diary, 10 December 1816, 263.

87. "Lamb" was a "common Moravian term for Jesus" and often included a diminutive such as "dear" or "little" (Nelson, vol. 2, 388). The Moravian seal, which dates at least from the sixteenth century and probably earlier, features the Lamb of God at its center with a cross on a staff. "From the staff hangs the banner of victory." The inscription in Latin (*Vicit agnus oster, eum Sequamur*) means "Our Lamb has conquered, let us follow Him." The Moravian motto is "In essentials, unity; in nonessentials, liberty; in all things, love." It dates probably from the sixteenth century, was dormant for several centuries, and began to appear again in the 1850s (Adelaide Fries, *Customs and Practices of the Moravian Church*, 22-23).

88. Nelson, vol. 2, 381.

89. Ibid, 395.

90. Ibid, 381.

91. Fries, *Records*, vol. 6, 2715.

92. Nelson, vol. 2, 393.

93. Fries, *Records*, vol. 4, 1579.

94. Fries, *Records*, vol. 5, Memorabilia, 1780, 1515.

95. Nelson, vol. 2, 389.

96. Vangie Roby Sweitzer, *Christmas in Bethlehem: A Moravian Heritage* (Bethlehem, Pennsylvania: Central Moravian Church, 2000) 23.

97. James Henry, *Sketches of Moravian Life and Character* (Philadelphia: J.B. Lippincott, 1859) 155.

98. Fries, *Records*, vol 5, 2112.

99. C. Daniel Crews, *Records*, vol. 13, 24 December 1870, 6935.

100. Nelson, vol. 2, 389.

101. Nelson, *The Bethlehem Diary*, 206, 204

102. Fries, *Records*, vol. 1, 201.

103. Nelson, 188.

104. Ibid, 29 January 1745, 208.

105. Fries, *Moravian Customs*, 24.

106. Peter Wolle Diary, 18 December 1814, 5.

107. Christmas, 1909 Source, no other identification.

108. Peter Wolle Diary, 16 December 1816, 264.

109. Ibid, 22 December 1816, 266.

110. Nelson, vol. 2, 389-90.

111. Ibid, vol. 2, 321.

112. David, 13.

113. Nelson, vol. 2, 321.

114. C. Daniel Crews and Richard Starbuck, *With Courage for the Future* (Winston-Salem, North Carolina: Moravian Church in America, Southern Province, 2002) 141-142.

115. George F. Bahnson Diary, 1 February 1835, 257.

116. Originally printed in *The Academy, A Monthly Journal of Salem Academy*, first published in 1879.

117. Ibid.

118. Margaret Blair McCuiston, *John Fries Blair, "Recollections of My Brother"* (Chapel Hill: North Caroliniana Society, Inc., 1983) 12.

119. Crews, *Records*, vol. 13, Salem Diary, 25 December 1868.

120. Griffin, 92.

121. George F. Bahnson Diary, 1 January 1835, 356-357.

122. A typed script, no origin, date, or location given, but attributed to Frances Griffin. Griffin included in *Less Time for Meddling* a description of this dialogue, pages 92-94.

123. Eliza Vierling Kremer, Reminiscences, Salem College Library. Also, Fries and Rights, *Records*, vol. 8, 3790-3791.

124. Letterbook, 1819, Lenoir papers, Southern Historical Collection, Wilson Library, Chapel Hill, NC.

125. Ibid.

126. Miranda Miller Scarborough, October 1890, Rare Book Room, Salem College Library.

127. Crews, *Records*, vol. 13, 26 December 1868, 6819.

128. Ibid, 25 December 1871, 6947.

129. Springplace Correspondence, Gambold to Van Vleck, 4 January 1816.

130. Fries, *Moravian Customs*, four Lectures delivered before the Woman's Auxiliary of the Home Moravian Church, 1936, 24.

131. Ibid.

132. Paul S. Larson, *An American Musical Dynasty: A Biography of the Wolle Family of Bethlehem, Pennsylvania* (Bethlehem, PA: Lehigh University Press, 2002) 62.

133. Ibid.

134. Old Salem Museums & Gardens Christmas Interpretive Material, 2002.

135. Letter, 1857, J.A. Freibele to "Dear Christian Friends," Moravian Archives, Winston-Salem, NC.

136. John Adam Friebele, *Diary of the Small Negro Congregation In and Around Salem*, trans. Elizabeth Marx, Book IV, 25, Moravian Archives, Winston-Salem, NC.

137. "Negro Project Around Salem," Book V, 19 March 1843, 4, 4734. Unpublished typescript, Old Salem Museums & Gardens.

138. *Records*, 28 December 1881, unpublished, Moravian Archives, Winston-Salem, North Carolina.

139. F. H. Fries, *The History of the Fries Family A.D. 810-1930*, manuscript at Old Salem Museums & Gardens Research Center, 193-94 .

140. The Candle Tea program, distributed to visitors, December 2005, prepared by the Committee.

141. Gene Capps, Christmas Interpretative material 2002, Old Salem Museums & Gardens.

142. Conversation with Allen Goslen, 2005 chairman of the project, 13 December 2005.

143. Christmas Box, Folder #2, "A Brief History of the Candle Tea" by Margaret Leinbach Kolb, 1954, Moravian Archives, Winston-Salem, NC.

144. Fries, *Customs and Practices*, 51.

145. Springplace Correspondence, John Gambold, 5 February 1816. "First Fruits" was a term for those first members baptized in a mission. Author McClinton thinks that Zinzendorf believed that Christ would choose certain leaders as the "first fruits," and with the exceptional qualities of these people exhibited, the others would naturally follow later. Not necessarily adhering to this premise, the Bethlehem missionaries postponed the idea for four years after the count's death. "First fruits" was of enough interest to the count that he commissioned the artist John Valentine Haidt to paint twenty-one people from various origins and cultures as an example. Three versions exist in Herrnhut, Zeist, and Bethlehem (Rowena McClinton, Dissertation Thesis, Ph. D.: *The Moravian Mission Among the Cherokees at Springplace, Georgia* (Lexington: University of Kentucky: 1996) 40).

146. Fries, *Customs and Practices of the Moravian Church*, 57.

147. Rondthaler, 1 December 1907, church records, Moravian Archives, Winston-Salem, North Carolina.

148. "Moravian Christmas," *Journal & Sentinel*, Sunday morning, 20 December 1936, by Col. William A. Blair. Christmas Box, Folder 6, Q645:6, Moravian Archives, Winston-Salem, NC.

Bibliography

Books

Louisa May Alcott, *The Novels of Louisa May Alcott* (Ann Arbor, MI: State Street Press, 2001).

The American Heritage Songbook (New York: American Heritage, 1969).

American Tract Society, The Publications of the American Tract Society, Vols. 4 and 7 (New York: American Tract Society, n.d.).

Hans Christian Andersen, *The Christmas Tree and Other Stories* (New York: McLoughlin Brothers, n.d.).

Peter Andrews, ed., *Christmas in Germany* (Chicago: World Book Encyclopedia, 1974).

William H. Armstrong, Paula Locklair, and Bruce Shull, *Splendid Service: The Restoration of David Tannenberg's Home Moravian Church Organ* (Winston-Salem, NC: Old Salem, 2004).

Arnold Arnold, *Pictures and Stories from Forgotten Children's Books* (New York: Dover, 1969).

William Attmore, *Journal of a Tour to North Carolina, 1787*, edited by Lida Tunstall Rodman (Chapel Hill: University of North Carolina Press, 1922; published under the direction of The North Carolina Historical Society: The James Sprunt Historical Publications, vol. 17, no. 2).

Craig D. Atwood, *Community of the Cross: Moravian Piety in Colonial Bethlehem* (University Park: Pennsylvania State University Press, 2004).

Craig D. Atwood and Peter Vogt, eds., *The Distinctiveness of Moravian Culture: Essays and Documents in Moravian History in Honor of Vernon H. Nelson on his Seventieth Birthday* (Nazareth, PA: Moravian Historical Society, 2003).

Captain Charles Frederic Bahnson, *Bright and Gloomy Days: The Civil War Correspondence of Captain Charles Frederic Bahnson, A Moravian Confederate,* edited by Sarah Bahnson Chapman (Knoxville: University of Tennessee Press, 2003).

James Barnett, *The American Christmas: A Study in National Culture* (New York: Arno Press, 1976).

Theodor Bechler, trans., *Ortsgeschichte von Herrnhut: mit besonderer Berucksichtigung der alteren Zeit* (Herrnhut, Germany: Verlag der Missionsbuchhandlung, 1922).

Catherine E. Beecher and Harriet Beecher Stowe, *American Woman's Home or Principles of Domestic Science; Being a Guide to the Formation and Maintenance of Economical, Healthful Beautiful and Christian Homes* (New York: J. B. Ford & Co., 1869; reprint Hartford, CT: The Stowe-Day Foundation, 1994).

Randall Bedwell, *Christmas in the South: Yuletides Not Forgotten* (Nashville, TN: Spiridon, 1998).

Louise Belden, *The Festive Tradition: Table Decoration and Desserts in America, 1650-1900* (New York: W. W. Norton & Co., 1983).

John Bivins Jr. and Paula Welshimer, *Moravian Decorative Arts in North Carolina: An Introduction to the Old Salem Collection* (Winston-Salem, NC: Old Salem, 1981).

James Boeringer, *Morning Star: The Life and Works of Francis Florentine Hagen (1815-1907), Moravian Evangelist and Composer* (Cranbury, NJ: Associated University Presses, 1986).

Gerry Bowler, *The World Encyclopedia of Christmas* (Toronto: McClelland & Stewart, 2000).

Anne M. Boylan, *Sunday School: The Formation of An American Institution, 1790-1880* (New Haven, CT: Yale University Press, 1988).

Robert Brenner, *Christmas Revisited* (West Chester, PA: Schiffer, 1986).

Carl Bridenbaugh, *Myths & Realities: Societies of the Colonial South* (New York: Atheneum, 1980).

Dale W. Brown, *Understanding Pietism* (Grand Rapids, MI: William B. Eerdmans, 1978).

Peter Brown, *The Keeping of Christmas: England's Festive Tradition, 1760-1840* (York, England: York Civic Trust, 1999).

George Buday, *The History of the Christmas Card* (London: Rockliff, 1954; reprint London: Spring Books, 1964).

Flora Ann L. Bynum, *The Christmas Heritage of Old Salem* (Williamsburg, VA: Williamsburg Publishing, 1983).

Creighton Lee Calhoun Jr., *Old Southern Apples* (Blacksburg, VA: McDonald and Woodward, 1995).

Simon Callow, *Dickens' Christmas: A Victorian Celebration* (New York: Harry N. Abrams, 2003).

Rosalie Stier Calvert, *Mistress of Riversdale: The Plantation Letters of 1795-1821*, edited by Margaret Law Callcott (Baltimore: John Hopkins University Press, 1991).

Lydia Child, *The American Frugal Housewife* (Boston: Carter, Hendee, and Co., 1833).

L. Maria Child, *The Girl's Own Book* (London: Thomas Tegg, 1844; reprint Carlisle, MA: Applewood Books, 1992).

Christmas in Dickens (Garden City, NY: Garden City Publishing, 1941).

Ronald M. Clancy, *Best-Loved Christmas Carols* (North Cape May, NJ: Christmas Classics, 2000).

John Amos Comenius, *The Orbus Pictus* (Syracuse, NY: C. W. Bardeen, 1887; reprint Detroit, MI: Singing Tree Press, 1968).

John Amos Comenius, *The School of Infancy,* edited by Ernest M. Eller (Chapel Hill: University of North Carolina Press, 1956).

C. Daniel Crews, *Faith and Tears: The Moravian Mission Among the Cherokee* (Winston-Salem, NC: Moravian Archives, 2000).

C. Daniel Crews, *Johann Friedrich Peter and His Times* (Winston-Salem, NC: Moravian Music Foundation, 1990).

C. Daniel Crews, *Mountain Gospel* (Winston-Salem, NC: Moravian Archives, 1993).

C. Daniel Crews, *Neither Slave Nor Free: Moravians, Slavery, and a Church that Endures* (Winston-Salem, NC: Moravian Archives, 1998).

C. Daniel Crews and Lisa D. Bailey, *Records of the Moravians in North Carolina, 1856-1866*, Vol. 12 (Raleigh: North Carolina Department of Archives and History, 2000).

C. Daniel Crews and Lisa D. Bailey, *Records of the Moravians in North Carolina, 1867-1876*, Vol. 13 (Raleigh: North Carolina Department of Archives and History, 2006).

C. Daniel Crews and Richard W. Starbuck, *With Courage for the Future: The Story of the Moravian Church, Southern Province* (Winston-Salem, NC: Moravian Church in America, Southern Province, 2002).

Hans T. David, *Musical Life in the Pennsylvania Settlements of the Unitas Fratrum*, Moravian Music Foundation Publications No. 6 (Winston-Salem, NC: Moravian Music Foundation, 1959).

Chester S. Davis, *Moravians in Europe and America, 1415-1865: Hidden Seed and Harvest* (Winston-Salem, NC: Wachovia Historical Society, 2000).

Gerard Del Re and Patricia Del Re, *Twas the Night Before Christmas: The Story of Clement Clarke Moore and the Best-Loved Poem of Yuletide* (Tarrytown, NY: Wynwood Press, 1991).

Charles Dickens, *A Christmas Tree* (Sydney, Australia: P.I.C. Printing, 2001).

Charles Dickens, *The Annotated Christmas Carol*, edited by Michael Patrick Hearn (New York: W. W. Norton, 2004).

Dorcas Co-Workers of the Salem Home, comps., *Pages from Old Salem Cook Books* (Winston-Salem, NC: Dorcas Service League, 1931, reprinted 1947).

Elaine Dow, *Christmas, a Potpourri: The story of Christmas, the origins of favorite traditions, directions for meaningful decorations, holiday recipes, personal reflections, and other miscellanea* (Topsfield, MA: Historical Presentations, 1986).

Earnest McNeill Eller, *Salem Star and Dawn* (Winston-Salem, NC: Woman's Fellowship of the Moravian Church, Southern Province,1962).

Jock Elliott, *Inventing Christmas: How Our Holiday Came to Be* (New York: Harry Abrams, 2001).

Encyclopaedia Britannica, fifteenth edition (Chicago: William Benton, 1974).

Carl Engel, *Discords Mingled* (Freeport, NY: Books for Libraries Press, 1931; reprinted 1967).

L. D. Ettlinger and R. G. Holloway, *Compliments of the Season* (London: Penguin Books, 1947).

Fanny Fern, *Little Ferns for Fanny's Little Friends* (Auburn, NY: Derby & Miller, 1854).

Philip Vickers Fithian, *Journal and Letters of Philip Vickers Fithian: A Plantation Tutor of the Old Dominion, 1773-1774*, edited by Hunter Dickinson Farish (Charlottesville: University of Virginia Press, 1983).

Fletcher, *The Letters of Elijah*, edited by Martha von Brieson (Charlottesville: University of Virginia Press, 1965).

Daniel J. Foley, *The Christmas Tree: An Evergreen Garland Filled with History, Folklore, Symbolism, Tradition, Legends and Stories* (Philadelphia and New York: Chilton Book Division, 1960).

Don Foster, *Author Unknown: On the Trail of Anonymous*, Chapter 6: "Yes, Virginia, There *Was* a Santa Claus" (New York: Henry Holt, 2000).

Damon Lee Fowler, ed., *Dining at Monticello* (Monticello, VA: Thomas Jefferson Foundation Inc., 2005).

Adelaide Fries, *Customs and Practices of the Moravian Church* (Bethlehem, PA: Interprovincial Board of Communication, Moravian Church in North America, 2003).

Adelaide L. Fries, ed., *Records of the Moravians in North Carolina*, Vols. 1-7 (Raleigh: North Carolina Historical Commission, 1922-1947).

Adelaide L. Fries and Douglas LeTell Rights, eds., *Records of the Moravians in North Carolina*, Vol. 8 (Raleigh: State Department of Archives and History, 1954).

Phebe Earle Gibbons, *Pennsylvania Dutch & Other Essays* (Philadelphia: J. B. Lippincott & Co., 1882; reprint Mechanicsburg, PA: Stackpole Books, 2001).

Nada Gray, *Holidays: Victorian Women Celebrate in Pennsylvania* (Lewisburg, PA: Oral Traditions Project of the Union County Historical Society, 1983).

Thomas Gray, *The Old Salem Toy Museum* (Winston-Salem, NC: Old Salem, 2005).

Frances Griffin, *Less Time for Meddling: A History of Salem Academy and College, 1772-1866* (Winston-Salem, NC: John F. Blair, 1979).

Frances Griffin, ed., *Three Forks of Muddy Creek*, Vol. 7, "Lisetta's Journey" (Winston-Salem, NC: Old Salem, 1980).

Tanya Gulevich, *Encyclopedia of Christmas* (Detroit: Omnigraphics, 2000).

W.D. Haley, *Johnny Appleseed* (Sandwich, MA: Chapman Billies, 1994).

Mrs. Basil Hall (Margaret Hunter), *The Aristocratic Journey: Being the Outspoken Letters of Mrs. Basil Hall Written During a Fourteen Months' Sojourn in America 1827-1828*, edited by Una Pope-Hennessy (New York: G.P. Putnam's Sons, 1931).

Herbert Halpert and G. M. Story, eds., *Christmas Mumming in Newfoundland: Essays in Anthropology, Folklore, and History* (Toronto: University of Toronto Press for Memorial University of Newfoundland, 1969).

Kenneth G. Hamilton, trans. and ed., *The Bethlehem Diary*, Vol. 1 (Bethlehem, PA: Archives of the Moravian Church, 1971).

Kenneth G. Hamilton, ed., *Records of the Moravians in North Carolina, 1841-1851*, Vol. 10 (Raleigh: North Carolina State Department of Archives and History, 1966).

Kenneth G. Hamilton, ed., *Records of the Moravians in North Carolina, 1852-1879*, Vol. 11 (Raleigh: North Carolina State Department of Archives and History, 1969).

Anneliese Harding, *John Lewis Krimmel: Genre Artist of the Early Republic* (Winterthur, DE: Henry Francis du Pont Winterthur Museum, 1994).

Marion Harland, *Marion Harland's Complete Cookbook* (St. Louis, MO: The Marion Co., 1906).

Marion Harland, *The Christmas Holly* (New York: Sheldon and Co., 1867).

Deborah Harper, *Discover Yuletide at Winterthur* (Winterthur, DE: Henry Francis du Pont Winterthur Museum, 1998).

Francis Bret Harte, *The Luck of Roaring Camp and Other Sketches*, "How Santa Claus Came to Simpson's Bar" (Chicago: The Fountain Press, 1965).

Peter J. Hatch, *The Fruits and Fruit Trees of Monticello* (Charlottesville: University of Virginia Press, 1998).

James Henry, *Sketches of Moravian Life and Character* (Philadelphia: J.B. Lippincott, 1859).

Heinrich Hoffmann, *Slovenly Peter or Cheerful Stories and Funny Pictures For Good Little Folks* (Philadelphia: John C. Winston Co., n.d.)

The Holy Bible, I Corinthians: 13 (New York: Oxford University Press, n.d.).

Richard James Hooker, *Food and Drink in America: A History* (Indianapolis, IN: Bobbs-Merrill, 1981).

Washington Irving, *Diedrich Knickerbocker's History of New-York* (New York: The Heritage Press, 1940).

Washington Irving, *The Sketch Book of Geoffrey Crayon, Gent.* (New York: The Heritage Press, 1939).

Harriet Jacobs, *Incidents in the Life of a Slave Girl: Written by Herself* (Cambridge, MA: Harvard University Press, 1987).

George Johnson, *Christmas Ornaments, Lights, and Decorations*, Vols. 1-3 (Paducah, KY: Collector Books, 1997).

George Johnson, *Pictorial Guide to Christmas Ornaments & Collectibles* (Paducah, KY: Collector Books, 2004).

Kathleen Karr, *The Great Turkey Walk* (New York: Farrar, Straus & Giroux, 1998).

Harnett Kane, *The Southern Christmas Book* (New York: David McKay, 1958).

John F. Kasson, *Rudeness & Civility: Manners in Nineteenth Century Urban America* (New York: Hill and Wang, 1990).

Sally Kevill-Davies, *Yesterday's Children: The Antiques and History of Childcare* (Woodbridge, Suffolk, England: Antique Collectors' Club, 1991; reprinted 1998).

Constance King, *Christmas: Antiques, Decorations and Traditions* (Woodbridge, Suffolk, England: Antique Collectors' Club, 1999).

Winifred Kirkland, *Where the Star Still Shines* (Winston-Salem, NC: Woman's Auxiliary, Home Moravian Church, n.d.).

Nola Reed Knouse, "Gott sah zu seiner Zeit": *A Moravian Chorale from the 1544 Gesangbuch der Bruder in Behemen und Merherrn,* in *The Distinctiveness of Moravian Culture,* edited by Craig Atwood and Peter Vogt (Nazareth, PA: Moravian Historical Society, 2003).

Kriss Kringle's Christmas Tree: A Holiday Present for Boys and Girls (New York and Philadelphia: E. Ferrett, 1846).

Frank Glenn Lankard, *A History of the American Sunday School Curriculum* (New York: Abingdon Press, 1927).

Paul S. Larson, *An American Musical Dynasty: A Biography of the Wolle Family of Bethlehem, Pennsylvania* (Bethlehem, PA: Lehigh University Press, 2002).

Emily-Sarah Lineback, ed., *Preserving the Past: Salem Moravians' Receipts & Rituals* Boonville, NC: Carolina Avenue Press, 2003).

The Liturgy and Hymns of the American Province of the Unitas Fratrum, or The Moravian Church (Bethlehem, PA: Moravian Publication Office, 1895).

Robert Lynn and Elliott Wright, *The Big Little School, Two Hundred Years of the Sunday School* (Birmingham, AL: Religious Education Press, 1980).

Karal Ann Marling, *Merry Christmas: Celebrating America's Greatest Holiday* (Cambridge, MA: Harvard University Press, 2000).

Nancy H. Marshall, *The Night Before Christmas: A Descriptive Bibliography of Clement Clarke Moore's Immortal Poem* (New Castle, DE: Oak Knoll Press, 2002).

Joanne Martell, comp., *American Christmas* (Winston-Salem, NC: John F. Blair, 2005).

Margaret McCuiston, *Christmas Recollections of Margaret McCuiston* (Winston-Salem, NC: John F. Blair, 1980).

Margaret Blair McCuiston, "Recollections of My Brother" in *John Fries Blair* (Chapel Hill, NC: North Caroliniana Society, 1983).

Salley G. McMillen, *To Raise Up the South: Sunday Schools in Black and White Churches (1865-1915)* (Baton Rouge: Louisiana State University Press, 2001).

H. L. Mencken, *The American Language* (New York: Alfred A. Knopf, 1957).

Robert M. Merck, *Deck the Halls* (New York: Abbeville Press, 1992).

Merriam-Webster's Collegiate Dictionary, eleventh edition (Springfield, MA: Merriam-Webster, 2003).

Clement Miles, *Christmas Customs and Traditions* (New York: Dover, 1976).

Katherine Milhous, *Snow Over Bethlehem* (New York: Charles Scribner's Sons, 1945; reprint Bethlehem, PA: Kemerer Museum of Decorative Arts, 2000).

Judith Miller and Martin Miller, *Miller's Traditional Christmas* (London: Mitchell Beazley International, 1992).

Lewis Miller, *Sketches and Chronicles: The Reflections of a Nineteenth Century Pennsylvania German Folk Artist* (York, PA: The Historical Society of York County, 1966).

Clement Moore, *The Night Before Christmas* (New York: Raphael Tuck & Sons, n.d.).

Moravian Daily Texts: Bible Texts with Hymn Verses and Prayers for Every Day in the Year (Bethlehem, PA, and Winston-Salem, NC: The Moravian Church in America, 2002).

Jedediah Morse, *Geography Made Easy: Being an Abridgement of the American Universal Geography* (Boston: Thomas & Andrews, 1816).

Kay Moss and Kathryn Hoffman, *The Backcountry Housewife: A Study of Eighteenth-Century Foods,* Vol. 1 (Gastonia, NC: Schiele Museum, 1985 & 1994).

Mother Goose's Melodies (Boston: Munroe & Francis, 1833; reprint New York: Dover, 1970).

Richmond E. Myers, *Christmas Traditions* (Bethlehem, PA: Acorn Graphics of Oaks Printing Co., 1985).

Richmond E. Myers, *Sketches of Early Bethlehem* (Bethlehem, PA: Moravian College Alumni Association, 1981).

Milo Naeve, *John Lewis Krimmel: An Artist in Federal America* (Newark: University of Delaware Press, 1987).

Thomas Nast, *Thomas Nast's Christmas Drawings for the Human Race* (New York: Harper & Row, 1971).

Vernon H. Nelson, ed., Kenneth G. Hamilton, trans., and Lothar Madeheim, trans., *The Bethlehem Diary, Vol. II. January 1, 1744 - May 31, 1745* (Bethlehem, PA: The Moravian Archives, 2001).

Stephen Nissenbaum, *The Battle for Christmas* (New York: Alfred A. Knopf, 1997).

Penelope Niven, *Old Salem: The Official Guidebook* (Winston-Salem, NC: Old Salem, 2004).

Libbey Hodges Oliver and Mary Miley Theobold, *Four Centuries of Virginia Christmas* (Richmond, VA: Dietz Press, 2000).

Mary Barrow Owen, ed., "The Vierling House" in *Old Salem, North Carolina* (Winston-Salem, NC: The Garden Club of North Carolina, 1941; reprinted 1946).

Oxford-Duden German Dictionary, second edition, edited by Werner Scholze-Stubenrecht, et al. (Oxford: Oxford University Press, 1999).

Rachel Theresa Paris, *Silk Stocking Street* (Atlanta, GA: Cherokee Publishing Company, 1972).

Samuel White Patterson, *The Poet of Christmas Eve: A Life of Clement Clarke Moore, 1779-1863* (New York: Morehouse-Gorham, 1956).

The Pennsylvania German Folklore Society, Vols. 3, 4, and 6 (Allentown, PA: Pennsylvania German Folklore Society, 1938, 1939, 1941).

The Pennsylvania German Society, Vol. 7 (Breinigsville, PA: Pennsylvania German Society, 1973).

Julia Peterkin, *A Plantation Christmas* (Marietta, GA: Larlin, 1987).

Michael Pollan, *Botany of Desire: A Plant's-Eye View of the World* (New York: Random House, 2001).

Random House Webster's College Dictionary (New York: Random House, 2001).

Rev. Levin T. Reichel, *The Moravians in North Carolina: An Authentic History* (Salem, NC: O. A. Keehln, 1857 and Philadelphia: J. B. Lippincott and Co, 1857).

William C. Reichel, *A History of the Moravian Seminary for Young Ladies* (Philadelphia: J.B. Lippincott & Co., 1858).

Penne Restad, *Christmas in America: A History* (New York: Oxford University Press, 1995).

Katharine Lambert Richards, *How Christmas Came to the Sunday-Schools: The observance of Christmas in the Protestant church schools of the United States, an historical study* (New York: Dodd, Mead & Co., 1934).

Richard de Rochemont, *Eating in America* (New York: William Morrow & Co., 1976).

Katharine Rockwell, *How Christmas came to the Sunday-schools* (New York: Dodd Mead, 1934).

S. Scott Rohrer, *Hope's Promise: Religion and Acculturation in the Southern Backcountry* (Tuscaloosa: University of Alabama Press, 2005).

W. J. Rorabaugh, *The Alcoholic Republic: An American Tradition* (New York: Oxford University Press, 1979).

Salem Academy and College Through the Years (Winston-Salem, NC: Salem College Alumnae Association, 1951).

William Sandys, *Christmas Carols, Ancient and Modern* (London: Richard Beckley, 1833).

William Sandys, *Christmastide: Its History, Festivities and Carols* (London: John Russell Smith, 1852).

William Sansom, *A Book of Christmas* (New York: McGraw-Hill, 1968).

Leigh Eric Schmidt, *Consumer Rites: The Buying and Selling of American Holidays* (Princeton, NJ: Princeton University Press, 1995).

Rev. Dr. Edmund Schwarze, *History of the Moravian Missions Among Southern Indian Tribes of the United States* (Bethlehem, PA: Times Publishing Co. for Transactions of the Moravian Historical Society, Special Series, Vol. 1, 1923).

Jon Sensbach, *A Separate Canaan: The Making of an Afro-Moravian World in North Carolina, 1763-1840* (Chapel Hill: University of North Carolina Press, 1998).

Jon Sensbach, *African-Americans in Salem* (Winston-Salem, NC: Old Salem, 1991).

Alfred L. Shoemaker, *Christmas in Pennsylvania: A Folk-Cultural Study* (Kutztown, PA: Pennsylvania Folklife Society, 1959; reprint Mechanicsburg, PA: Stackpole Books, 1999).

Amelia Simmons, *American Cookery* (Hartford, CT: 1796; reprint Bedford, MA: Applewood Books, 1996).

William Gilmore Simms, *The Golden Christmas: A Tale of Lowcountry Life* (Columbia: University of South Carolina Press, 2005; originally published by Walker, Richards and Co. as *The Golden Christmas: A Chronicle of St. John's, Berkeley, Compiled from the Notes of a Briefless Barrister*, 1852).

William Gilmore Simms, "Maize in Milk" in *The Writings of William Gilmore Simms*, Vol. 5, edited by John Guilds (Columbia: University of South Carolina Press, 1974).

Lissa Smith and Dick Smith, *Christmas Collectibles: A Guide to Selecting, Collecting and Enjoying the Treasures of Christmas Past* (Secaucus, NJ: Chartwell Books, 1993).

Minnie J. Smith, ed., *Records of the Moravians in North Carolina*, Vol. 9 (Raleigh: North Carolina State Department of Archives and History, 1964).

Phillip V. Snyder, *The Christmas Tree Book: The History of the Christmas Tree & Antique Christmas Tree Ornaments* (New York: The Viking Press, 1976).

Phillip V. Snyder, *December 25* (New York: Dodd, Mead, & Co., 1985).

August Gottlieb Spangenberg, *An Exposition of Christian Doctrine, as Taught in the Protestant Church of the United Brethren, or Unitas Fratrum*, translated by Benjamin La Trobe (Winston-Salem, NC: Southern Province of the Moravian Church, 1959).

Rick Steves and Valerie Griffith, *European Christmas* (Emeryville, CA: Avalon Travel, 2005).

William Studwell, *The Christmas Carol Reader* (New York: The Haworth Press, 1995).

Jim L. Sumner, *A History of Sports in North Carolina* (Raleigh: North Carolina Department of Cultural Resources, Division of Archives and History, 1990).

Jerry Surratt, *Gottlieb Schober of Salem: Discipleship and Ecumenical Vision in an Early Moravian Town* (Macon, GA: Mercer University Press, 1983).

Vangie Roby Sweitzer, *Christmas in Bethlehem: A Moravian Heritage* (Bethlehem, PA: Central Moravian Church, 2000).

Joe Gray Taylor, *Eating, Drinking, and Visiting in the South: An Informal History* (Baton Rouge: Louisiana State University, 1982).

Ella Gertrude Clanton Thomas, *The Secret Eye: The Journal of Ella Gertrude Clanton Thomas, 1848-1889*, edited by Virginia Ingraham Burr (Chapel Hill: University of North Carolina Press, 1990).

Basil Armstrong Thomasson, *The Diary of, North Carolina Yeoman, 1853-1862*, edited by Paul D. Escott (Athens: University of Georgia Press, 1996).

Alexander Tille, *Yule and Christmas: Their Place in the Germanic Year* (London: David Nutt, 1899).

Maguelonne Toussaint-Samat, *History of Food*, translated by Anthea Bell (New York: Barnes & Noble, 1998).

Henry Van Dyke, *The Story of the Other Wise Man* (Mount Vernon, NY: Peter Pauper Press, n.d.).

Herman J. Viola, *The Indian Legacy of Charles Bird King* (Washington, DC: Smithsonian Institution Press, 1976).

Herman J. Viola, *Thomas L. McKenney: Architect of America's Early Indian Policy: 1816-1830* (Chicago: Swallow Press, 1974).

Charles Vogler, ed., *Descendants of Philipp Christoph Vogler,* Books I and II (Camden, ME: Penobscot Press for Philip Christoph Vogler Memorial Inc., 1994).

John Walker, *A Critical Pronouncing Dictionary and Expositor of the English Language* (Hartford, CT: Silas Andrus, 1828).

F. Addison Warner, *Memoir of F. Addison Warner of Athens, Pennsylvania* (Philadelphia: American Sunday School Union, n.d.).

Nathan Warren, *The Holidays: Christmas, Easter, and Whitsuntide, Their Social Festivities, Customs, and Carols* (New York: Hurd and Houghton, 1868).

George Washington, *The Diaries of George Washington, 1771-1785*, Vol. 2, edited by John C. Fitzpatrick (Boston and New York: Houghton Mifflin Co., 1925).

William Woys Weaver, *America Eats: Forms of Edible Folk Art* (New York: Harper & Row, 1989).

William Woys Weaver, *The Christmas Cook: Three Centuries of American Yuletide Sweets* (New York: Harper Perennial, 1990).

William Woys Weaver, *Sauerkraut Yankees: Pennsylvania German Foods & Foodways* (Philadelphia: University of Pennsylvania Press, 1983; reprint Mechanicsburg, PA: Stackpole Books, 2002).

Noah Webster, *The American Spelling Book; Containing The Rudiments of the English Language for the Use of Schools in the United States* (Philadelphia: Jacob Johnson & Co., 1805).

Gavin Weightman and Steve Humphries, *Christmas Past* (London: Sidgwick & Jackson, 1987).

John R. Weinlick, *Count Zinzendorf* (Nashville, TN: Abingdon Press, 1956).

Joe Wheeler and Jim Rosenthal, *St. Nicholas: A Closer Look at Christmas* (Nashville, TN: Thomas Nelson Inc., 2005).

Dr. George Follett Wilson, *The Journal of Dr. George Follett Wilson: April 27, 1828 - September 30, 1830*, edited by Evelyn Hubbard Wilson (Greenville, SC: A Press, 1984).

Jean Fagan Yellin, *Harriet Jacobs: A Life: The Remarkable Adventures of the Woman Who Wrote Incidents in the Life of a Slave Girl* (New York: Basic Civitas Books, 2004).

Joanna B. Young, *Christmas in Williamsburg* (Williamsburg, VA: Colonial Williamsburg Foundation, distributed by Holt, Rinehart and Winston Inc., New York, 1970).

Yuletide at Winterthur: Tastes and Visions of the Season (Winterthur, DE: Henry Francis du Pont Winterthur Museum, 1992).

Periodicals

The Academy, A Monthly Journal of Salem Academy, Salem College, Winston-Salem, NC.

Colonial Williamsburg: The Journal of Colonial Williamsburg Foundation, 2005 Christmas Edition, Colonial Williamsburg Foundation, Williamsburg, VA.

Early American Life, Vol. 37, Christmas 2006.

Food History News, edited by Sandra Oliver, Autumn 1991.

Adelaide Fries, "Our Christmas" booklet, 1920, Christmas Folder, Moravian Archives, Winston-Salem, NC.

Adelaide Fries, "Moravian Customs: Our Inheritance" booklet, 1936, Salem College Library, Winston-Salem, NC.

Harper's New Monthly Magazine, Vol. 27 (June to November 1863).

Arthur Hosking, "Is Santa Claus an American?" *Liberty* (magazine), 30 December 1933.

Journal and Sentinel, "Moravian Christmas in Salem," 20 December 1936, Winston-Salem, NC.

Roy Ledbetter, "Moraviana: Christmas Eve," *The Moravian,* December 1996.

Donald M. McCorkle, "The Unknown Century of American Classical Music," news bulletin of the Moravian Music Foundation, Vol. 4, No. 2, Spring-Summer 1960, Winston-Salem, NC.

Donald M. McCorkle, "The *Collegium Musicum Salem*: Its Music, Musicians and Importance," Moravian Music Foundation, October 1956; reprinted from *The North Carolina Historical Review*, Vol. 33, No. 4, October 1956, p. 487.

The Moravian, "Christmas in Philadelphia," 1 January 1863, Vol. 8, No.1, p. 1.

"Moravian Christmas Practices, 1753-1859," Christmas Folder, Moravian Archives, Winston-Salem, NC.

People's Press, 25 November 1859, Francis W. Meller advertisement.

St. Nicholas, An Illustrated Magazine for Young Folks, edited by Mary Mapes Dodge, 1881-1882, Vols. 9 and 10.

The Wachovia Moravian, Vol. 7, No. 83 (January 1900), p. 10.

Unpublished Materials

George Frederick Bahnson, *Personal Diary of George Frederick Bahnson, 1834-1838*, transcribed by Alice North Henderson and Dr. Peter Meyers, Old Salem Museums & Gardens, Winston-Salem, NC.

Charles Brietz, Memoir, Old Salem Museums & Gardens, Winston-Salem, NC.

Cherokee Mission Papers, Folder #4, Springplace Letters, 1804-1805, 27 January, Gottlieb Byhan to Gotthold Reichel, Moravian Archives, Winston-Salem, NC.

Christmas Folder, all categories, Moravian Archives, Winston-Salem, NC.

Cookbook, early-eighteenth-century manuscript recipes found in the house of Doctor Lumpkin, Mechanicsville, VA, 26 May 1862, Old Salem Museums & Gardens, Winston-Salem, NC.

Dialogues, Christmas Folder 1, Q645.1, Moravian Archives, Winston-Salem, NC.

Diary of the African Church in Salem, James Hall, pastor, Christmas excerpts, p. 1, 26 December 1879 (prepared for the author by Richard Starbuck), Moravian Archives, Winston-Salem, NC.

J. A. Freibele, Letter to "Dear Christian Friends," 1857, Moravian Archives, Winston-Salem, NC.

Fries-Bahnson Correspondence, 1887, Moravian Archives, Winston-Salem, NC.

Fries-Bahnson Correspondence, 6 January 1888, Moravian Archives, Winston-Salem, NC.

Lisetta Vogler Fries, Daybook, 25 December 1846, Old Salem Museums & Gardens, Winston-Salem, NC.

Mary E. Fries, Diary, 31 August 1863 – 14 June 1864, Salem, NC, copied from original given by Mary Patterson Fisher for preservation in the Southern Historical Collection, University of North Carolina, Chapel Hill, NC.

Fries and Shaffner Papers, Series B: 1864, Vol. 3, #4046. Southern Historical Collection, University of North Carolina, Chapel Hill, NC.

The Holiday Journal, "edited by the Holiday Club," numbers 11 through 21, November, 1882 - February, 1883 (this hand-made journal was conceived by local Salem NC children, with the future Moravian archivist "Addie" Fries serving as one of the editors), Moravian Archives, Winston-Salem, NC.

Susannah Kramsch, Diary, Moravian Archives, Winston-Salem, NC.

Eliza W. (Vierling) Kremer, Bits of Old Salem Gossip, Salem College Library, Rare Books. Winston-Salem, NC.

Johann Leinbach, Journal, Old Salem Museums & Gardens, Winston-Salem, NC.

Regina E. Leinbach, Autograph Book, MS 6:4//MC 9:I, Moravian Archives, Winston-Salem, NC.

Louisa Lenoir, Letterbook, Lenoir Papers, Southern Historical Collection, University of North Carolina, Chapel Hill, NC.

Rowena McClinton, *The Moravian Mission Among the Cherokees at Springplace, Georgia*, dissertation (Ph.D.), 1996, University of Kentucky.

Alexander Campbell McIntosh, McIntosh Family Letters, 1848-1849, #1212, Southern Historical Collection, University of North Carolina, Chapel Hill, NC.

Albert Oerter, *Diary of the Colored Church in Salem*, Moravian Archives, Winston-Salem, NC.

Karsten Petersen, Memory Book, 1807-1813, Old Salem Museums & Gardens, Winston-Salem, NC.

Salem Boys School, "Day Books," 1-7 April 1818, Thomas Schulz, teacher, Moravian Archives, Winston-Salem, NC.

Jon F. Sensbach, *A Separate Canaan: The Making of an Afro-Moravian World in North Carolina, 1763-1856*, dissertation (Ph.D.), 1991, Duke University, Department of History.

Mary Senseman, Autograph Book given to her by her uncle (Elias Alexander Vogler), 25 December 1857, Salem, NC, Old Salem Museums & Gardens, Winston-Salem, NC.

Elisabeth Sommer, Research Report on Toys in Salem 1785-1900, 10 May 2001, Old Salem Museums & Gardens, Winston-Salem, NC.

Springplace Correspondence, Gambold to Van Vleck, 4 January 1816, Moravian Archives, Winston-Salem, NC.

Louisa Hagen Sussdorff, Diary, Old Salem Museums & Gardens, Winston-Salem, NC.

Elias Alexander Vogler, Letter Book, 1857-1860. Moravian Archives, Winston-Salem, NC.

Lisetta M. Vogler, Ode, Old Salem Museum & Gardens, Winston-Salem, NC.

Sarah "Sallie" Vogler, Album: *Forget Me Not*, 1861, MS 16:2, Mc 81 XIII, Moravian Archives, Winston-Salem, NC.

Peter Wolle, *The Peter Wolle Diaries*, 1809-1821. Translated by Peter S. and Irene P. Seadle. Old Salem Museums & Gardens Research Center, Winston-Salem, NC.

Yuletide Christmas Interpretive Manual, "Christmas: Trees in American Homes," Henry F. DuPont Winterthur Museum, Winterthur, DE.

Photography Credits

Photographs are identified by position as left (l.) or right (r.) or by Roman numeral (i, ii, iii, etc.) clockwise from the top.

Front cover, Vogler House, Old Salem Museums & Gardens (OSMG); back cover, Vierling House, OSMG; contents, Salem Square, Virginia R. Weiler (VRW); Preface, p. xi, OSMG.

Chapter One

Frontispiece, OSMG; p. 1, stock photography; p. 2, l., Belsnickel candy container, collection of Old Salem Toy Museum, acc. 4561; OSMG, r., Old Salem Historic Photograph Collection, Old Salem Museums & Gardens (OSHPC), s-245; p. 3, OSMG; p. 4, OSMG; p. 5, North Carolina State Archives; p. 6, OSMG; p. 7; OSMG; p. 8, i. ii, OSHPC, s-23761, s-23760, iii, Moravian Archives, Herrnhut, Germany; p. 9, OSMG; p. 10, OSMG, acc. 1090.3; p. 11, OSMG; p. 12, OSMG; p. 14, OSMG; p. 15, OSMG; p. 16, OSMG; p. 17, OSMG.

Chapter Two

p. 18, traditional Christmas tree decorations from MESDA's Winter Pleasures program, OSMG; p. 19, Christmas tree at the Vogler House, OSMG; p. 20, OSMG, acc. 2873; p. 21, i, OSMG, acc. 2873, ii, Moravian Archives, Bethlehem, Pennsylvania; p. 22, OSMG; p. 23, pyramid from MESDA's Winter Pleasures program, OSMG; p. 24, Winterthur Library; p. 25, York County Heritage Trust, York, PA; p. 26, OSMG, acc. m-137; p. 27, OSMG; p. 28, OSMG; p. 30, OSMG; p. 32, OSHPC, s-21842; p. 33, OSHPC, s-18391; p. 34, OSMG, acc. 4973; p. 36, i, ii, OSMG, acc. 5265.5; p. 37, OSHPC, s-26828.

Chapter Three

p. 38, Gary Albert; p. 39, twentieth-century die cut decoration, author's collection, OSMG; p. 40, OSMG; p. 41, OSMG, acc. 750.1; p. 42, OSMG, s-28256; p. 43, i, stock photography, ii, OSHPC, s-21982; p. 44, OSMG; p. 46, mantel from the Salem Tavern, OSMG; p. 47, OSHPC, s-15276; p. 49, OSHPC, s-15277; p. 50, i, ii, OSMG; p. 51, OSMG, acc. 5194.1; p. 52, OSMG; p. 53, i, Moravian Music Foundation doorway, Salem, OSMG, ii, OSMG; p. 55, OSMG; p. 56, OSMG, acc. 4502.8; p. 57, OSMG.

Chapter Four

p. 58, OSMG: p. 59, author's collection, OSMG; p. 61, i, ii, OSMG; p. 62, OSMG; p. 64, New-York Historical Society; p. 65, OSMG; p. 66, OSMG; p. 67, OSMG; p. 68, OSMG, acc. 2801; p. 69, OSMG; p. 71, OSMG, acc. 3183.2; p. 72, OSMG, acc. P-59; p. 75, OSMG; p. 76, i, ii, OSMG; p. 77, OSMG, s-2957a; p. 78, i, ii, OSMG, acc. 2873; p. 79, OSMG; p. 80, OSMG; p. 81, OSMG; p. 82, OSMG; p. 83, i, ii, OSMG; p. 84, OSMG.

Chapter Five

p. 86, Salem Tavern, OSMG; p. 87, stock photography; p. 88, York County Heritage Trust, York, PA; p. 89, OSMG; p. 90, York County Heritage Trust, York, PA; p. 92, Criss-Cross Hall during the Winter Pleasures program, OSMG; p. 93, from MESDA's Winter Pleasures program, OSMG; p. 94, York County Heritage Trust, York, PA; p. 95, from MESDA's Winter Pleasures program, OSMG; p. 96, OSMG; p. 99, OSHPC, s-27330; p. 100, York County Heritage Trust, York, PA; p. 101, OSMG; p. 102, OSMG, acc. 260.7; p. 103, OSMG; p. 105; Moravian Archives, Winston-Salem, NC; p. 106, from MESDA's Winter Pleasures program, OSMG; p. 107, OSMG, s-30742; p. 109, OSMG; p. 110, VRW; p., 111, i, ii, OSMG; p. 113, OSMG.

Chapter Six

p. 114, Vierling House, OSMG; p. 115, OSMG; p. 116, OSHPC, s-27985; p. 117, VRW; p. 118, OSMG; p. 119, i, ii, OSMG; p. 120, OSMG, acc. 2608; p. 121, Moravian Music Foundation, Winston-Salem, NC; p. 123, OSMG; p. 124, Moravian Archives, Herrnhut, Germany; p. 125, OSMG, acc. P-570; p. 127, OSHPC, s-21657; p. 129, doorway of Salem's Anna Johanna Vogler House, OSMG; p. 130, Salem's Single Brothers' Workshop, VRW; p. 131, Salem's Home Moravian Church, OSMG; p. 132, OSMG; p. 133, Moravian Archives, Herrnhut, Germany; p. 134, i, ii, OSMG; p. 135, Salem's Third and Fourth houses, VRW; p.136, Salem's Home Moravian Church, OSMG.

H

Hagen, Francis F., 54, 75, 115, 121, 122, 145, 154, 159; *see also* "Morning Star"

Haidt, John Valentine, 8, 72, 133, 153

Hale, Sarah Josepha, 29

ham, ix, 87, 89; *see also* hogs

Harland, Marion, 2, 9, 61, 137, 138, 143, 155

Harper's Weekly, 12, 31, 58, 62, 79, 96

Hauser, Martin, 16, 121

Henry, James, 40, 48, 52, 139, 141, 152, 156

Herrnhut, ix, xii, 6, 8, 25, 33, 35, 39, 54, 124, 125, 126, 133, 139, 140, 153, 154, 160

hogs, 91, 92, 100, 111, 147; *see also* butchering

Holland, xii, 60

Home Moravian Church, xv, 3, 16, 38, 39, 40, 42, 43, 52, 53, 78, 81, 107, 122, 123, 133, 134, 135, 138, 142, 151, 152, 154, 156, 160

    Candle Tea, 3, 52, 53, 122, 133, 134, 135, 153

    Ladies' Auxiliary (Home Moravian Church), 133

    Woman's Auxiliary (Home Moravian Church), 16, 133, 138, 142, 152, 156

"Home Sweet Home," 9, 98

Hope (North Carolina), viii, x, xi, xiii, 47, 59, 69, 78, 83, 139, 149, 157

Huss, John (Jan Hus), xii, 122

hymn, 4, 35, 54, 72, 108, 115, 116, 118, 119, 121, 122, 125, 130, 132, 135, 141, 156

hymnbook, 121, 132

I

illuminations, 35, 41, 43, 48

Industrial Revolution, xv, 9

instruments (musical), xiv, 115, 116, 120, 122, 124

    bassoon, 119, 120

    clavichord, 120

    clavier, 120

    organ, 118, 122, 123, 124, 128, 135, 151, 152, 154

    piano, 45, 119, 120, 130

    trombone, 2

    trumpet, 77, 117

    violin, 95, 120

Irving, Washington, 13, 65, 143, 156

J

Jackson, Andrew, xiv, 31, 158

Jefferson, Thomas, 98, 110, 124, 150, 155

Jerusalem, 4

Jesus, xii, 1, 3, 5, 6, 16, 20, 29, 35, 40, 42, 43, 48, 54, 56, 68, 71, 72, 110, 115, 117, 126, 129, 135, 141, 152; *see also* Christ, Prince of Peace

Joseph of Arimathea, 26

K

Kalends, 27, 68, 146

Kirkland, Winifred, 16, 50, 54, 138, 142, 156

Klemm, Gottlob, 122

Kramsch, Susanna, 11, 35, 74, 99, 102, 106, 140, 145, 147, 148, 149, 150, 159

Kremer, Eliza Vierling, 39, 75, 129, 145, 152

Krimmel, John Lewis, 24, 26, 139, 155, 156

Kringle, Kriss, 2, 13, 14, 27, 30, 60, 63, 65, 138, 140, 143, 156; *see also* Gift Bringer

Krippe, 39, 45, 52, 53, 141

Kriss Kringle's Christmas Tree, 13, 14, 27, 30, 138, 140, 156

L

Ladies' Auxiliary (Home Moravian Church), 133; *see also* Home Moravian Church

lamb, 5, 75, 125, 152

Lancaster, 24, 36, 45, 56

Lapland, xii

Latvia, 28

Lehigh River, vii, 4, 137, 152, 156

Lenoir, Louisa, 43, 129, 141, 152, 159

Lind, Jenny, 30, 31, 140

liquor, 93, 95, 96, 98; *see also* alcohol

Linnean, 21

Lititz, xiii, 20, 29, 35, 119

Little Women, 15, 78, 81, 145

Locklair, Paula, ix, 22, 151, 154

lot, the, xiv

lotteries, 12

Louisiana, 31, 146, 156, 157

lovefeast, xii, xv, 1, 2, 6, 19, 20, 47, 54, 70, 73, 75, 76, 87, 101, 106, 107, 108, 109, 110, 111, 112, 117, 118, 120, 124, 125, 126, 127, 128, 133, 150

lovefeast buns, 87, 108, 111, 150

Luther, Martin, xii, 27, 60, 69, 72

Lutheran, xii, 132, 145

M

McIntosh, Alexander Campbell, 95, 150, 159

McKenney, Thomas, ix, x, 22, 139, 158

Magi, The, 28, 54, 68, 110

maxims, 7, 61, 124

maypole, 27

Meller, F. W., 68, 83, 104, 149

memoir, 21, 110, 149, 158

MESDA (Museum of Early Southern Decorative Arts), ix, xv, 10, 16, 68, 76, 144, 145, 149, 150, 160

metzel soup, 91

Middle Ages, 26, 27, 39, 45, 52, 53, 60, 68, 69

milk, 2, 63, 67, 69, 87, 96, 98, 100, 101, 104, 108, 109, 112, 138, 150, 157

mill, xiii, 46, 70, 92, 135

Miller, Lewis, x, 19, 25, 88, 90, 94, 100, 138, 156

Milton, John, iii, 10

mission, vii, xii, xiii, xiv, xv, 6, 11, 19, 20, 21, 22, 23, 31, 32, 37, 40, 45, 47, 71, 72, 78, 81, 85, 89, 107, 108, 111, 112, 122, 127, 129, 137, 138, 139, 144, 146, 149, 150, 151, 153, 154, 158, 159

Missionary Society, xiv, 78, 81, 112

Mississippi, 31

mistletoe, 42, 146

Moore, Clement, 13, 66, 67, 138, 143, 155, 156, 157

Moravia, xii, 53

Moravian Archives, ix, xv, 8, 21, 105, 108, 124, 133, 137, 138, 139, 140, 141, 142, 145, 146, 147, 148, 149, 150, 151, 152, 153, 154, 155, 156, 158, 159, 160

Moravian Church, ii, vii, viii, xiii, xiv, xv, 1, 3, 12, 13, 16, 38, 39, 40, 42, 43, 45, 52, 53, 54, 55, 68, 78, 81, 84, 106, 107, 108, 115, 116, 122, 123, 125, 126, 130, 132, 133, 134, 135, 137, 138, 140, 141, 142, 144, 149, 150, 151, 152, 153, 154, 155, 156, 157, 160

    Calvary Moravian Church, 68

    choir, xiv, 2, 3, 6, 46, 47, 54, 122, 126, 128, 132

    Herrnhut, ix, xii, 6, 8, 25, 33, 35, 39, 54, 124, 125, 126, 133, 139, 140, 153, 154, 160

    Home Moravian Church, xv, 3, 16, 38, 39, 40, 42, 43, 52, 53, 78, 81, 107, 122, 123, 133, 134, 135, 138, 142, 151, 152, 154, 156, 160

    Huss, John (Jan Hus), xii, 122

    lot, the, xiv

    lovefeast, xii, xv, 1, 2, 6, 19, 20, 47, 54, 70, 73, 75, 76, 87, 101, 106, 107, 108, 109, 110, 111, 112, 117, 118, 120, 124, 125, 126, 127, 128, 133, 150

    Moravian Archives, ix, xv, 8, 21, 105, 108, 124, 133, 137, 138, 139, 140, 141, 142, 145, 146, 147, 148, 149, 150, 151, 152, 153, 154, 155, 156, 158, 159, 160

    Northern Province (Moravian Church, North America), xii, xv

Oeconomie, xiii

    Southern Province (Moravian Church, North America), xv, 78, 84, 137, 149, 152, 155, 157

    Spangenberg, August Gottlieb, xiii, 5, 137, 157